Do Black Lives Matter?

Do Black Lives Matter?

How Christian Scriptures Speak to Black Empowerment

Edited by
Lisa M. Bowens *and*
Dennis R. Edwards

Foreword by Love L. Sechrest

CASCADE *Books* · Eugene, Oregon

DO BLACK LIVES MATTER?
How Christian Scriptures Speak to Black Empowerment

Cascade Books
An Imprint of Wipf and Stock Publishers
199 W. 8th Ave., Suite 3
Eugene, OR 97401

www.wipfandstock.com

PAPERBACK ISBN: 978-1-6667-0541-6
HARDCOVER ISBN: 978-1-6667-0542-3
EBOOK ISBN: 978-1-6667-0543-0

Cataloguing-in-Publication data:

Names: Bowens, Lisa M., editor. | Edwards, Dennis R., editor.

Title: Do black lives matter? : how Christian Scriptures speak to black empowerment / Edited by Lisa M. Bowens and Dennis R. Edwards.

Description: Eugene, OR: Cascade Books, 2023 | Includes bibliographical references and index.

Identifiers: ISBN 978-1-6667-0541-6 (paperback) | ISBN 978-1-6667-0542-3 (hardcover) | ISBN 978-1-6667-0543-0 (ebook)

Subjects: LCSH: Race relations—Religious aspects—Christianity. | United States—Race relations. | Anti-racism—United States.

Classification: E184.A1 D60 2023 (print) | E184 (ebook)

06/09/23

The essay "Hearing Scripture as Protest and Resistance" appeared previously in *Word & World Journal* Special Edition on Race, *Word & World*, 41 Special Issue (2021) 4–12, and appears here with permission and with revisions. The essay "White Supremacy is a Script We're Given at Birth" originally appeared in *The Christian Century* (September 15, 2020) and appears here with permission. The poem by Tammie Denyse, "The Women Gather," appears here with permission of the author. The "Hagar Poem" by Hanna Watson is used with permission of the author.

Unless otherwise indicated, all Scripture quotations are taken from the New Revised Standard Version Bible, copyright © 1989 the Division of Christian Education of the National Council of the Churches of Christ in the United States of America. Used by permission. All rights reserved.

For Past, Present, and Future Believers—We are surrounded
with a great cloud of witnesses (Hebrews 12:1)

For the resilient who confronted the world's
hatred with tenacious faith (1 John 3:13)

Contents

**Section Two: Theological Reflections and
Expressions of Black Empowerment**

Section Three: Sermons on Blackness

Foreword

I WAS LOCKED IN a bedroom sick with COVID in the summer of 2020, longing for vaccines that would not be available for over a year. Though my flu-like symptoms subsided in a few days, I did not know that my health would be impaired for a long time afterward. Just months into the pandemic we were already beginning to see the toll that that disease would have on Black life. I dreaded the results of the "blackening" of the pandemic, the early observations that Black and Indigenous people especially were susceptible to COVID-19 sickness and death. The politicization of simple public health measures and later resistance to life-saving vaccines and treatments resulted in an astonishing indifference to the toll of over 1.3 million dead Americans, essentially, I believe, because it had come to be seen as *Black* death. I too was shocked by the televised lynching of George Floyd. We bore witness to Floyd's pleas for help and his cries for his dead mother in the moments before he died. We watched White police officer Derek Chauvin kneel on Floyd's neck with all his body weight, supremely unmoved by the sound of Floyd's suffering.

I could not participate in the explosion of spontaneous activism to chant "Black Lives Matter!" with the inspiring multiracial and multigenerational crowds across the globe. Quarantined in my bedroom, I was working on a decade-long exploration of how Black folk read, love, and live with the Bible, building a responsible method for biblical reflection on our broken interactions on race and gender. Over the years, I had discerned how African American Bible readers and preachers imaginatively read themselves into biblical stories using the power of analogical reasoning. However, as a seminary professor, I have also seen the harm that can emerge from irresponsible use of this reading strategy. Not surprisingly, the chapter I wrote that summer would forever bear the marks of the pandemics of protest, racism, and disease raging all around.

This powerful book likewise emerges from those explosive months of massive protests in the middle of the pandemic. In the aftermath of this epoch-shaping moment, the editors convened scholars in Bible, theology, ethics, church history, education, homiletics, and practical theology to develop a thick theological consideration of the Black Lives Matter (BLM) movement and the racism that it resists. Now in the years after those momentous events, the contributors were writing in a period when the battle cry of "BLM!" was contending with the reactive declaration that "All Lives Matter." By then, they were fully aware of the fleeting nature of the expressions of solidarity and the promises to do better made in the heat of those extraordinary days. The backlash to progress in Black civil life, the obligatory backward leap taken for every two steps forward, was right on schedule following the extraordinary multiracial solidarity of the protests against police brutalization of Black men, women, and children and the legal police impunity that implies that Black lives don't matter.

These scholars are credentialed and educated by some of the finest institutions in the world. Some preach or teach at evangelical or evangelical-friendly institutions, while others represent the voices of their people in mainline, mainstream, or other predominantly White contexts. They represent a range of viewpoints across the landscape of Black religious thought. I may not know how they vote, but their essays fully exhibit their devotion to the God of the exodus, the Christ of the Jubilee, and the Spirit of Pentecost freedom.

The work I do in describing and exhibiting analogical reasoning would have been right at home among these scholars, many of whom I count as friends. Readers who want to see the Bible come alive through connections between the biblical narratives and the BLM movements will love reading about how African Americans have long connected their stories with the people of the exodus, protesting their conditions as enslaved people for as long as the United States has been a nation. In a different essay, we see the heteroglossia of Acts 2 associated with code-switching among contemporary Black prophets. Some readers will catch the analogy between the BLM movement and the great Old Testament prophets on the one hand and between the biblical description of false prophets and those performing the All Lives Matter backlash on the other. Others will be convicted as I was by a correspondence between evangelical disdain for civil rights protests and the Philippian merchants of Acts 16 who turned on Paul and Silas for threatening their profits and way of life. One essay describes bricolage, a penchant among bricklayers to use whatever is at hand to accomplish their goals, as a metaphor for the construction of White supremacy, before going on to problematize "notions of protest that situate inclusion as the primary aim," thus inadvertently accepting the dominance, exclusions, and erasures of the status quo.

Those who want to know how the Bible empowers Black bodies, Black words, and Black protest movements for liberation will also appreciate the second section of the book. These essays explore the power of Black art, the global reach of the Black church, a definition of White supremacy that centers theological reflection on human nature and anthropology, and an essay that likens attacks on Black speech like #SayHerName and #BLM with attacks on Black humanity. Another essay touches on how the prophetic speech of the BLM movement is triggering for those who have been formed by White supremacy.

The last section of sermons explores BLM protests with audiences in different contexts by exemplifying the analogical reasoning at home in so much Black preaching. The first sermon addresses mainline Protestants, exhorting them to engage people on the margins by reminding them that Jesus himself was a marginalized subject crushed by a brutal empire. In response, they should "embrace blackness and every single Black life." The second sermon in this section draws an analogy between Harriet Tubman and contemporary protesters. Just as Tubman believed in direct revelation and the power of dreams, visions, and signs, so too should contemporary protesters expand their understanding of God's presence while seeking liberty in a new context. A sermon to evangelicals has an explicit defense of BLM using Exodus 3:7–10, drawing a correspondence between BLM protestors and God's ability to empower Moses' speech. The section ends with a sermon on James 2 about the criminalization of blackness and poverty. This closing sermon sees an analogy between James, a no-nonsense, brutally honest preacher called by a God who hates bigotry, and the voices of modern Black prophets like James Baldwin, Malcolm X, Angela Davis, Cornel West, Michelle Alexander, and Ibram Kendi.

The church needs leaders prepared to lead Christians in deep reflection on the racism tearing our country apart. The church needs this book because these days demand it.

Love Lazarus Sechrest, PhD
Associate Provost and Professor of Theology
Mount St. Mary's University
Author of *Race and Rhyme: Rereading the New Testament*

Acknowledgments

THERE ARE A NUMBER of people to thank for the publication of this volume coming to fruition, especially in the midst of a global pandemic, which complicates life on so many levels. We are extremely grateful to all of the contributors who provided their time, expertise, and patience as we navigated the publication process. A special thank you to Dr. Love Sechrest for her powerful foreword. We are also grateful to Michael Thomson of Cascade Books, whose patience, insight, and expertise have been invaluable to bringing this book to completion. We are also thankful to Ken Bendickson, David King, and Jackson Reynolds, research assistants who helped with editing, proofreading, and formatting. In addition, we extend thanks to Stephanie Bowens for her proofreading expertise. And, finally, we say a special thank you to our families, whose love and support are always crucial to the work we do, but especially now in the age of multiple pandemics.

Lisa and Dennis

Contributors

Vince Bantu is assistant professor of church history and Black church studies, Fuller Theological Seminary.

Brian Bantum is Neal F. and Ila A. Fisher Professor of Theology, Garrett Evangelical Theological Seminary.

Lisa Bowens is associate professor of New Testament, Princeton Theological Seminary.

Marcia Clarke is adjunct faculty, Fuller Theological Seminary.

David Daniels III is professor of church history, McCormick Theological Seminary.

Antonia Michelle Daymond is adjunct faculty, McCormick Theological Seminary.

Dennis Edwards is dean and vice president for church relations, North Park Theological Seminary.

Danjuma Gibson is professor of pastoral care, Calvin Theological Seminary.

Antipas L. Harris is an independent scholar.

Y. Joy Harris-Smith is senior lecturer in communication and ministry, Princeton Theological Seminary.

Jamal-Dominique Hopkins is associate professor of Christian Scriptures, George W. Truett Theological Seminary.

Jennifer Kaalund is associate professor of New Testament, Pittsburgh Theological Seminary.

Valerie Landfair is adjunct faculty, McCormick Theological Seminary.

Donyelle McCray is associate professor of homiletics, Yale Divinity School.

Angela Parker is assistant professor of New Testament and Greek, McAfee School of Theology at Mercer University.

Luke Powery is dean of Duke University Chapel and associate professor of homiletics, Duke Divinity School.

Joseph Scrivner is dean of chapel at Stillman College and pastor of Brown Memorial Presbyterian Church (USA), Tuscaloosa, Alabama.

Efrem Smith is pastor of Midtown Church, Sacramento, California.

Jaime Waters is associate professor of Old Testament, Boston College School of Theology and Ministry

Reggie Williams is professor of Christian ethics, McCormick Theological Seminary.

Introduction

THE IDEA FOR THIS volume, *Do Black Lives Matter?: How Christian Scriptures Speak to Black Empowerment,* came about because of the murder of George Floyd, an unarmed black man, by police officers in Minneapolis, Minnesota, in May 2020. This murder occurred in the middle of a COVID-19 global pandemic and sparked ensuing protests in this country and around the world.[1] The images and sounds of George Floyd begging for air and calling for his dead mother while the white police officer, Derek Chauvin, nonchalantly pressed his knee upon Floyd's neck, ignoring Floyd's and bystanders' cries for help, are images and sounds seared into the minds, ears, and consciences of millions. Three other police officers participated in Floyd's murder and, at the time of this writing, are awaiting trial. Derek Chauvin received a guilty verdict and a prison sentence of twenty-two years. Floyd's murder occurred amidst other murders of unarmed black people: Ahmaud Arbery, Breonna Taylor, and Elijah McClain. In addition, the global pandemic of COVID-19 continues, and statistics reveal that this virus disproportionately affects black Americans due to existing racial disparities in the healthcare system.[2]

America's history informs us that in this nation black lives have often been considered expendable, insignificant, and criminal. This understanding of black people manifested in a plethora of ways historically and continues in the present, such as in mass incarceration, racial disparities

1. Protests occurred around the world in a number of countries, such as Germany, France, the United Kingdom, Tunisia, Australia, Brazil, Lebanon, and Chile, thereby indicating the global impact of Floyd's death upon millions.

2. For example, research indicates that blacks die from COVID at twice the rate than their white counterparts. https://www.brookings.edu/blog/up-front/2020/06/16/race-gaps-in-covid-19-deaths-are-even-bigger-than-they-appear/.

in education and healthcare, and racial profiling. As this volume goes to press, two significant events have greatly affected communities around the nation. First, a self-avowed white supremacist launched another attack on black lives. The recent mass killing of ten black people in a Buffalo, New York grocery store by a white teenager who wanted to incite a race war demonstrates that the ideology of white supremacy is still present in the nation—and not only present but fueling violent attacks upon African Americans. However, such attacks upon black Americans are not new. Indeed, since the founding of this country, white supremacist ideology provided the basis for viewing black lives as not as important as white lives. Samuel Miller, one of the first professors of Princeton Seminary and a leading theologian of his time, believed that equality between blacks and whites could never exist. African Americans could "never . . . associate with the whites on terms of equality . . . They will be treated and they will feel as inferiors."[3] Thomas Jefferson promoted a similar point of view, writing that blacks "are inferior to the whites in the endowments both of body and mind."[4] Historical documents indicate the prevalence of such views and present incidents, such as those discussed above, demonstrate that this history is still present with us and manifesting in deadly violence. After all, if black inferiority is upheld and ingrained in societal structures, killing and attacking black people is not deemed consequential. Thus, the rhetoric of and belief in white supremacy leads to dangerous realities for African Americans. Whether jogging down the street like Ahmaud Arbery, walking home like Elijah McClain, going to the grocery store like the Buffalo ten, sleeping in one's apartment like Breonna Taylor, or attending a Bible study like the Emanuel nine in Charleston in June 2015, black people are not safe.

The second significant event is the murder of Tyre Nichols, an unarmed black man, at the hands of black police officers in Memphis, Tennessee. Communities across the nation are wrestling with the reality that black police officers murdered "one of their own" for no apparent reason.[5] The violence of the officers' attack and their neglect to render

3. Samuel Miller, *A Sermon Preached at March 13th, 1808, For the Benefit of the Society Instituted In The City of New York, For The Relief Of Poor Widows With Small Children* (New York: Hopkins and Seymour, 1808), 13.

4. Thomas Jefferson, *Notes on the State of Virginia* (Philadelphia: Pritchard & Hall, 1787), 153.

5. At the time of this writing, leadership in the Memphis Police Department related that "an investigation found no evidence that Nichols had, in fact, been driving

aid to Nichols makes this case especially difficult to fathom. Were their actions about power and being powerful? Were their actions about an internalization of self-hatred? Has black life been deemed so inconsequential that some black officers believe that they too can participate in the narrative of black insignificance and get away with it? Or, were their actions born out of police culture and training? Is it all of the above and/or much more? Are there undercurrents to this tragedy not yet known or revealed? The relatively recent nature of this event means that conversations are ongoing and will continue for some time. Many people are still trying to process all that has transpired, especially as they anticipate difficult days ahead in the trials of those involved.

Remarkably, in the midst of such ongoing realities, African Americans have found Scripture an empowering source and resource to fight oppression, racism, and white supremacy. Throughout the centuries, numerous black activists utilized Scripture to claim and proclaim their humanity, their significance, and their equality. Against voices throughout the nation who wanted to de-emphasize black life and target black lives with violence, black Christians have called out those voices and used Scripture to denounce those acts. This volume highlights black resilience and the importance of Scripture to this resilience. It also forefronts the significance of Scripture to the black struggle for justice and brings together prominent and gifted black scholars in biblical studies, ethics, history, and theology, all of whom employ their expertise, their research, and their writings as tools for the struggle. Like those before them, such as David Walker, Maria Stewart, James Pennington, and Jarena Lee, these black scholars understand the crucial role that Scripture and writing about Scripture plays in the black protest tradition.

The volume consists of three sections: "Biblical Analyses of Blackness," "Theological Reflections and Expressions of Black Empowerment," and "Sermons on Blackness." This first section includes essays by black biblical scholars of the Old and New Testaments. In "Hearing Scripture as Protest and Resistance," Lisa Bowens provides a brief historical review of how some blacks, specifically Lemuel Haynes, Richard Allen, and Fannie Lou Hamer, utilized Scripture to protest racism and oppression in their contexts. Bowens argues for the importance of Scripture's voice for the voices of these black interpreters. Joseph Scrivner, in "Black Lives Matter:

---

recklessly before he was stopped." See https://www.npr.org/2023/02/17/115776023/memphis-tyre-nichols-police-officers-court-charges. All five of the officers have pled not guilty, however.

A Hermeneutics of Text and History," exegetes what a "biblically informed call for justice" looks like by examining the discussions of race and poverty after the March on Washington in 1963. Scrivner demonstrates the importance of such an examination to the current issue of police brutality. In "The Empire Will Fail: Paul's Vision for the Church Then and Now in Romans 8," Angela Parker employs a Womanist New Testament lens to Romans 8 and argues for the significance of familial imagery for solidarity across bodies in the midst of a failing empire that refuses to see the worth of black life. The theme of the body continues in Jennifer Kaalund's essay in "The Stories Our Bodies Tell: Black Bodies that Matter, Black Lives That Matter." Kaalund investigates the intrinsic value of the body to the discourse of mattering—specific bodies are deemed those that matter while others, like black bodies, are devalued and left out of the conversation. Kaalund discusses the liminal space that black bodies often inhabit and how they are frequently omitted in the discourse of whose bodies and lives matter. In the essay "Prophetic Tenacity," Jaime Waters explores the prophetic tenacity prevalent in Old Testament prophetic literature and how this tradition of prophetic tenacity "speaks to black empowerment initiatives of today," including initiatives that address economic injustice and the removal of Confederate monuments. Dennis R. Edwards, with "Protesting Police Brutality and Criminal Injustice with Paul and Silas," issues a clarion call for "Bible readers to resist the status quo" of police brutality. The actions of Paul and Silas in Acts 16:35–40 offer a model or analogue for our times as to what "challenging policing might mean." In the last essay of this section, "Biblical Accounts of Racial Profiling and the Social Death of Black Lives," Jamal-Dominique Hopkins reflects on the murder of Tyre Nichols as social death and examines racial profiling in the biblical text and contemporary contexts.

"Theological Reflections and Expressions of Black Empowerment" titles the second section of this volume and features scholars in theology, practical theology, ethics, and history. Danjuma Gibson, in "Black Lives Moved by the Bible: Moving from the Love of Power to the Power of Love," puts forth a black biblical imagination that resists the abuse of the Bible, an abuse that ends in destruction of black lives. Gibson provides a "practical theological reflection" on the internalization of black self-hate that derives from abuse of Scripture and offers a counter way of reading Scripture that can provide healing and redemption for black people.

In "Hagar's Lament: Affirming Black Lives Matter through Resilience, Interconnectivity, Spirituality, and Expectancy," Valerie Landfair reads Hagar's story in Genesis and Galatians through a Pentecostal Womanist lens with a view toward focusing on African American Pentecostal prayers. Landfair sees in Hagar's narrative a powerful trajectory that moves from despair to hope and analyzes the implications of this potent movement for the contemporary reader. Antonia Daymond, in "Toward a Theology of Revolutionary Protest," argues for the significance and relevance of Christian theology in taking on and dismantling systemic racism. Although the "merger of Enlightenment philosophy and Christianity" promoted white identity and imperialism, Daymond asserts that a deep look at the history of Christian theology, as demonstrated in the protest of the Protestant Reformation, can speak powerfully to present protest movements. The "art" of protest is the subject of "Black Bodies, Art, and Community," an essay by Brian Bantum, who investigates the importance of the arts and visuality to black protests historically and in the present moment. Bantum sees a dialogue taking place between the icon, black flesh, black life, and black art. This dialogue is black articulation promoting black life and the power of black life in the midst of a society where black destruction continually takes place.

Do we really know what white supremacy means and what such a view entails? In his contribution, "White Supremacy Is A Script We're Given at Birth," Reggie Williams argues that although the terms *xenophobia*, *prejudice*, and *white supremacy* are often used interchangeably, they are not the same. Williams defines white supremacy and explores its connection to anthropology—what does it mean to be human? Williams goes on to delineate the details of the script of white supremacy we receive at birth and how the script replays itself in various forms historically and in the present.

Y. Joy Harris, in "Communicating Culture: The Beauty in Black Speech," discusses the power and beauty of black discourse in songs, poems, and stories, as well as the ability of African American speech to give and create life, an ability that echoes God's creative speech in Genesis. The theme of black beauty continues in Vince Bantu's essay, "I Am Black and Beautiful: A Biblical Haymanot (Theology) of Blackness," in which he examines both Old and New Testament passages to argue that despite the way the ancient world may have "denigrated Black skin," God in Scripture portrays black skin and black people as beautiful. This affirmative portrayal of black people indicates that Scripture both condemns white supremacy and offers a valuable counternarrative to white supremacist beliefs.

Marcia Clarke explores the significance of Pentecostalism as a global movement in "Migration, Adaptability, and the Utilization of Media: Black Pentecostalism Goes Global," by using the Church of Pentecost (CoP) as an example of a black church that does not have its origin in Western Christianity. With membership of over three million people in over one hundred and twenty countries, the CoP contradicts the notion that the West is the Christian epicenter whose missionaries gave rise to Christianity in Africa. Rather, Clarke argues that the CoP is an example of black Christians as principal actors in Christianity without the West.

In the final essay in this section, "Black Protest Theology: Considering Bourdieu's *Habitus* Theory with A Comparative Analysis of Protest Approaches in the Civil Rights Movement and the Hip-Hop Generation," Antipas Harris utilizes Pierre Bourdieu's *Habitus* theory to demonstrate an "interplay of structures and experience" that bridges both the civil rights and hip-hop eras. Harris asserts that examining and outlining such an interplay may offer ways to foster collaboration between those who locate themselves in the civil rights movement and those who see themselves as belonging to the hip-hop world.

The reader will note that at the end of each essay, discussion questions follow. We anticipate the use of this book in Bible study groups, small groups, and Sunday school classes, as well as seminary and divinity school classrooms, and we hope that all of these constituencies find this volume useful and the questions generative for conversations around race, racism, white supremacy, and Christianity. The aim of these questions is to evoke deep thought and engagement with the authors' respective contributions.

This book ends with the section entitled "Sermons on Blackness" and includes four powerful sermons by four renowned preachers. In "Jesus and the Borders," Luke Powery declares that while borders and margins are often overlooked, the gospel calls us to attend to the margins, the borders, and their significance to God and our existence. Efrem Smith, in "Rise of the Liberating Church," proclaims a biblical foundation for God's care of black bodies and asserts that the cry "Black lives matter" aligns with the mission of the liberating God. Donyelle McCray's sermon, "Feast Day for Saint Harriet," asks the reader to consider bringing black people into our liturgical calendars as exemplars of the Hall of Faith as found in Hebrews 11. McCray also asks the reader to think about what it would mean to have a Feast Day for Saint Harriet and to reflect upon what Harriet's confidence in God can teach us about our own faith. In the final sermon in this unit, "A Decriminalizing Gospel and Empowering Maneuvers," David Daniels III asserts that Scripture speaks to the important issues raised by the Black Lives Matter movement. Daniels calls upon believers to be intentional about exegeting and preaching Scripture in a way that shows that the "gospel demands the decriminalization of black people" as well as the creation of a "society that values black bodies and lives."

In each of these essays and sermons, the reader will find affirmative answers to the query, "Do black lives matter?" Our hope is that this volume will provide glimpses into the black Christian tradition, a tradition rich in Scripture, ethics, history, and theology, which has always seen and heard a divine yes to this question.

Section One

Biblical Analysis of Blackness and Expressions of Black Empowerment

Hearing Scripture as Protest and Resistance[1]

LISA M. BOWENS

Introduction

AFRICAN AMERICAN BIBLICAL INTERPRETATION often utilizes protest and resistance hermeneutics. This essay will provide snapshots into the historical, biblical, and theological realities in which blacks found themselves and the ways in which they utilized Scripture to counter their oppressive contexts.[2] We will look briefly at three African American interpreters—Lemuel Haynes, Richard Allen, and Fannie Lou Hamer—all of whom engage in a protest and resistance hermeneutic.

Historical, Biblical, and Theological Nexus

As early as the 1700s, African Americans were utilizing Scripture to argue for their freedom from slavery and to assert their humanity in a

---

1. This essay appeared previously in *Word & World*, 41, Special Issue on Race (2021) 4–12. It appears here with permission. My thanks to *Word and World*. It has been revised for the present volume.

2. There is an enormous body of literature regarding African American biblical interpretation. Some important starting points are Blount, Felder, Martin, and Powery, eds., *True to Our Native Land*; Bowens, *African American Readings of Paul*; Braxton, *No Longer Slaves*; Callahan, *Talking Book*); Edwards, *Might From the Margins*; Felder, ed., *Stony the Road We Trod*; McCaulley, *Reading While Black*; Powery and Sadler, *Genesis of Liberation*); Weems, *Just a Sister Away*.

society that declared blacks nonhuman. Historical documents, such as narratives of the enslaved and texts written by proslavery writers, relate how Scripture was often used to justify the mistaken belief in black inferiority and blacks as less than human. For instance, white preachers often used Genesis 9:18–27, the Ham narrative, to proclaim to the enslaved that God created them to be slaves, inferior to whites, and that in order for them to experience salvation, they had to obey the slave owner. Peter Randolph, a formerly enslaved African who absconded and became a preacher, described those times for the enslaved: "The gospel was so mixed with slavery, that the people could see no beauty in it, and feel no reverence for it."[3] In addition, white ministers utilized the Pauline texts of Ephesians 6:5 and Colossians 3:22 to justify their erroneous notions of black subservience. The role of Scripture, in the slavery debate and in the repeated declarations of whites regarding their supposed divinely ordered supremacy to blacks, cannot be overestimated. Such notions were prevalent realities in newspapers (the social media of the day), in churches, and in the nation's laws, which codified such beliefs. For example, in 1787, the Constitution stated that a black person was three-fifths of a human being. In 1857, the Supreme Court's decision in the Dred Scott case further espoused this erroneous view, stating that blacks, whether enslaved or free, were not and could not be citizens of the United States. They were property void of rights in federal court. In the landmark 1896 *Plessy v. Ferguson* case, the US Supreme Court upheld the constitutionality of racial segregation under the "separate but equal" doctrine.

Views of blacks as nonhuman, inferior, and devoid of citizenship rights were not limited to the South but occurred throughout the nation. These views included stereotypes of blacks as dangerous. One illustration of this occurs in discussions of Kansas's new state constitution, in which residents in the Kansas territory opposed having free African Americans within their state "because they were 'terribly frightened at the idea of being overrun by negroes. They hold to the idea that negroes are *dangerous* to the State and a nuisance, and measures have to be taken to prevent them from migrating to the territory.'"[4] Many whites saw blacks as dangerous and therefore sought to control and limit blacks' movement.

Coupled with this notion of blacks as dangerous was the idea of blacks as criminals. This belief led to the idea that whites needed to

3. Randolph, "Plantation Churches," 64.

4. Berwanger, "Negrophobia in Northern Proslavery and Antislavery Thought," 271 (emphasis added).

surveil blacks, so the implementation of "patrols" became central to monitoring blacks' movement as they traveled from one place to another. When stopped by such "patrols," African Americans had to present written documentation from whites that gave them permission to travel. Furthermore, African Americans were denied political involvement. After all, if one is deemed nonhuman, dangerous, and not even a citizen, then of course participation in the political process is considered nonsensical. Eugene Berwanger writes that even as late as 1860, the *Illinois State Register* did not support African Americans' involvement in the political process, stating, "Negroes have no voice whatever in [this nation's] political affairs . . . They are an inferior race, and must remain so, politically forever."[5] Blacks, then, experienced dehumanization through scriptural interpretation, laws, denial of citizenship, stereotypes, patrol surveillance, and explicit rejection of their participation in politics. What, then, did African Americans have to say to these things?

In reading essays, sermons, autobiographies, and conversion narratives of enslaved and free African Americans, black hermeneuts had quite a lot to say to these things. They protested and resisted every aspect of this dehumanization and believed Scripture to be central to their protest and resistance. For these African Americans, Scripture was sacred, and this sacredness meant that the justice and liberation called for in Scripture was just as sacred. For a "Christian" nation to deny justice and liberation to those who inhabited its borders was egregious, transgressing the faith it claimed to embrace. So, how did these interpreters go about the task of scriptural protest and resistance to white supremacy? African American interpreters are not monolithic in the way they interpret Scripture, so there is no one way or method that characterizes all black scriptural interpretation. Yet, the following brief analysis will provide some insight into how three African American interpreters—Lemuel Haynes, Richard Allen, and Fannie Lou Hamer—used Scripture to protest the racial injustice happening in their contexts.

Lemuel Haynes

African Americans asserted their humanity and refused to believe that they were inferior to whites or that God destined them for slavery. Around

5. (Springfield Illinois State Register, September 28, 1860.) Quoted in Berwanger, "Negrophobia," 272.

1776, Lemuel Haynes, an early African American pastor and preacher, in an essay titled "Liberty Further Extended," decried those who tried to justify their participation in the slave trade by stating that when they buy African Americans from merchants, they are not told whether or not they have been stolen. Haynes proclaims, why should having this information matter? He writes, "If I buy a man, whether I am told he was stole, or not, yet I have no right to Enslave him, Because he is a human Being: and the immutable Laws of God, and indefeasible Laws of nature, pronounced him free."[6] Haynes appeals to the unchangeable nature of God found in Scripture to argue that African Americans are human beings, and therefore, no one should deny their creation as free human beings by enslaving them. In an earlier part of the essay, Haynes writes, "Liberty is a Jewel which was handed Down to man from the cabinet of heaven, and is Coaeval with his Existence. And as it proceed from the Supreme Legislature of the univers, so it is he which hath a sole right to take away; therefore, he that would take away a mans Liberty assumes a prerogative that Belongs to another . . ."[7] In such statements, Haynes protests whites' beliefs that they have the right to declare another human being inferior or to assert their own superiority. Because liberty and humanity originate from God, no human being has the right to rescind either. For Haynes, those who deny the liberty of African Americans presume a role that belongs only to God. The "Supreme Legislature" overrules a nation's laws and practices when the nation blatantly goes against divine decrees.

Haynes also protests such actions by pronouncing judgment upon America, and he utilizes Scripture, specifically Judges and Revelation, to indicate that such judgment would align with God's character. After citing the examples of Adoni-bezek, Ahab, Jezebel, the prophet Elijah's pronouncement upon the latter two, and the judgment that occurs in Revelation, Haynes takes up a prophetic office like that of Elijah, declaring, "I say this is often God's way of Dealing, by retaliating Back upon men the Same Evils that they unjustly Bring upon others."[8] Here, Haynes takes up a prophetic stance to the rest of the nation, boldly declaring that if it does not cease its involvement with the practice of oppressing black minds and bodies, the nation would suffer dangerous consequences. For

6. Haynes, "Liberty Further Extended," 23.

7. Haynes, "Liberty Further Extended," 18. I have chosen to keep the author's original spelling and wording in this quote and in all quotes to follow from all remaining authors.

8. Haynes, "Liberty Further Extended," 28.

Haynes, such judgment would be just because, as he stated earlier, whites put themselves in the place of God in their treatment of their black sisters and brothers, since they presume to be the arbiters of what comes only from the Divine.

Richard Allen

Richard Allen, founder and bishop of the African Methodist Episcopal denomination in 1794, compared blacks' enslavement to that of Israel, writing to slaveholders, "I do not wish to make you angry, but excite attention to consider how hateful slavery is, in the sight of that God who hath destroyed kings and princes, for their oppression of the poor slaves . . . Men must be wilfully blind, and extremely partial, that cannot see the contrary effects of liberty and slavery upon the mind of man . . . We wish you to consider, that God himself was the first pleader of the cause of slaves."[9] Like Haynes, Allen pronounces that God works on the side of the oppressed; those suffering enslavement are those for whom God fights. This depiction of African Americans as enslaved Israelites is a frequent one in black protest literature of this period, in which blacks see America as Egypt, not the promised land, which is the way whites often described it.[10] Consequently, Allen's use of Scripture at this point to counter the white ideal of America as a promised land is an important one for a number of reasons: 1) it foregrounds the suffering taking place within the nation and refuses to ignore it; 2) it counters the nation's perception of itself as a land of liberty and freedom when all within its borders were not free; 3) it centers the God of Scripture as the One who advocates liberty, not enslavement, a view that we have seen defies that of slaveholders and their ministers; 4) it refuses to relegate Scripture as sanctioning the notions of blacks as nonhuman, inferior, and subservient, and 5) it links blacks' identity with scriptural history in a way that deems them important and significant to the divine realm.

Once slavery ended, views of black inferiority and black subservience persisted. Jacquelyn Grant writes of the predicament of African Americans after the Civil War and Reconstruction periods: "The end of slavery as a formal, legal institution brought neither change in the image

---

9. Allen, *Life, Experience, and Gospel Labours*, 45–46.

10. For the classic treatment of this dichotomy, see Raboteau, *Fire in the Bones*, 17–36; 57–76.

of, nor significant change in the condition of Black people in the United States. The image that Blacks were inferior and that they were intended to service white America remained intact. Consequently, when freed blacks, sought work they were relegated in the labor market to the same service jobs and menial work which had been forced upon them during slavery."[11] If we fast-forward to the 1960s, we encounter the persistence of racial inequality pointed out by Grant and the continual existential crisis faced by African Americans. Yet, we also encounter blacks' sustained use of Scripture to protest and resist racial inequality.

Fannie Lou Hamer

In her essay "Sick and Tired of Being Sick and Tired," Fannie Lou Hamer, civil rights activist, writes of her struggles due to her participation in voting rights in Mississippi in the 1960s. "I have been brutally beaten and permanently injured by white men while I was in jail for no other crime than trying to get citizens of Mississippi to register and vote. But I do not say that every white man in the country would do the same thing to me that a handful of white men did in Mississippi . . . But we have a question to raise to America today, because America must wake up and learn the truth about itself and racism . . ."[12] Hamer details what racism looks like up close for her, her family, and all those who dare to fight against the white supremacy machine. She experiences terrorism at the hands of the KKK as well as threats to her life, and the loss of her job and home because of her involvement in voting rights. After detailing the trials and tribulations of those like her who pursue racial justice, she turns to churches. "Just as it's time for America to wake up, it is long *past* time for the churches to wake up. The churches have got to say that they will have no more talk that 'because your skin is a little different, you're better than they are.'"[13] For Hamer, it is time for churches across America to recognize their complicity in the racist structures of the country and to refuse to be a part of it anymore. The color of one's skin does not make one person better than another. For churches to sit idly by and do nothing while African Americans suffer is what she calls hypocritical, for they betray the very gospel they profess. Hamer goes on to say:

11. Grant, *White Women's Christ and Black Women's Jesus*, 197.
12. Hamer, "Sick and Tired," 171.
13. Hamer, "Sick and Tired," 179.

We have to realize just how grave the problem is in the United States today, and I think the 6th chapter of Ephesians, the 11th and 12th verses, helps us to know how grave the problem is, and what it is we are up against. It says, "Put on the whole armor of God, that ye may be able to stand against the wiles of the devil. For we wrestle not against flesh and blood, but against principalities, against powers, against the rulers of the darkness of this world, against spiritual wickedness in high places." This is what I think about when I think of my own work in the fight for freedom . . . So we are faced with a problem that is not flesh and blood, but we are facing principalities, and powers and spiritual wickedness in high places: that's what St. Paul told us. And that's what he meant. America created this problem . . . But we're looking for this check now, that's long past due, to let us have our share in political and economic power, so that we can have a great country, together.[14]

Hamer characterizes the entrenched powers of injustice, oppression, and racism as the presence of spiritual powers and wickedness. Racist inequality is so grave that it has supernatural elements to it; indeed, cosmic entanglements. Such characterizations mean that fighting racism is a spiritual war and an ongoing struggle against which human beings need God's help to protest and resist. For Hamer, however, such characterization does not let America off the hook, for "America created this problem." And in order for America to get rid of the problem, the nation and its churches need to recognize the demonic source of racism and oppression and fight it. Part of that fight involves recognizing African Americans' equality in every area, including making sure they have equal access to politics and economics, arenas denied to them since the country's founding. The exorcism required, then, involves restoring to African Americans what racial inequality stole from them.

Hamer, following in the footsteps of Richard Allen, who critiques America by comparing it to Egypt, protests America by demanding it "learn the truth about itself and racism." In order for America to rectify the race issue, it must be honest about its racism and face it head-on. This reckoning with its past is also part of the nation's exorcistic process. Only then can America truly be what it can and should be—one unified nation. She prophetically writes, "A nation that's divided is definitely on the way out. We have the same problems from coast to coast. The future for black

14. Hamer, "Sick and Tired," 180.

people in America is the same as the future for white people in America. Our chances are the same. If you survive, we will too. If we crumble, you are going to crumble too."[15] For Hamer, all rise or fall together, for the destinies of everyone are interwoven.

Some Implications for Moving Forward

Racism "is the combination of racial privilege, prejudice, plus power. Racism requires that one racial group possesses the power to impose its racial prejudices on another group; it can make the other racial group be treated as inferior."[16] This brief foray into the use of Scripture by three African Americans to protest racial injustice provides some insight into the ways in which Scripture empowered these interpreters to resist racism in all of its forms. Their use of Scripture also sheds light into the ongoing struggle with racism in the nation today. First, these interpreters believed that the nation had to face its racist history and not try to cover it up, gloss over it, and/or pretend it was not that bad, for historical documents and evidence prove otherwise. These documents also demonstrate the centrality of Scripture in justifying racist practices, laws, and behavior. To deny this history or to sugarcoat it is to deny opportunity for real progress and change to happen. James Baldwin once said, "Not everything faced can be changed but nothing can be changed unless it is faced."[17] As believers, our Scripture is filled with times in which God confronted individual people and nations regarding their sin. Such confrontations were opportunities for repentance, not just in belief but in actions. The interpreters discussed above called out America and demanded a change in its behavior and actions.

Second, and relatedly, these interpreters call upon the *nation* to change. Too many times, racism is seen as an individual problem or the problem of a few (if it is recognized at all), but these interpreters recognized that racial inequality was not just about a few bad apples; it was systemic and needed addressing in a wholistic manner. As Haynes declares, the entire nation will be held accountable for its actions. Such

---

15. Hamer, "Sick and Tired," 182.

16. Daniels, "Transcending the Exclusionary Ecclesial Practices of Racial Hierarchies of Authority," 139.

17. This quote comes from James Baldwin's unfinished manuscript, *Remember This House.*

declarations counter the individualistic notions prevalent in American society in his day and ours, a society that often opts for individuality over corporate identity. These interpreters lift up that the corporate is just as important as the individual and cannot be ignored. As Hamer related, we rise and fall together.

Third, Hamer speaks of the spiritual wickedness of racial injustice and how evil powers play a role in fomenting injustice. Forces of evil do not relinquish easily. Thus, to see racial inequality in this light is important because to fight this battle requires divine assistance, godly ingenuity, and divine strategies. When one thinks about the civil rights movement of the twentieth century, this movement was innovative in introducing protest strategies that the nation had not seen before. Recognition of the spiritual element to justice work is significant because one needs spiritual insight as to what type of strategies work for the twenty-first century, strategies that include the old methods but build upon them for the present struggle. Believers, through the power of the Holy Spirit, have what they need to overcome the principalities and powers of this world and can partner with God in concrete actions that bring forth justice to the earth.

Concluding Thoughts

For too long black lives have been deemed less valuable than other lives; the vestiges of the nation's past linger in societal behavior, structures, and laws. Although God so loved the world (John 3:16), history shows that the church has too often refused to see black people as part of the world that God loves. The phrase "All lives matter" as a retort to "Black lives matter" misconstrues the issue. When we look back historically, blacks have had to fight repeatedly to be included in the "all." When the founders of this country wrote the phrase "All men are created equal," this did not include black men because these writers deemed the black person three-fifths of a human being. Blacks were excluded. When the phrase "liberty and justice for all" became part of the American discourse, that ideal did not apply to black people because they did not have freedom and equality. Blacks were excluded. Historical evidence belies the claim that "all lives matter." Again, blacks have had to fight repeatedly to be included in the "all."

Consequently, to claim "black lives matter" does not mean that other lives do not matter. In the 1960s, black men carried signs as they protested that said, "I Am A Man." This assertion did not mean that men of other races were not men, but black men needed to assert their humanity in a country that continually denied them that. When black people yelled in the 1960s and 1970s that "Black is beautiful," this did not mean that other people were not beautiful. Blacks had to assert their own beauty and worth, because for centuries they were told that black is ugly, inferior, and insignificant. The assertion that black lives matter is another chapter in the enduring black struggle to affirm the significance of black life. So, while it is true that all lives matter, for centuries blacks were never included in the "all," and this is so even now, for if all lives truly mattered, George Floyd, Ahmaud Arbery, Breonna Taylor, Manuel Ellis, Eric Garner, Sean Bell, Sandra Bland, Trayvon Martin, and countless others would still be alive. Until this reality changes, the phrase "All lives matter" will just be a pithy phrase echoed by those who neither understand the history of this country nor the depth of the historical trauma and pain systematically inflicted upon their black sisters and brothers, including the anguish bestowed with the word "all."

Before the year 2020 began, some proclaimed that 2020 would be the year of 20/20 (or perfect) vision. For many, the murder of George Floyd opened their eyes to the existence of systemic racism, the continued presence of white supremacy, and the daily reality of police brutality that African Americans face. Seeing a human being call for his dead mother and beg to be allowed to breathe and then denied that most basic human right given to all human beings since Genesis 2:7 caused many to lament and cry out for justice.

May God's Spirit breathe upon the church afresh as we live and move in this next decade of the twenty-first century, and may we continue to hear Scripture's call to protest and resist the death-dealing powers of racism and white supremacy. The African American interpreters who lived before us, from the 1700s onward, who echoed Scripture's voice not to neglect justice (Luke 11:42) but to *do* justice, and to love kindness, and to walk humbly with our God (Micah 6:8), beckon us to continue to join our voices with theirs. The vision of hope of our forebearers resounds in the words of Hamer: "I do have faith, as bad as the situation is now, for faith is the substance of things hoped for and evidence of things not seen."[18]

18. Hamer, "Sick and Tired," 171.

Discussion Questions

1. Were any of these interpreters new to you? If so, who and what did you learn about them? If not, did this essay affirm what you already knew about them, or did you learn something new about someone you had already heard of before?

2. How do these interpreters utilize Scripture to protest racism?

3. What are some similarities and differences between these interpreters and their use of Scripture?

4. Why are these figures important to know for understanding American history, and why is it important to learn about the significance of Scripture for the struggle against injustice?

Works Cited

Allen, Richard. *The Life, Experience, and Gospel Labours of the Rt. Rev. Richard Allen. To Which is Annexed the Rise and Progress of the African Methodist Episcopal Church in the United States of America. Containing a Narrative of the Yellow Fever in the Year of Our Lord 1793: With an Address to the People of Colour in the United States: Electronic Edition*, 45–46. Documenting the American South, University of North Carolina at Chapel Hill Digitization Project. https://docsouth.unc.edu/neh/allen/allen.html.

Baldwin, James. *Remember This House.* Unfinished manuscript, 1987.

Berwanger, Eugene H. "Negrophobia in Northern Proslavery and Antislavery Thought." *Phylon* 33, no. 3 (Fall 1972) 266–75.

Blount, Brian, Cain Hope Felder, Clarice J. Martin, and Emerson Powery, eds. *True to Our Native Land: An African American New Testament Commentary.* Minneapolis: Fortress, 2007.

Bowens, Lisa. *African American Readings of Paul: Reception, Resistance, and Transformation.* Grand Rapids: Eerdmans, 2020.

Braxton, Brad. *No Longer Slaves: Galatians and African American Experience.* Collegeville, MN: Liturgical, 2002.

Callahan, Allen Dwight. *The Talking Book: African Americans and the Bible.* New Haven: Yale University Press, 2006.

Daniels, David D. "Transcending the Exclusionary Ecclesial Practices of Racial Hierarchies of Authority: An Early Pentecostal Trajectory." In *Ecclesiology and Exclusion: Boundaries of Being and Belonging in Postmodern Times*, edited by Dennis Doyle, Timothy Furry, and Pascal Bazzell, 137–54. New York: Orbis, 2012.

Edwards, Dennis R. *Might From the Margins: The Gospel's Power to Turn the Tables on Injustice.* Harrisonburg, VA: Herald, 2020.

Felder, Cain Hope, ed. *Stony the Road We Trod: African American Biblical Interpretation.* Minneapolis: Fortress, 1991.

Grant, Jacquelyn. *White Women's Christ and Black Women's Jesus: Feminist Christology and Womanist Response*. Atlanta: Scholars, 1989.

Hamer, Fannie Lou. "Sick and Tired of Being Sick and Tired." In *Can I Get A Witness? Prophetic Religious Voices of African American Women An Anthology*, edited by Marcia Riggs, 170–81. New York: Orbis, 1997.

Haynes, Lemuel. "Liberty Further Extended: Or Free thoughts on the illegality of Slave-keeping; Wherein those arguments that Are useed [*sic*] in its vindication Are plainly confuted. Together with an humble Address to such as are Concearned in the practise." In *Black Preacher to White America: The Collected Writings of Lemuel Haynes, 1774–1833*, edited by Richard Newman, 17–30. Brooklyn: Carlson, 1990.

McCaulley, Esau. *Reading While Black: African American Biblical Interpretation As An Exercise in Hope*. Downers Grove, IL: IVP Academic, 2020.

Powery, Emerson, and Rodney Sadler. *The Genesis of Liberation: Biblical Interpretation in the Antebellum Narratives of the Enslaved*. Louisville: Westminster John Knox, 2016.

Raboteau, Albert. *A Fire in the Bones: Reflections on African-American Religious History*. Boston: Beacon, 1995.

Randolph, Peter. "Plantation Churches: Visible and Invisible." In *Slave Cabin to the Pulpit, The Autobiography of Reverend Peter Randolph: The Southern Question Illustrated and Sketches of Slave Life*. Boston: James H. Earle, 1893. Reprinted in *African American Religious History: A Documentary Witness*, edited by Milton Sernett, 63–68. Durham, NC: Duke University Press, 1999.

Weems, Renita. *Just a Sister Away: A Womanist Vision of Women's Relationships in the Bible*. San Diego: LuraMedia, 1988.

Black Lives Matter

A Hermeneutics of Text and History

Joseph F. Scrivner

To be a Negro in this country and to be relatively conscious is to be in
a state of rage almost, almost all of the time—and in one's work. And
part of the rage is this: It isn't only what is happening to you. But it's
what's happening all around you and all of the time in the face of the
most extraordinary and criminal indifference, indifference of most
white people in this country, and their ignorance. Now, since this is
so, it's a great temptation to simplify the issues under the illusion that
if you simplify them enough, people will recognize them. I think this
illusion is very dangerous because, in fact, it isn't the way it works. A
complex thing can't be made simple. You simply have to try to deal
with it in all its complexity and hope to get that complexity across.[1]

—JAMES BALDWIN

JAMES BALDWIN'S QUOTE IS an appropriate point of departure for a reflection on the Bible and the claim, "Black Lives Matter!" First, the Baldwin
quote begins with rage against racial injustice. This certainly corresponds

1. Baldwin et al., "Negro in American Culture," 205–24. The final two sentences
about complexity are edited out of this transcript, but the audio can be heard here:
www.youtube.com/watch?v=jNpitdJSXWY.

to what is intended when one exclaims, "Black Lives Matter!" It is infuriating that it has to be said in response to another heartbreaking murder and to incessant indifference about it. The first section of this essay will address this aspect, contending that it is obvious that an interpretation of the Bible rooted in the Golden Rule supports "Black Lives Matter!"

Second, the other half of Baldwin's quote indicates the way that rage can short-circuit a thorough analysis. Rage can lead to a mistaken simplicity. Yet, the issues are complex, and one cannot shrink back from this complexity. This will be the focus of the second section. Specifically, I will detail how race and poverty were discussed by key civil rights leaders and government officials after the March on Washington in 1963. In my judgment, this is crucial for at least three reasons: (a) these historical details are rarely presented; (b) this historical period repeats and reinforces how racial stigma functions to avoid aggressive action on poverty and unemployment; and (c) how one interprets this period will predict how one understands the larger context in which police brutality takes place. I contend that police killings are one component of a much larger set of issues that our government has failed to address since the mid-1960s. Emphasizing this failure regarding black life for nearly sixty years is required by a biblically informed call for justice.

A Hermeneutics of Text

The social media hashtag #BlackLivesMatter was created by Alicia Garza, Patrisse Cullors, and Opal Tometi after the acquittal of Trayvon Martin's murderer, George Zimmerman, on July 13, 2013.[2] It is a protest against the unjust killing of black Americans at the hands of vigilantes or police. In 2014, this hashtag expanded beyond social media and became a persistent protest slogan as black Americans were repeatedly killed by police or died while in police custody. Tragically, many of these victims have become household names: Eric Garner, Michael Brown, Tanisha Anderson, Tamir Rice, Walter Scott, Sandra Bland, Philando Castile, Terrence Crutcher, Atatiana Jefferson, Breonna Taylor, and George Floyd. To the degree these deaths indicate a devaluing of black life, people understandably protested, "Black Lives Matter!"

Building on the resonances of the protest movement, Garza, Cullors, and Tometi founded a nonprofit organization, Black Lives Matter

2. www.blacklivesmatter.com.

Global Network, Inc.[3] It is decentralized with a reported forty chapters in the United States, Canada, and the United Kingdom. In 2015, Black Lives Matter leaders met with other organizations focused on racial justice. This meeting resulted in the formation of a distinct advocacy organization titled "Movement for Black Lives" (MFBL), which issued a policy platform under the heading "A Vision for Black Lives." A long list of policy positions includes abolition of prisons, an end to the death penalty, ending cash bail, demilitarization of police, ending the War on Drugs, and an affirmation of trans, intersex, queer, and gender noncon-forming (LBGTQ+) people.[4]

For many Christians, the affirmation of human worth conveyed by "Black Lives Matter" corresponds to what the Bible affirms about human dignity and worth. The Bible begins with the proclamation that God created humanity "in the image of God" (Gen 1:27). One psalmist also teaches that humans are made "a little lower than God" (Ps 8:5). Another exclaims that humanity is "fearfully and wonderfully made" (Ps 139:14). In addition, the biblical law is clear that God requires protection of the vulnerable. The Mosaic code prohibits oppression of the resident alien, the orphan, and the widow (Exod 22:21–24; Deut 27:19). It also com-mands the Golden Rule (Lev 19:18).

The prophets repeatedly convey the stern message that God rejects worship when injustice is rampant. This is the context of Amos's oracles to Israel: "I hate, I despise your festivals, and I take no delight in your solemn assemblies" (Amos 5:21). The reason for this rejection is made clear a few lines later: "Take away from me the noise of your songs; I will not listen to the melody of your harps. But let justice roll down like waters, and righteousness like an ever-flowing stream" (5:23–24). One finds the same point in Isaiah: "Look, you serve your own interests on your fast day, and oppress all your workers" (Isa 58:3). "Is not this the fast that I choose: to loose the bonds of injustice, to undo the thongs of the yoke, to let the oppressed go free, and to break every yoke?" (58:6). These and many other prophetic proclamations are nicely summarized in the famous verse from Micah: "He has told you, O mortal, what is good; and what does the Lord require of you but to do justice, and to love kindness, and to walk humbly with your God?" (Mic 6:8).

---

3. *Encyclopedia Britannica*, "Black Lives Matter."
4. www.m4bl.org.

The emphasis on justice in Scripture continues with Jesus and the writers of the NT. In fact, Jesus quotes Isaiah 61 in Luke 4, where Jesus is presented as standing in the synagogue proclaiming that he has come "to bring good news to the poor" and "to let the oppressed go free" (Luke 4:18). Similarly, Jesus exalts the importance of society's most vulnerable in Matthew's Gospel, going so far as to identify himself with them: "Truly, I tell you, just as you did it to one of the least of these who are members of my family, you did it to me" (Matt 25:40). Moreover, Jesus repeatedly interprets the Scriptures to make the point that God gave them to show that God is most concerned about human well-being (Mark 2:23–28; 3:1–6; Luke 14:1–6). Jesus' condemnation of injustice and his affirmation of compassion are clear and unequivocal, summarized in the Golden Rule (Matt 7:12) and in his teaching about the two greatest commandments (Matt 22:35–40; Mark 12:28–34; Luke 10:27). The epistles emphasize the Golden Rule within the body of Christ (Gal 6:7–10; Rom 13:8–10). The writer of James is more explicit, condemning favoritism toward the rich (Jas 2:1–13), inaction in response to a human need (2:14–26), and the oppression of the poor by the rich (5:1–6).

Accordingly, when one sees the biblical theme of justice, the history of racism in the US, and the disproportionate killing of black Americans by police, it should be uncontroversial to assert that the Bible supports the claim, "Black Lives Matter!"[5] Again, the statement simply affirms black worth, black dignity, and black humanity. When protestors proclaim this statement, they are saying: "I matter!" "My children matter!" "My spouse matters!" "You cannot kill us with impunity!" "You cannot kill us and not face justice!" "You cannot shoot us and discard us!" "We are black!" "Our lives matter!" "Black Lives Matter!"[6]

---

5. This recent debate about the Bible and Black Lives Matter follows a tragic trajectory in which far too many white Christians read the Bible to protect their socioeconomic position in relation to blacks and others. Black Christians have developed a distinctive hermeneutical tradition as an appropriate response. The literature is extensive. See, for example, the following and the literature cited there: Scrivner, "African American Interpretation"; Junior, *Introduction to Womanist Biblical Interpretation*; Smith, ed., *I Found God in Me*; Gafney, *Womanist Midrash*; Edwards, *What Is the Bible and How Do We Understand It?*; Bowens, *African American Readings of Paul*; McCaulley, *Reading While Black*.

6. On the disproportionate killing of blacks by police, see the police shooting database developed by the *Washington Post*, www.washingtonpost.com. Police killings disproportionately affect blacks and Latinos. But it is also an issue more generally. See McWhorter, "Police Kill Too Many People—White and Black."

Now, if someone wants to debate the particular views of the founders of the organization, their public statements, or the policy positions advocated by MFBL, they have every right to do so. But it must be immediately said in response that none of these issues are directly related to the claim "Black Lives Matter!" I can affirm and repeat that claim without any connection to or affirmation of any position by anyone on this or that topic. Indeed, the affirmation of "Black Lives Matter" puts no one under any burden to affirm or deny anything other than the worth and dignity of black life.

Furthermore, any attempt to create such a burden demonstrates a lack of genuine concern for the death of black life under protest. Such attempts are distractions, and they have a long, ugly history in response to black activism for freedom and equality. Most famously, during the civil rights movement, many opponents of the movement tried to smear the Rev. Dr. Martin Luther King, Jr. with the charge of Communism.[7] This was an attempt to discredit him and the movement instead of dealing with the righteous protest for justice he and others represented.

As it was then, so it is now—making charges about Marxism and debating human sexuality are not germane to the simple question of whether one agrees that black life is devalued when black Americans are killed unjustly by police.[8] The Christian call to solidarity in suffering should be overwhelmingly prioritized over any disagreements Christians may have about a plethora of contemporary issues. Unfortunately, this indifference to the real issues at stake takes us back to Baldwin's quote and how these modern strategies of avoidance were shaped in the mid-1960s.

A Hermeneutics of History

The employment of skin pigmentation as a rationalization for economic profit began shortly after Europeans transported Africans across the Atlantic. Over the next three hundred years, they were exchanged and exploited for financial gain.[9] Such exploitation had always existed in human

7. Garrow, "FBI and Martin Luther King."

8. Corley, "Black Lives Matter Fights Disinformation to Keep the Movement Strong."

9. The justly famous *1619 Project* published by *The New York Times* emphasizes 1619 because it was the year Africans arrived in the first British colony of Jamestown in Virginia. The project was published in 2019 for the four hundreth anniversary. Yet, Europeans brought Africans to North America at various points before 1619. For

history, but the use of skin color as a justification was relatively new.[10] It arose in the seventeenth to nineteenth centuries to resolve the contradiction between white-skinned espousal of liberty and equality, on the one hand, and withholding the extension of those ideals to the black-skinned slave, on the other.[11] Slowly but surely, the slave trade became interwoven into American life.[12]

After slavery's abolition, the era of Reconstruction promised equality for black citizens. But this era was short-lived, and its gains quickly and severely limited.[13] Accordingly, the stigma of black skin continued into the twentieth century. This stigmatization was policed and reinforced with violence.[14] In the South, legal segregation, debt peonage, and racial terrorism marked the next half-century.[15] This racial terrorism included more than four thousand lynchings and the unconscionable use of bombs.[16] In the North, blacks were locked into pockets of concentrated poverty, and their lives threatened for venturing into restricted white spaces.[17] Then, when those conditions conspired to create an increase in crime among dispirited residents, black perpetrators were viewed as inherently violent because of their race. Meanwhile, comparable violence among white immigrants was seen as a product of an impoverished environment, not as something conveyed by skin color.[18]

---

instance, the Spanish imported Africans to Florida in 1565, and perhaps earlier. Accordingly, I count three centuries from 1565 to the end of slavery in 1865. See Gausco, "Misguided Focus on 1619"; Ellis, "Forget What You Know about 1619."

10. On the development of proto-racism in the ancient Greco-Roman world as a precursor to modern racism, see Isaac, *Invention of Racism in Classical Antiquity.*

11. Fields, "Slavery, Race, and Ideology in the United States of America," reprinted in Fields and Fields, *Racecraft,* 111–48.

12. Rothman, "Deep Cruelty of the U.S. Traders of Enslaved People Didn't Bother Most Americans"; see also Rothman, *Ledger and the Chain.*

13. DuBois, *Black Reconstruction in America*; Foner, *Reconstruction*; Foner, *Second Founding.*

14. Maxouris, "100 Years Ago, White Mobs Across the Country Attacked Black People." See also Krugler, *1919, The Year of Racial Violence.*

15. Blackmon, *Slavery by Another Name.*

16. See Stevenson et al., "Lynching in America: Confronting the Legacy of Racial Terror," a report by the Equal Justice Initiative. See also Dray, *At the Hands of Persons Unknown.* On bombings, see, for example, Gray, "Bombingham."

17. Purnell and Theoharis, eds., with Woodard, *Strange Careers of the Jim Crow North*; Sugrue, *Origins of the Urban Crisis.*

18. Muhammad, *Condemnation of Blackness.*

To undo the legal framework for this racial caste system, it would take ten years of nonviolent protests by the activists in the civil rights movement. These protests were often met with a vast array of violent attacks.[19] Nevertheless, the civil rights movement achieved the passage of three historic laws: the Civil Rights Act of 1964, the Voting Rights Act of 1965, and the Civil Rights Act of 1968. This was the end of *de jure* segregation. Yet, many civil rights leaders realized that these laws were just the beginning of what was needed to address three centuries of slavery and a century of *de jure* and *de facto* segregation.

In fact, the organizers of the "March on Washington" in 1963 understood that justice for black Americans included economic issues, not just access to public accommodations and the protection of voting rights. This is clearly evident in the full title for that historic event: "The March on Washington for Jobs and Freedom."[20] Accordingly, A. Philip Randolph, a longtime union leader and one of the march's organizers, said this in his speech at the march on August 28, 1963.

> We have no future in a society in which 6 million black and white people are unemployed and millions more live in poverty. Nor is the goal of our civil rights revolution merely the passage of civil rights legislation. Yes, we want all public accommodations open to all citizens, but those accommodations will mean little to those who cannot afford to use them. Yes, we want a Fair Employment Practice Act, but what good will it do if profit-geared automation destroys the jobs of millions of workers black and white?[21]

This economic aspect of the protest march in 1963 is often overlooked as people only recall the last words of King's speech, "I Have a Dream." But it was indispensable for many of the march's key leaders. In 1966, Bayard Rustin, the march's organizer, pointed out that school segregation, comparable wages, and unemployment had all worsened for black Americans since the *Brown v. Board of Education* decision in 1954. He observed, "To put all of this in the simplest and most concrete terms: the day-to-day lot

---

19. One standard history of the civil rights movement is this well-regarded trilogy: Branch, *Parting the Waters*; *Pillar of Fire*; *At Canaan's Edge*.

20. See, for example, the Martin Luther King, Jr. Research and Educational Institute, "March on Washington for Jobs and Freedom."

21. Austin, "Unfinished March." Randolph's seven-minute speech can be heard here: https://www.youtube.com/watch?v=SZGroHBk5kE.

of the ghetto Negro has not been improved by the various judicial and legislative measures of the past decade."[22]

Accordingly, this economic emphasis led to Randolph and Rustin proposing "A Freedom Budget for All Americans." This budget included provisions for a federal jobs guarantee, a basic income, and universal healthcare. The budget was released in January of 1967, with more than one hundred signatures of support, and was circulated in black neighborhoods with a foreword by King.[23] Similarly, in November of 1967, King announced the "Poor People's Campaign," with a multiracial coalition seeking economic measures understood to be essential to any legitimate definition of freedom and equality.[24]

Of course, these things did not materialize. King was assassinated in Memphis on April 4, 1968. Riots in response to King's murder decimated major cities in the spring and summer of 1968, following the earlier racial riots in 1965 and 1967, in Watts and Detroit, respectively. The violent destruction of property by black citizens in the mid-to-late 1960s combined with an emerging argument about poverty among blacks. Specifically, in 1965, Daniel Moynihan, then undersecretary in President Lyndon Johnson's administration, issued a report, *The Negro Family: The Case for National Action*.[25] While Moynihan intended to support an economic program for black Americans, he also framed black poverty in terms of unwed mothers and made debatable associations between poverty and welfare.[26] This framing fed into racially biased rhetoric about a unique cultural dysfunction among poor blacks. Still, Moynihan believed that the government should do more to address unemployment among black Americans. He helped craft a speech given by President Lyndon Johnson at Howard University on June 4, 1965, in which Johnson proclaimed, "Freedom is not enough." Johnson emphasized that the recent civil rights legislation was not enough to establish freedom. Economic policies were also needed.[27]

22. Rustin, "'Black Power' and Coalition Politics."

23. Randolph and Rustin, "How the Civil-Rights Movement Aimed to End Poverty."

24. See, for example, the Martin Luther King, Jr. Research and Educational Institute, "Poor People's Campaign."

25. Moynihan, *Moynihan Report*.

26. See Geary, "Moynihan Report."

27. Patterson, *Freedom Is Not Enough*.

But the controversy surrounding Moynihan's report, which became public later that summer, merged with protests about the Vietnam War and the Watts Riot in 1965 to derail additional legislation aimed at black unemployment.[28] Consequently, the Economic Opportunity Act of 1964, the Food Stamp Act of 1964, and the Social Security Act of 1965, which created Medicare and Medicaid, would be the extent of what became known as Johnson's "War on Poverty." While these laws were important steps in social policy, they fell far short of what Randolph, Rustin, and King had envisioned, and as they and others predicted, they did not meet the economic challenges of the moment.[29] None of this was lost on Moynihan himself. In 1967, Moynihan lamented "the moment lost."

> Few groups in the nation have much to complain about in terms of how they fared during those thirty-six months [1963 to 1966]; few can point to large and clearly formulated expectations that have been left unsatisfied. With one exception. For Negro Americans the election [midterm congressional election of 1966] may turn out to have been a calamity. For the second time in their history, the great task of liberation has been left only half-accomplished. It appears that the nation may be in the process of reproducing the tragic events of the Reconstruction: giving to Negroes the forms of legal equality, but withholding the economic and political resources which are the bases of social equality.[30]

Sad to say, Moynihan was correct. The window of opportunity for aggressive economic action to address worsening black poverty had closed. Randolph, Rustin, and King tried to pry it back open with the "Freedom Budget for All" in 1967 and with King's "Poor People's Campaign" in 1968. But the devastating events of 1968—the riots in multiple cities, the assassination of King, the assassination of Robert Kennedy, continual fallout from the Vietnam War, and the violence at the Democratic Convention—painted that window shut.[31]

In addition, even before his death, King's moral influence had waned as his commitment to a nonviolent philosophy began to fall on

28. Patterson, *Freedom Is Not Enough*, 65–86.

29. Reed, *Toward Freedom*, 77–100.

30. Moynihan, "President and the Negro."

31. On protests against the Vietnam War, see Zimmerman, "Four Stages of the Antiwar Movement"; see also Zimmerman, *Troublemaker*. On the Democratic Convention in 1968, see, for example, Kusch, *Battleground Chicago*.

deaf ears. Younger blacks, inside and outside the South, began to listen to what seemed to them to be a more self-respecting call—Black Power and black self-determination. In 1966, Stokely Carmichael, who later became Kwame Ture, introduced "Black Power" in Mississippi.[32] Similarly, that same year, Bobby Seale and Huey P. Newton advocated for black self-defense in the midst of incessant police brutality. They created the Black Panther Party in Oakland.[33]

Indeed, a sense of rage emerged as more blacks lost faith in the nation's willingness to do more to address the plight of too many black Americans seemingly trapped in poor communities with insufficient educational and economic opportunities.[34] This rage deepened as police departments ramped up their patrols with a corresponding abuse of power as poverty worsened and crime increased.[35] The clash of black militancy and police abuse perhaps reached a symbolic climax in 1969 with the FBI-supported, Chicago Police assassination of Black Panther leader Fred Hampton as he lay in his bed in the wee hours of a cold December morning.[36]

Meanwhile, as whites witnessed this violence in predominantly black spaces, many processed it through their racial prejudices, further reducing their capacity for empathy. These prejudices and fears were most likely deepened as news turned to black resistance in prisons. Soledad Prison in California and Attica Prison in New York are two illustrative episodes. On January 16, 1970, in Soledad Prison, a white prison guard named John Mills was killed after another three white guards were exonerated for the killing of three black inmates. A month later, three black inmates, George Jackson, Fleeta Domingo, and John Clutchette, were charged with killing Mills. They became known as the "Soledad Brothers."[37]

On August 7, 1970, George Jackson's seventeen-year-old brother, Jonathan Jackson, armed himself and held up a courtroom during the trial of James McClain, another inmate who was charged with attempted murder of a prison guard. The younger Jackson freed three prisoners; he

32. Ture and Hamilton, *Black Power.*

33. Bloom and Martin, *Black Against Empire.*

34. On how the mid-to-late 1960s played a role in the birth of black liberation theology, see Cone, *Said I Wasn't Gonna Tell Nobody.*

35. On the increase of crime from the 1960s forward, see Forman, *Locking Up Our Own*; Usmani, "Did Liberals Give Us Mass Incarceration?"

36. Williams, *From the Bullet to the Ballot.*

37. Weisman, "'Soledad' Story Opened in Death."

also took the presiding judge, the district attorney, and three jurors as hostages in demand for the release of the Soledad Brothers. Jackson, Mc-Clain, the judge, and a freed inmate were killed in the attempted escape.

This case led to criminal charges against Angela Davis, who had purchased the guns used by the younger Jackson. She immediately went into hiding and was placed on the FBI's Most Wanted List. She was caught two months later and held in prison for eighteen months. Her imprisonment made her an international symbol of black resistance to anti-black violence perpetuated by the state. As she waited for her day in court, more violence ensued. George Jackson attempted an armed escape from the San Quentin prison on August 21, 1971. Three prison guards and three inmates were killed, including Jackson.[38]

Two weeks later, on September 9, more than twelve hundred inmates took control of Attica prison in New York. After four days of negotiations, Governor Nelson Rockefeller ordered police to regain control of the prison. On September 13, 1971, the state police dropped tear gas and without warning, opened fire indiscriminately, killing twenty-nine inmates and nine hostages. The final count totaled forty-three deaths. It was one of the deadliest days in American history.[39] In March of 1972, the two living Soledad Brothers were acquitted of the original murder charge.[40] Three months later, on June 4, 1972, Davis was also acquitted of murder, kidnapping, and criminal conspiracy.[41]

Implications

I have recounted this history in some detail for three reasons. First, outside of academic circles, most people are not aware of what I have described here regarding the debate about large-scale government action to address poverty among black Americans in the mid-1960s. Knowing this history helps dispel a common narrative that presents the civil rights legislation as the climax of American repentance about racism. Indeed, the best minds of the time were unambiguous that the new laws were only half of the task required. In short, the narrative we commonly hear is soaked in racially biased selectivity.

38. Turner, "'Soledad Brother' and 5 are Killed in Prison Battle."
39. *Time*, "War at Attica."
40. Caldwell, "2 Soledad Blacks Cleared in Killing of Prison Guard."
41. Caldwell, "Angela Davis Acquitted on All Charges."

Second, the interpretation of violence in this period clearly demonstrates how racial stigma works so that whites and some blacks feel no moral burden for more comprehensive action regarding poverty and unemployment in predominantly black communities. Remember that white government officials and the police under their control regularly engaged in savage violence against black protests for the most basic civil rights. Yet, somehow, all of this is forgiven and forgotten. There is no talk about white dysfunction. Or white brokenness. The government under predominantly white control can commit all manner of horrible violence and it is almost never interpreted as a poor reflection on whites in general.

But the same is most certainly not the case when blacks are the perpetrators of violence. Black protestors were model citizens for ten years, between the Montgomery Bus Boycott, which began in 1955, to the Selma March for voting in 1965. Again, this was in the face of unbelievable violence of every kind. Yet, when black rioters outside the South erupted in rage due to police brutality and poor living conditions, the nation essentially decided it had done enough, and many returned to their self-righteous views about black family breakdown and criminality. This is racial stigma. The actions of a group that is not stigmatized are viewed with some level of empathy and compassion while also rightly condemning individual actions that are immoral or unlawful. This is the exact opposite of what takes place with black Americans. The entire racial group or some subgroup is seen as fundamentally dysfunctional and outside the reach of any government action.[42] Responding to the debates following Moynihan's report, King described this phenomenon precisely. What he says here applies generally and repeatedly: police brutality, riots, poverty, unemployment, education, etc.

> As public awareness of the predicament of the Negro family increases there will be dangers and opportunities. The opportunity will be to deal fully rather than haphazardly with the problem as a whole—to see it as a social catastrophe and meet it as other disasters are met, with an adequacy of resources. The danger

---

42. Glenn C. Loury identifies racial stigma as operating in the following situation: "I argued, if observers refuse to see the *systemic* and *endogenous* interactions that lead to bad social outcomes for African Americans, and if they instead attribute those results to *exogenous* factors that are taken to be internal to the group and beyond political remedy" (*Anatomy of Racial Inequality*, xvii).

will be that problems will be attributed to innate Negro weaknesses and used to justify neglect and rationalize oppression.[43]

The danger King identified leads to a third and final point, one that reaches
back to Baldwin's words about complexity. The poverty and violence we
are now familiar with in predominantly black communities were already
troubling realities when King said, "I Have a Dream." Recall Randolph's
words at the march in 1963: "We have no future in a society in which 6
million black and white people are unemployed and millions more live
in poverty." Likewise, remember what Moynihan said in 1967: "It appears
that the nation may be in the process of reproducing the tragic events
of the Reconstruction: giving to Negroes the forms of legal equality, but
withholding the economic and political resources which are the bases
of social equality." These statements correct the common misperception
that things somehow fell apart after the 1960s. That President Johnson's
"War on Poverty" played some significant role in creating allegedly dysfunctional families that were heretofore mostly unknown. Nothing could
be further from the truth.

Rather, the failure to act aggressively nearly sixty years ago simply
made matters much worse. The white middle class continued to leave
urban areas, followed shortly by the black middle class. Likewise, deindustrialization continued to move better paying jobs out of urban centers
in search for lower labor costs elsewhere. This means that black unemployment and underemployment continued to rise. Meanwhile, heroin
and crack cocaine moved into these communities, and the War on Drugs
began in 1971.[44] Violent crimes and homicides also continued to rise
from the 1960s to the 1990s.[45] Thus, in addition to everything else, you
have added the devastation of familial and communal life wrought by
mass incarceration.[46]

It is in this larger context that we also have overly aggressive policing
of these urban spaces. Yet, the policing issue, as immoral and murderous
as it undoubtedly is, is actually a symptom of this much larger problem of
inexcusable neglect of predominantly black communities for more than

43. King, *Where Do We Go from Here*, 116. Note the similarity in logic between
King's words in 1967 and Loury's words in the previous footnote.

44. *Encyclopedia Britannica*, "War on Drugs."

45. On drugs and crime, see Forman, *Locking Up Our Own*. On the homicide rate
in predominantly black communities, see Currie, *Peculiar Indifference*.

46. Johnson, "Panthers Can't Save Us Now"; Clegg and Usmani, "Economic Origins of Mass Incarceration."

half a century. In fact, "Black Lives Matter" in the broadest sense would mean that we care enough about black life to finally do what should have been done when Randolph, Rustin, and King proposed "the Freedom Budget for All" in 1967, demanding a federal jobs program, a guaranteed income, and universal healthcare.

It is only this kind of large-scale action that would address the root causes of high unemployment, educational underachievement, unconscionable homicide rates, and unjustified murders by police. We as a nation found the will to do so during the Great Depression with the New Deal.[47] Similarly, we invested in Europe's redevelopment after World War II with the Marshall Plan.[48] We should do the same for communities suffering decades of depressed conditions.[49] We have certainly had enough tax cuts and wars to have paid for it many times over. Yet, we prefer to focus on the perceived shortcomings of those in these communities so we can avoid acknowledging our own greater complicity. Glenn Loury describes our denial eloquently.

> The tacit association in the American public's imagination of "blackness" with "unworthiness" or "dangerousness" has obscured a fundamental ethical point about responsibility, both collective and individual, and promoted causal misattributions: when confronted by the facts of racially disparate achievement, racially disproportionate crime rates, and racially unequal school achievement, observers will have difficulty identifying with the plight of a group of people whom they (mistakenly) think are simply "reaping what they have sown." Thus, the enormous racial disparity in the imposition of social exclusion, civic ex-communication, and lifelong disgrace has come to seem legitimate, even necessary: we fail to see how our failures as a collective body are implicated in this disparity. We shift all the responsibility onto their shoulders, only by irresponsibly—indeed, immorally—denying our own. And yet, this entire

---

47. *Encyclopedia Britannica*, "New Deal."

48. *Encyclopedia Britannica*, "Marshall Plan."

49. In recent years, we have learned what we should have known all along—black poverty is not so distinctive. In fact, as whites have experienced the effects of deindustrialization and challenges with highly addictive drugs, many of the statistics used to identify alleged dysfunction have increased significantly among those whites with lower incomes. See Murray, *Coming Apart*; Vance, *Hillbilly Elegy*; Metzl, *Dying of Whiteness*; Case and Deaton, *Deaths of Despair and the Future of Capitalism*.

dynamic has its roots in past unjust acts that were perpetrated on the basis of race.[50]

Consequently, until we as a nation repent of this monstrous, malevolent neglect, we are the guilty ones identified in a Victor Hugo quote often cited by King: "If the soul is left in darkness, sins will be committed. The guilty one is not he who commits the sin, but he who commits the darkness."[51]

Questions for Discussion

1. Do you agree or disagree with the claim that the Golden Rule in the Bible is consistent with what is intended by the protest, "Black Lives Matter"?

2. Did you know that Rev. Dr. Martin Luther King, Jr. was often accused of being a Communist? Do you see similarities and differences now when people make claims about Black Lives Matter and Marxism?

3. How do you respond to the argument that police killings of black Americans is connected to the larger issue of longtime, malevolent neglect of predominantly black communities?

4. Is the quote from Glenn Loury at the end of this essay similar to what a biblical prophet would say in terms of pointing out how the people are guilty when they are inclined to see themselves as righteous?

---

50. Loury, *Race, Incarceration, and American Values*, 35–36. See this additional quote (33): "Society at large is implicated in an individual person's choices because we have acquiesced in—perhaps actively supported through our taxes and our votes, words and deeds—social arrangements that work to our benefit and his detriment, and which shape his consciousness and sense of identity in such a way that the choices he makes, which we may condemn, are nevertheless compelling to him—an entirely understandable response to circumstance. Closed and bounded social structure—like racially homogenous urban ghettos—create contexts where 'pathological' and 'dysfunctional' cultural forms emerge, but these forms are neither intrinsic to the people caught in these structures nor independent of the behavior of people who stand outside them."

51. King, "Crisis in America's Cities."

Works Cited

Austin, Algernon. "The Unfinished March: An Overview." The Economic Policy Institute, June 18, 2013. https://www.epi.org/publication/unfinished-march-overview/.

Baldwin, James, Emile Capouya, Lorraine Hansberry, Nat Hentoff, Langston Hughes, and Alfred Kazin. "The Negro in American Culture." CrossCurrents 11, no. 3 (Summer 1961) 205–24.

Blackmon, Douglas A. Slavery by Another Name: The Re-Enslavement of Black Americans from the Civil War to World War II. New York: Anchor, 2008.

Bloom, Joshua, and Waldo E. Martin, Jr. Black Against Empire: The History and Politics of the Black Panther Party. Oakland, CA: University of California Press, 2016.

Blount, Brian K., Cain Hope Felder, Clarice Jannette Martin, and Emerson B. Powery. True to Our Native Land: an African American New Testament Commentary. Minneapolis: Fortress, 2007.

Bowens, Lisa M. African American Readings of Paul: Reception, Resistance, and Transformation. Grand Rapids: Eerdmans, 2020.

Branch, Taylor. Parting the Waters: America in the King Years, 1954–63. New York: Simon and Schuster, 1989.

———. Pillar of Fire: America in the King Years, 1963–65. New York: Simon and Schuster, 1999.

———. At Canaan's Edge: America in the King Years, 1965–68. New York: Simon and Schuster, 2007.

Caldwell, Earl. "2 Soledad Blacks Cleared in Killing of Prison Guard." New York Times, March 28, 1972. https://www.nytimes.com/1972/03/28/archives/2-soledad-blacks-cleared-in-killing-of-prison-guard-2-soledad.html.

———. "Angela Davis Acquitted on All Charges." New York Times, June 5, 1972. https://www.nytimes.com/1972/06/05/archives/angela-davis-acquitted-on-all-charges.html.

Case, Ann, and Angus Deaton. Deaths of Despair and the Future of Capitalism. Princeton: Princeton University Press, 2020.

Clegg, John, and Adaner Usmani. "The Economic Origins of Mass Incarceration." Catalyst 3, no. 3 (Fall 2019) 9–53. https://catalyst-journal.com/2019/12/the-economic-origins-of-mass-incarceration.

Cone, James. Said I Wasn't Gonna Tell Nobody. Maryknoll, NY: Orbis, 2018.

Corley, Cheryl. "Black Lives Matter Fights Disinformation to Keep the Movement Strong." National Public Radio, May 25, 2021. https://www.npr.org/2021/05/25/999841030/black-lives-matter-fights-disinformation-to-keep-the-movement-strong.

Currie, Elliott. A Peculiar Indifference: The Neglected Toll of Violence on Black America. New York: Metropolitan, 2020.

DuBois, W. E. B. Black Reconstruction in America: An Essay Toward a History of the Part Which Black Folk Played in the Attempt to Reconstruct Democracy in America, 1860–1880. New York: Oxford University Press, 2007.

Dray, Philip. At the Hands of Persons Unknown: The Lynching of Black America. New York: Random House, 2002.

Edwards, Dennis R. What Is the Bible and How Do We Understand It? Harrisonburg, VA: Herald, 2019.

Ellis, Nicquel Terry. "Forget What You Know about 1619, Historians Say. Slavery Began a Half-Century before Jamestown." *USA Today*, December 16, 2019. https://www.usatoday.com/in-depth/news/nation/2019/12/16/american-slavery-traces-roots-st-augustine-florida-not-jamestown/4205417002/.

Encyclopedia Britannica. "Black Lives Matter." Accessed August 13, 2020. https://www.britannica.com/topic/Black-Lives-Matter.

———. "Marshall Plan." Accessed January 27, 2020. https://www.britannica.com/event/Marshall-Plan.

———. "New Deal." Accessed July 28, 2021. https://www.britannica.com/event/New-Deal.

———. "War on Drugs." Accessed July 23, 2020. https://www.britannica.com/topic/war-on-drugs.

Fields, Barbara J. "Slavery, Race, and Ideology in the United States of America." *New Left Review* 181 (May 1990) 95–118. Reprinted in Karen E. Fields and Barbara J. Fields, *Racecraft: The Soul of Inequality in American Life*, 111–48. New York: Verso, 2014.

Foner, Eric. *Reconstruction: America's Unfinished Revolution, 1863–1877.* New York: Harper Perennial Modern Classics, 2014.

———. *The Second Founding: How the Civil War and Reconstruction Remade the Constitution.* New York: W. W. Norton and Company, 2020.

Forman James, Jr. *Locking Up Our Own: Crime and Punishment in Black America.* New York: Farrar, Straus, and Giroux, 2017.

Gatney, Wilda C. *Womanist Midrash: A Reintroduction to the Women of the Torah and the Throne.* Louisville: Westminster John Knox, 2017.

Garrow, David J. "The FBI and Martin Luther King." *Atlantic* (July–August 2002: 80–88. https://www.theatlantic.com/magazine/archive/2002/07/the-fbi-and-martin-luther-king/302537/.

Gausco, Michael. "The Misguided Focus on 1619 as the Beginning of Slavery in the U.S. Damages Our Understanding of History." *Smithsonian*, September 13, 2017. https://www.smithsonianmag.com/history/misguided-focus-1619-beginning-slavery-us-damages-our-understanding-american-history-180964873/.

Geary, Daniel. "The Moynihan Report: An Annotated Edition." *Atlantic*, September 15, 2015. https://www.theatlantic.com/politics/archive/2015/09/the-moynihan-report-an-annotated-edition/404632/.

Gray, Jeremy. "Bombingham: Racist Bombings Captured in Chilling Photos." July 24, 2018. https://www.al.com/news/erry-2018/07/f39190a3553390/bombingham.html.

Isaac, Benjamin. *The Invention of Racism in Classical Antiquity.* Princeton: Princeton University Press, 2004.

Johnson, Cedric. "The Panthers Can't Save Us Now." *Catalyst* 1, no. 1 (Spring 2017) 57–85. https://catalyst-journal.com/2017/11/panthers-cant-save-us-cedric-johnson.

Junior, Nyasha. *An Introduction to Womanist Biblical Interpretation.* Louisville: Westminster John Knox, 2015.

King, Martin Luther, Jr. "The Crisis in America's Cities." 1967. Reprinted in *Atlantic*, March 31, 2018. https://www.theatlantic.com/magazine/archive/2018/02/martin-luther-king-jr-the-crisis-in-americas-cities/552536/.

———. *Where Do We Go from Here: Chaos or Community?* Boston: Beacon, 1967.

Krugler, David F. *1919, The Year of Racial Violence: How African Americans Fought Back*. New York: Cambridge University Press, 2014.

Kusch, Frank. *Battleground Chicago: The Police and the 1968 Democratic Convention*. Chicago: University of Chicago Press, 2008.

Loury, Glenn C. *The Anatomy of Racial Inequality*. Cambridge: Harvard University Press, 2021.

———. *Race, Incarceration, and American Values*. Cambridge: MIT Press, 2008.

The Martin Luther King, Jr. Research and Educational Institute. "March on Washington for Jobs and Freedom." https://kinginstitute.stanford.edu/encyclopedia/march-washington-jobs-and-freedom.

———. "Poor People's Campaign." https://kinginstitute.stanford.edu/encyclopedia/poor-peoples-campaign.

Maxouris, Christina. "100 Years Ago, White Mobs Across the Country Attacked Black People. And They Fought Back." July 27, 2019. https://www.cnn.com/2019/07/27/us/red-summer-1919-racial-violence/index.html.

McCaulley, Esau. *Reading While Black: African American Biblical Interpretation As An Exercise in Hope*. Downers Grove, IL: IVP Academic, 2020.

McWhorter, John. "Police Kill Too Many People—White and Black." *Time*, July 14, 2016. https://time.com/4404987/police-violence/.

Metzl, Jonathan. *Dying of Whiteness: How the Politics of Racial Resentment is Killing America's Heartland*. New York: Basic, 2019.

Moynihan, Daniel Patrick. *The Moynihan Report—The Negro Family: The Case for National Action*. New York: Cosimo Classics, 2018.

———. "The President and the Negro: The Moment Lost." *Commentary* (February 1967) 31–45. https://www.commentary.org/articles/daniel-moynihan/the-president-the-negro-the-moment-lost/.

Muhammad, Khalil G. *The Condemnation of Blackness: Race, Crime, and the Making of Modern Urban America*. Cambridge: Harvard University Press, 2019.

Murray, Charles. *Coming Apart: The State of White America, 1960–2010*. New York: Crown Forum, 2012.

Patterson, James T. *Freedom Is Not Enough: The Moynihan Report and America's Struggle Over Black Family Life from LBJ to Obama*. New York: Basic, 2010.

Purnell, Brian, and Jeanne Theoharis, eds., with Komozi Woodard. *The Strange Careers of the Jim Crow North: Segregation and Struggle Outside the South*. New York: New York University Press, 2019.

Randolph, Philip A., and Bayard Rustin. "How the Civil-Rights Movement Aimed to End Poverty." *Atlantic* (MLK Special Edition; April 2, 2018) 67–71. https://www.theatlantic.com/magazine/archive/2018/02/a-freedom-budget-for-all-americans-annotated/557024/.

Reed, Touré F. *Toward Freedom: The Case against Race Reductionism*. New York: Verso, 2020.

Rothman, Joshua D. "The Deep Cruelty of the U.S. Traders of Enslaved People Didn't Bother Most Americans." *Washington Post*, April 14, 2021. https://www.washingtonpost.com/outlook/2021/04/14/deep-cruelty-us-traders-enslaved-people-didnt-bother-most-americans/.

———. *The Ledger and the Chain: How Domestic Slave Traders Shaped America*. New York: Basic, 2021.

Rustin, Bayard. "'Black Power' and Coalition Politics." *Commentary* (September 1966) 7–13. https://www.commentary.org/articles/bayard-rustin-2/black-power-and-coalition-politics/.

Scrivner, Joseph. "African American Interpretation." In *The Oxford Encyclopedia of Biblical Interpretation*, edited by Steven L. McKenzie, 1–8. New York: Oxford University Press, 2013.

Smith, Mitzi, ed. *I Found God in Me: A Womanist Biblical Hermeneutics Reader*. Eugene, OR: Cascade, 2015.

Stevenson, Bryan, Jennifer Taylor, Andrew Childers, John Dalton, Aaryn Urell, Sia Sanneh, Josh Cannon, Noam Biale, Bethany Young, Ian Eppler, Kiara Boone, and Imani Lewis. "Lynching in America: Confronting the Legacy of Racial Terror." 3rd ed. The Equal Justice Initiative. 2017. https://eji.org/reports/lynching-in-america/.

Sugrue, Thomas J. *The Origins of the Urban Crisis: Race and Inequality in Postwar Detroit*. Princeton: Princeton University Press, 2004.

Time Magazine. "The Nation: War at Attica: Was There No Other Way?" September 27, 1971. https://content.time.com/time/subscriber/article/0,33009,910027-1,00.html.

Ture, Kwame, and Charles V. Hamilton. *Black Power: The Politics of Liberation in America*. New York: Vintage, 1992.

Turner, Wallace. "'Soledad Brother' and 5 are Killed in Prison Battle." *New York Times*, August 22, 1971. https://www.nytimes.com/1971/08/22/archives/-soledad-brother-and-5-are-killed-in-prison-battle-george-jackson.html.

Usmani, Adaner. "Did Liberals Give Us Mass Incarceration?" *Catalyst* 1, no. 3 (Fall 2017) 168–83. https://catalyst-journal.com/2017/12/did-liberals-give-us-mass-incarceration.

Vance, J. D. *Hillbilly Elegy: A Memoir of a Family and Culture in Crisis*. New York: Harper, 2016.

"War at Attica: Was There No Other Way?" *Time* September 27, 1971, 18–26. http://content.time.com/time/magazine/article/0,9171,910027,00.html.

Weisman, Steven. "The 'Soledad' Story Opened in Death." *New York Times*, August 22, 1971. https://www.nytimes.com/1971/08/22/archives/the-soledad-story-opened-in-death.html.

Williams, Jakobi. *From the Bullet to the Ballot: The Illinois Chapter of the Black Panther Party*. Chapel Hill: University of North Carolina Press, 2013.

Zimmerman, Bill. "The Four Stages of the Antiwar Movement." *New York Times*, October 24, 2017. https://www.nytimes.com/2017/10/24/opinion/vietnam-antiwar-movement.html.

———. *Troublemaker: A Memoir from the Front Lines of the Sixties*. New York: Doubleday, 2011.

The Empire Will Fail

*Paul's Vision for the Church Then
and Now in Romans 8*

Angela N. Parker

Introduction

ON THE SAME DAY that Derek Chauvin, the Minnesota police officer who murdered George Floyd, was found guilty, police in Ohio shot and killed fifteen-year-old foster child Ma'Khia Bryant. Friends, let that sink in. As soon as a semblance of justice was about to occur in one part of the United States of America, a young Black girl was shot and killed by another police officer. This young girl had a knife in her hand, so I am not sure even if anyone will face charges regarding her death.

First, I am a Black mama who would be angered and horrified if my child experienced such an assault. Second, I am a Womanist New Testament scholar who takes seriously the experiences of Black women and girls as valid theoretical frameworks for reading biblical texts. Third, I am a critically thinking Black woman. I believe that had the child been white-presenting and living in a white neighborhood, the police officer may have been more apt to fire a warning shot in the air and actually try to talk to that child.

As I ponder recent violence against Black and brown bodies in the years 2020 and 2021 in the United States of America, I am compelled to argue that while Black lives may not matter to certain sectors of the police force or even certain sects of ecclesial communities, Black lives do matter to God.[1] Moreover, in the context of this essay entitled "The Empire Will Fail," I argue that the Empire fails precisely because Black lives matter to God even when they do not necessarily matter to the Empire. The thesis of this essay is that solidarity across bodies must occur so that those who have the Spirit of Christ residing in them can bring about the transformation of society in the midst of a failing Empire. Accordingly, where do we go to the Pauline corpus in order to begin to pull these strands together? Attention to Romans 8 may be one area to show that the Empire will fail as long as the vision of the church stays focused on language of solidarity as opposed to the familial imagery. While I do not want to necessarily dismantle and deconstruct the image of family as a metaphor for the family of God in this essay, I will argue that family imagery coupled with solidary across differences may be a way to bring about transformation with the whole economy of God that is not based on patriarchal identities alone. This essay will argue that solidarity is slightly different than "familial" language in that solidarity with Christ and with one another as adopted children of God allows solidarity across identities. While familial language is important, the ways that family language has been co-opted by evangelical Christianity, along with Black folks who still reside in evangelical Christianity, provides difficulty for complete transformation in the midst of a failing Empire. Thus, attention to Paul's vision for the church then and now *must* be built upon solidarity within the body of Christ for transformation in a failed imperial world.

Interpretive Methods for Engaging Paul's Letter to the Church at Rome

Generally, scholars have three ways of engaging Paul's letter to the church at Rome: traditional, empire-critical, and through the New Perspective on Paul (NPP).[2] When scholars engage a traditional reading of Paul, such a reading often stems from an "enlightened" or "decontextualized" reading that tends to lean toward spiritualization. For example, I describe to students that when evangelicals use the "Romans Road" method to

---

1. There have been a number of Black and brown bodies dying as a result of police violence: George Floyd, Angelo Quinto, Ma'Khia Bryant, Sincere Pierce, Jonathan Price, and others. See Marco della Cava, "After George Floyd, Other Families Demand Justice After Police Killings."

2. I have a stamp in my office that says, "You down with NPP? Yeah, you know me!" My stamp was gifted as a reminder to the song "You Down with OPP!"

evangelization, such a methodology is decontextualized and spiritual. In essence, the Romans Road way of engaging the Romans text is the way that a housewife would present "Jesus" to a person in the supermarket.

Second, an empire-critical method is often described as a way of reading Romans that takes seriously Paul's issues with the Roman Empire. How does Paul view Jesus as higher than the emperor? This methodology asks if Paul's writing is polemical against Empire or if Paul serves as an accommodation to Empire? As I engage the issue of Empire in this essay, I hold the Roman Empire as a societal reality in the era of Paul. The Roman Empire was based on the common principle of peace through victory. The guiding principle was the idea of piety, war (which included violence against "othered" bodies), victory, and peace. As I ponder and engage the Roman Empire in Paul's letter to the church at Rome, I will nuance an understanding of the United States of America as a postindustrial civilization that is comparable to Rome, which was, in Paul's time, the greatest preindustrial civilization.

Third, there is an outgrowth in Pauline scholarship that embraces the "New Perspective on Paul." The "New Perspective on Paul" began as an outgrowth of Krister Stendahl's landmark 1963 article entitled "The Apostle Paul and the Introspective Conscience of the West." In essence, Stendahl argues that, in Romans 7:19, Paul is not wrestling with some internal idea of personal shortcomings that Western civilization terms as "sin" (which is what Martin Luther wrestled with). Stendahl is correct that Paul's major "sin" was persecuting the church. However, this essay will operate under a combined understanding of empire-criticism with links to the NPP. In such a reading, Paul persecutes the newly established Jesus assemblies under the role of Empire since the Torah had been subsumed under rule of the Roman Empire. This is where an empire-critical reading converges and diverges from the New Perspective on Paul.

Additionally, as a Womanist New Testament scholar, I employ an interpretative approach that takes seriously the issues of Black bodies mattering in the context of an American empire that may have similar contours as the Roman Empire: similar but not equivalent. First, I interpret texts while taking seriously Katie Geneva Cannon's statement that a Womanist consciousness reads the Scriptures in order to struggle for human dignity, fight against white hypocrisy, and struggle for justice by understanding the prophetic tradition of Scriptures as a way to face formidable oppression.[3] Adding to Cannon's thought, I fight white consciousness with a counteracting Womanist consciousness.

Second, particular to a Womanist approach in this essay is the idea of a body-contextual hermeneutic, which, as Lisa Bowens identifies in her work, is an oppositional hermeneutic where African Americans declared the authority to determine their bodily status. Such a declaration belongs to Blacks across centuries and belongs to God. Highlighting the Spirit of adoption (Rom 8:15), Bowens shows that in early African American hermeneutical history, Black bodies belonged to God and to the Spirit.[4] This essay takes seriously the contours of African American hermeneutics as they develop in the United States of America while expanding Pauline scholarship and its implications for contemporary society in the age of the Black Lives Matter movement.

The Roman Historical Situation

Understanding the historical situation behind Paul's letter to the Romans is important in order to properly unpack and interpret Romans 8. First, Paul wants to share his circumstances and plans with the Roman church. In 1:10, 11, 15, Paul writes that he wants to visit them. He wants to go to Spain via the way of Rome to meet them. However, beforehand, Paul hopes to receive money from the Roman church via Phoebe for the collection for the saints in Jerusalem. (See Acts 20:1–5, 1 Cor 16:1–4.)

Second, we must know the background of the churches in Rome. These churches are house churches. There is debate in scholarly circles about the affluence of these house churches. Most scholars bring a "middle-classed" understanding to house churches, but commentator Robert Jewett sees more of an idea of a "tenement church." We do not know for certain, but it should always be a question in the background when we deal with an empire-critical study of Romans. Specifically, how does the idea of "tenement church" differ from more "affluent" house churches? Further, scholars agree that there was a large Jewish community in Rome, which may have dated back to 63 BC when Pompey brought Jewish captives. A large returning Jewish constituency also is relevant after the year 49 CE when Emperor Claudius expelled the Jews regarding riots over a person named "Chrestos." As a result, some scholars believe

---

3. Cannon, *Katie's Canon*, 47–56.
4. Bowens, *African American Readings of Paul*, 115.

Priscilla and Aquila returned to Rome when Claudius opened Rome back up to Jewish people. Jewett argues that it is clear from Acts 18:2 that both of them were banned from Rome at the time of the Edict of Claudius in 49 CE, which means that they were not Pauline converts in Corinth but had been leaders in the Roman church prior to meeting Paul for the first time.[5]

As a result of Jews returning to Rome, scholars note that the situation in Romans is slightly different than the situation in Galatians. In Galatians, Paul expresses his anger at Galatian folks who are "becoming Jewish." In Romans, it appears that there is competition or rivalry where Roman identities have an upper hand over Jewish identities within the ecclesial setting. Most scholars, in a traditional interpretation, see tensions between the Jewish and Gentile Christians. In essence, Roman Jesus followers think highly of themselves since they have been in the Roman churches longer than the Jewish Christians who are returning to Rome. Such an understanding of this background is important in the midst of my interpretation of solidarity over against family relationship.

The Background of Romans 8:1–11

Paul's argumentation in Romans 8 begins with his thesis statement that there is now no condemnation in Christ Jesus. The word translated as condemnation is *katakrima* (κατάκριμα). Paul's three uses of *katakrima* in Romans are the only occurrences in the New Testament. The word *katakrima* is important since it finds its antithesis in the word δικαίωμα in Romans 8:4. However, before proceeding to 8:4, I must note that Paul's argumentation begins with a juxtaposition of the "law of the spirit of life in Christ Jesus" and the "law of sin and death." More specifically, the law of the Spirit of Life in Christ Jesus frees Paul's auditors from the law of sin and death since they are created in the space that is *en Christo Iesou*. Momentarily, I will argue that the phrase *en Christo Iesou* is important for solidarity building across identities.

Continuing in Romans 8:3–8, Paul uses a coordinating conjunction *gar* in verse 3 to signify his transition from directly stating his thesis statement to the process of explaining his thesis statement. In Romans 8:3–8, Paul states that the law was unable to free those *en Christo Iesou* because it has been weakened by flesh (8:3). Accordingly, God sent God's

---

5. Jewett, Kotansky, and Epp, *Romans*, 95.

son in the likeness of flesh so that Jesus might condemn sin in the flesh since Jesus assumes the condemnation.[6] After said condemnation, the ones walking according to Spirit fulfill the regulation of the law (8:4). I believe that here Paul introduces the idea that bodily practices matter through the use of the term περιπατοῦσιν (walking) (8:4). The way that Jesus followers in Rome walk in their bodies matters to God and to one another.

As Paul continues his argumentation, he links the practices of the body with the practices of the mind through his repetitive use of the Greek word for "being" (*ontes*). As Paul writes, he repeats the use of *ontes* in 8:5 and 8:8 while using *ontes* as a word that bookends the Greek word for mind (*phronema*) in 8:6 and 8:7. As I read and interpret Paul's creative use of words that bookend and frame other words, I highlight that mindfulness/consciousness is not merely successive thinking within the ideas and thoughts of a person. Consciousness lies within the experiences of a self that is situated in a particular world and structured within a particular space and time. Paul is writing in the midst of Roman imperial consciousness being a part of the dominant worldview. Similarly, white hypocrisy, as Cannon articulates, is similar to a white supremacist consciousness, which is not just thinking, feeling, and perceiving the doctrine that the white race is inherently superior to other races and should have control over all peoples. White consciousness actually acts white supremacy out in the operation of brain, body, *and* living similarly to what Roman imperial consciousness would do.[7] Paul is attempting to transform both mind and bodily practices in his auditors.

What does this say about Paul's argument? For Paul, "being" in the Spirit ensures that one not only has bodily practices that show that they are in Christ, but their mind/thinking are related to "being" in life and peace and not the death that is rampant in the Roman imperial system. And for my argument, recognition of life and peace as connected to being jointed in mind and spirit is where the Empire fails. The Empire, in Paul's view, does not necessarily relate to life and peace in the same way that those who walk in the Spirit of Christ may think of life and peace. Imperial thinking is a direct enemy against God, according to 8:7. Additionally, the type of thinking (that leads to death and evidences itself in bodily practices [*ontes*, 8:8]) is not able to please God.

6. (The verb for "condemn" [κατέκρινεν] is a cognate of the word condemnation translated in 8:1.)

7. See Noë, *Out of Our Heads*, 10.

Moving to Romans 8:9–11, Paul builds his argument that bodily practices matter. Paul's language around the word οἰκέω, oikeō (8:9, 8:11), along with language that places Jesus and the Spirit "in" the community of believers argues that if Christ is "in you (plural)" (8:10), then the body is dead through sin but the spirit lives through righteousness. This last portion of Paul's argument introduces the concept of resurrection through his use of the verbs *egeirantos* (meaning "raised") (8:11) and *zōopoiēsei* (meaning "will give life") (8:11). The final clause of this verse allows Paul's auditors to know that their "subject-to-death" bodies will be made alive by the indwelling of Christ's Spirit. The indwelling of Christ into the plurality of bodies shows that bodies matter.

Family Language in Romans 8:12–17

As Paul moves from the language of Rom 8:1–11, he begins to discuss the issue of "adoption." Traditional and conventional scholarship on Romans 8:12–17 highlight Paul's "family" language. For example, Paul Achtemeier argues that becoming a member of the family confers certain privileges and responsibilities toward other members of that family. Family ties are among the closest of humanity's relations. Further, to be a member of a family means one shares with others a common life in mutual interdependence. Through God's Spirit, we are invited into family, and our status is changed.

While I agree with the ways that traditional scholarship highlights the family language, I would argue that it is oftentimes problematic the way "family" has been hijacked even within Western civilization. Recent works show that scholars connect evangelical politics and the issue of family values to lingering issues of race and racism in the United States. For example, Kristin Du Mez, in her work *Jesus and John Wayne,* highlights that the term "family values" was code for the white-identified family that was in the mind of the nuclear family. The nuclear family that dominates the mind and language of evangelical politics is steeped in patriarchy, where the husband rules (as God) and the woman is a "stay-at-home" mother who acquiesces to the rule of the father (husband?). Uncritical use of Romans' language of adoption into the family of God only upholds the patriarchal and problematic nature of evangelical surface readings of Scripture.

What does it mean to nuance our understanding of family to an expanded view of solidarity that extends beyond the above-referenced white-identified view of the rule of the father that is equivalent to a domineering patriarchal God? Additionally, how do we reconcile the transformation from "slave" to "son" (or "child" in our inclusive language?) God's Spirit does transform us into a sibling relationship with Jesus so that we can address God as "Abba" in the way that Roman patriarchal society understands father figures. However, is this only for transformation of ourselves while the Empire remains intact? I do not believe so. Serving a God who is Father of all humankind in the same patriarchal sense may arouse hostility on the part of some who recognize the problematic nature of evangelical surface readings of Scripture. However, my above reading of Paul's language in Romans allows me to argue that recognizing the perplexed attitude of Empire is actually the beginning of the failing of Empire. The failing of Empire begins to show forth as the new Spirit engages a multiplicity of bodies that matter and become unified against patriarchal understandings of becoming a part of the family of God.

Solidarity across Family in Romans 8:12–17

After Paul explains that God has made Jesus alive through resurrection and will also make his auditors' mortal bodies alive, he goes on to argue that *how* one lives in their mortal body matters. Paul's readers cannot live κατὰ σάρκα (according to the flesh; 8:12) but must put to death the practices (8:13) of *tou sōmatos/tns sarkos*[8] (the body/flesh) in order to live in the spirit of God. Paul names the sons/children of God as those who put the deeds of the body/flesh to death (and do it while being led by the Spirit of God) (8:14). This is the first mention of this phrase in Paul's letter as a referent to Paul's auditors.[9] The children of God did not receive the spirit of slavery again in fear but received the spirit of "sonship" (*huiothesias*—8:15).

Additionally, this same spirit bears witness with Paul's auditors' spirits that they "are children of God." The verb for "bears witness with" is the verb *symmartyrei*. This verb occurs three times in the New Testament, and those occurrences are only in the letter to the Romans. Normally the

---

8. Verse 13 is important to note because some manuscripts have *tes sarkos* instead of *tou somatos*. Text critics recognize that scribes were copying these texts over and over again, and in their copying, some scribes did not view the body as inherently evil. Rather, the "fleshly" mind was evil.

9. The first time the term occurs in Romans is at 1:4 and refers to Jesus' sonship only.

verb that New Testament writers use regarding "witnessing" is *martyreo* without the preposition *syn* added to the word. However, this is not the only time Paul adds this preposition to words. Careful readers of Paul begin to see that the Spirit of God joins in solidarity with the spirits of Paul's auditors in order to confirm that they are children of God. This solidarity also shows that just as they are children, they are also heirs.

Further, Paul uses the language of "co-heirs" when he uses the word *synklēronomoi*. Paul's auditors are not just heirs of God, but they are co-heirs with Christ (8:17). This use of the word *synklēronomoi* outlines a sibling relationship with Christ. Christ is not over Paul's auditors but is a brother who shares in the inheritance. In this word, Paul combines the best of family relationships along with solidarity across family identities. Finally, Paul continues the theme of solidarity with the idea that his auditors "co-suffer" (*sympaschomen*,[10] 8:17) and are "co-glorified" (*syndoxasthōmen*, 8:17) with Christ. These three terms show the solidarity that occurs in three relationships: (1) the Spirit and Paul's auditors; (2) Paul's auditors and Christ; and (3) Paul's auditors and God. However, the solidarity does not end there but extends into creation in later verses. Paul links this solidarity through his use of the words for suffering and glory as he moves to the subject of creation.

Solidarity with Creation in Romans 8:18–24

As we move through Romans 8, Paul focuses on solidarity, which he juxtaposes to Empire. Empire, however, not only breaks solidarity within the family of God but also causes a disconnect in solidarity between the people of God and creation. Paul begins the next section with his thesis statement that the sufferings of this world are not able to be compared to the glory that will be revealed. What is interesting about this suffering is the term that he uses for sufferings. In 8:17, Paul uses the verb *sympaschomen* (i.e., "co-suffer"), which is a cognate for the noun *pascha* (i.e., "suffer"—which could either mean the formal Passover meal *or* Jesus as the sacrifice, as Paul uses it in 1 Corinthians 5:7). Instead of *pascha* Paul uses *ta pathēmata* ("the sufferings"), as he did previously in Rom 7:5.[11]

---

10. Paul uses the idea of co-suffering in 1 Cor 12:26 to show solidarity in the Corinthian community but never uses the term for co-glorification again.

11. The Greek text of that verse is ὅτε γὰρ ἦμεν ἐν τῇ σαρκί, τὰ παθήματα τῶν ἁμαρτιῶν τὰ διὰ τοῦ νόμου ἐνηργεῖτο ἐν τοῖς μέλεσιν ἡμῶν, εἰς τὸ καρποφορῆσαι τῷ θανάτῳ·. However, most translations render τὰ παθήματα τῶν ἁμαρτιῶν as "sinful

While Jewett notes that this word would be known to the original Roman auditors as suffering related to the Roman Empire, one can also connect "the sufferings" to those which Jesus suffered at the hands of the Roman Empire on the cross. So even though Jesus suffered, God raised him, and just as Paul's auditors suffer, their glory is about to be revealed. Additionally, this suffering also shows solidarity with creation as well (as I will demonstrate in the following verses).

In verse 19, Paul depicts creation as eagerly awaiting the revelation of the sons of God through her co-groaning and co-suffering with the children of God. Paul further reveals, in verse 20, that creation has been subjected in vanity, not of her own free will, but through the one subjecting her, on the basis of hope, so that she will be freed from the slavery of decay/decomposition/corruption to the freedom of the glory of the children of God (8:21). Also, one must note that Paul reiterates themes from 8:2 (freedom [*ēleutherōsen*]) and 8:16 (slavery [*douleias*]) in 8:21, in order to show that the bodily practices of children/sons of God are related to creation.

Paul solidifies this argument when he states that creation co-groans and co-suffers birth pangs until the present time (8:22). The verbs *systenazei* (co-groans) and *synōdinei* (co-suffers) also contain the preposition *syn*. Paul began the practice of adding *syn* to words in 8:12–17 and continues it here, I believe, to show the solidarity that creation has with God, Christ, and the children/sons of God.

Further, Paul parallels the groaning of creation with the groaning of the children/sons of God as they await "sonship" (*huiothesian*, 8:23). Since the term "sonship" is not linked to the phrase *tēn apolytrōsin tou sōmatos hēmōn* (the redemption of our body) by any coordinating conjunction, a careful reader would surmise that "the redemption of our body" is an epexegetical phrase that further defines "sonship." For Paul, "sonship" occurs completely when God redeems/buys back "our (singular) body" (8:23). At this juncture in Paul's argument, the sons/children of God have the first fruits of the Spirit (8:23) and groan as they await redemption, just as creation groans. One can see, with this mention of the Spirit, that Paul links bodily practices to being in the Spirit (8:5, 8:9, 8:11, and 8:14), which is also part of what creation waits for (i.e., the revealing for the children/sons of God.) So again, Paul argues that the actions of

---

passions" and not "suffering of the sins through the law." See the NRSV, NAB, and NLT. Even if English translators use different words for translation, Paul wrote the same word.

the body are not only important, but they are also related to what happens to creation.

We should also notice the switch between "sons" and "children" that occurs in Romans 8:23. The change may be Paul's way of trying to include women in the text. Further, one should notice that Paul's auditors are awaiting the redemption of a singular "body" in 8:23. My argument throughout is that solidarity into one body means that the church then and now must purposefully unite in solidarity with those who undergo high levels of imperial suffering even when that includes creation whom interpreters rarely place within the language of the "family of God."

The final word that I would like to highlight as I tie the solidarity of God, Jesus, the children of God, and Creation together is found with the word *symmorphous* in 8:29. This word is another conjoined word (*syn* and *morphe*) and signifies that those who have the same form as Christ are the firstborn among many brothers. This verse shows, for a second time, that Christ is in a sibling relationship with Paul's auditors.[12] Those children/sons of God who are made with the image of God's son are the firstborn of many brothers (and sisters.)

Solidarity across Various Identities Today

Just as Paul has shown solidarity across the family of God and other identities (including creation), how should contemporary Jesus followers move forward in these solidarities today? Further, how do movements bring about the failure of Empire so that society can experience transformation and move out of "groaning"? In the age of Black Lives Matter, there is a collective consciousness that those who police Black and brown bodies must undergo a transformation. I think a turn to Paul's ending in Romans and his greetings to the varieties of people, while not providing a program on transformation, does begin to prompt followers of Christ today on how churches may engage in bringing about the fall of the Empire.

Romans 16 provides us with valuable information about Paul's audience. Scholars such as Jewett and Beverly Roberts Gaventa pay particular attention to Romans 16 as a way to begin to understand the community relationships in the Roman churches. Jewett, for example, highlights that Paul is struggling with cultural chauvinism in all its forms. Since the

---

12. The prior clue to a sibling relationship occurs when Paul uses the word συγκληρονόμοι, as referenced in my exegesis of 8:17.

Roman church is in a highly imperial context in the city, then the majority of people would be Greek-speaking including those from a Jewish background, who would be slaves or former slaves. Jewett opines that respect for original cultural origins and identity was a matter of importance.[13] As such, I also think that attention to Romans 16 provides an avenue to ponder solidarity in that community.

Gaventa's work is helpful for thinking through Paul's greetings in Romans 16 and how they may relate to our understanding of congregations today. Gaventa highlights the Pew Research Center's May 2015 study that confirmed anxiety in churches that the populations among self-identified Christians were declining. Said study intensified concerns among both clergy and laity, many of whom immediately set out to provide solutions in terms of new programs or strategies.[14]

I think that what is interesting for my argumentation around solidarity is the fact that Paul continues his usage of *syn* even in his greetings. Paul refers to Prisca and Aquila as *tou synergouv* ("my co-workers in Christ Jesus"). Jewett identifies this language as technical language for missionary colleagues. Citing scholars who show that *synergov* is a distinctive and unique Pauline expression that refers to a person "who works together with Paul as an agent of God in the common 'work' of missionary proclamation," the phrase implies the following. First, there is a shared divine commission. Second, the co-workers are working in a collegial manner with Paul in congregational activities. Third, there is a specifically missionary proclamation in their co-work. There is an egalitarian nature in this work that allows for transformation not only of the church but of the society in which the church finds itself. Hence, co-working leads to the Empire failing.[15]

Another pair that Paul greets in Romans 16 is Andronicus and Junia. Andronicus and Junia are not only compatriots but also "my fellow prisoners," probably indicating they had shared a particular prison experience with Paul. Jewett notes that the possessive pronoun "my" along with the prefix *syn-* ("with, fellow") indicate shared experience. Further, the idea of "fellow prisoner/prisoner of war" parallels Paul's language in Philemon 23 and Colossians 4:10 as referring to persons who were evidently sharing Paul's imprisonments at the times of writing. However,

---

13. Jewett, Kotansky, and Epp, *Romans*, 954.

14. Gaventa, *When in Romans*, 66.

15. Jewett, Kotansky, and Epp, *Romans*, 957.

Jewett notes that not all scholars want to identify Paul as being in prison but instead argue for an understanding of "fellow prisoner" as a metaphor in reference to militant struggle.[16]

Being housed in the Roman prison system would not have been a pleasant experience. Incarceration was not usually a tool of punishment but was used to secure persons while trying to coax confessions out of them. Male and female prisoners were typically kept together in confined spaces where the conditions of crowding, inadequate ventilation and sanitation, deprivation of nourishment and sleep, as well as violence among inmates were frequent causes of complaints. One can imagine the gendered violence that would occur against female prisoners. Guards often used iron chains and stocks in order to increase torture and punishment. Moreover, the prison system was administered largely by military authorities, so it would have been natural for Paul to call himself and his colleagues in ministry "fellow prisoners of war," thereby signifying the conflict between early Jesus followers and the Roman Empire. Since most of the Jewish community had been brought to Rome as prisoners of war to be purchased as slaves, the choice of this expression would have had an evocative connotation for some of Paul's audience while also solidifying the solidarity across marginalized identities.

Conclusion

So, what can we carry from the above understandings of Pauline literature today? The following are a few closing reflections on Pauline solidarity as related to the Empire failing. First, the Empire will fail when all congregations embrace the idea of understanding their own consciousness. The Empire will fail when congregations actually combine mindfulness and thinking with the bodily practices that lead to transformation in faith communities. The Empire will fail when all segments of congregations engage their own consciousness: whether it is body consciousness, white consciousness, Black consciousness, etc.

The Empire will fail when more churches preach about racial injustice. A recent study by the Pew Research Center stated that Black worshippers attend predominately Black congregations and see a role for religion in fighting racial injustice.[17] Moreover, the study highlighted that

16. Jewett, Kotansky, and Epp, *Romans*, 958.
17. Mohamed, "10 New Findings About Faith Among Black Americans."

there is a difference in preaching in these churches. Black Americans who attended Black Protestant churches related that they were more likely to hear messages from the pulpit regarding race relations and criminal justice reform. Black Protestant churchgoers who attended multiracial, white, or other race churches did not report a high incidence of hearing such sermons.

There is still a lack of solidarity across racial lines on how the gospel actually impacts and touches society for transformation. If we take Paul's language seriously about embracing solidarity, then the suffering of Black Americans as a result of watching Black lives fall due to police violence is not merely a Black Protestant churchgoer problem but should be a problem for members of all churches, no matter the racial or ethnic identity makeup. The Empire will fail when all congregations make fighting racism essential to faith.

The Empire will fail when we move from "color-blind" faith formation to solidarity across identities. Identities do not "melt away." Those with whom Paul was imprisoned remained "marked" by their shared prison experience. Similar identity formation occurs in contemporary times with Black and brown bodies being marked particularly for retention in the prison industrial complex. The Empire will fail when churches actually address these issues without delving into color-blind ideologies or trauma invoked from the shame around having members and loved ones in the prison system.

Discussion Questions

1. What are three ways that scholars interpret Romans?

2. What elements are important for interpreting Romans in a way that is empire critical?

3. Discuss the idea of solidarity building across identities. Why is this important in interpreting Romans and contesting the Empire?

Works Cited

Achtemeier, Paul J. *Romans*. Atlanta: John Knox, 1985.

Blount, Brian K., Cain Hope Felder, Clarice Jannette Martin, and Emerson B. Powery, eds. *True to Our Native Land: an African American New Testament Commentary.* Minneapolis: Fortress, 2007.

Bowens, Lisa M. *African American Readings of Paul: Reception, Resistance, and Transformation.* Grand Rapids: Eerdmans, 2020.

Cannon, Katie G. *Katie's Canon: Womanism and the Soul of the Black Community.* New York: Continuum, 1995.

Crossan, John Dominic, and Jonathan L. Reed. *In Search of Paul: How Jesus's Apostle Opposed Rome's Empire with God's Kingdom.* New York: HarperSanFrancisco, 2004.

Della Cava, Marco. "After George Floyd, Other Families Demand Justice After Police Killings." *USA Today.* May 24, 2021. https://www.usatoday.com/in-depth/opinion/2021/05/24/year-after-murder-george-floyd-americans-react-his-death/5080199001/.

Du Mez, Kristin Kobes. *Jesus and John Wayne: How White Evangelicals Corrupted a Faith and Fractured a Nation.* New York: Liveright, 2020.

Gaventa, Beverly Roberts. *When in Romans (Theological Explorations for the Church Catholic): An Invitation to Linger with the Gospel According to Paul.* Grand Rapids: Baker Academic, 2016.

Glancy, Jennifer. *Corporal Knowledge: Early Christian Bodies.* Oxford: Oxford University Press, 2010.

Howard-Brook, Wes. *"Come Out My People!": God's Call Out of Empire in the Bible and Beyond.* Maryknoll, NY: Orbis, 2010.

Jewett, Robert, Roy David Kotansky, and Eldon Jay Epp. *Romans: A Commentary.* Minneapolis: Fortress, 2007.

Keck, Leander E. *Romans.* Nashville: Abingdon, 2005.

Mohamed, Besheer. "10 New Findings About Faith Among Black Americans." February 16, 2021. https://www.pewresearch.org/fact-tank/2021/02/16/10-new-findings-about-faith-among-black-americans/.

Noë, Alva. *Out of Our Heads: Why You are Not Your Brain, and Other Lessons From the Biology of Consciousness.* New York: Hill and Wang, 2009.

Taylor, Keeanga-Yamahtta. *From #BlackLivesMatter to Black Liberation.* Chicago: Haymarket, 2016.

The Stories Our Bodies Tell

Black Bodies That Matter, Black Lives That Matter

JENNIFER KAALUND

To speak within these classical contexts of bodies that matter is not an idle pun, for to be material means to materialize . . . In this sense, to know the significance of something is to know how and why it matters, where "to matter" means at once "to materialize" and "to mean."

—JUDITH BUTLER, *Bodies That Matter*

BODIES ARE SITES WHERE identity is signified and negotiated. Body as place is never value-free, and the spaces that bodies occupy are often replete with social messages. Undoubtedly, different bodies matter differently. In her book *Bodies That Matter*, Judith Butler begins her exposition of matters of the body by asserting that what makes a body readable or recognizable is precisely what "matters" about that body. In the context of the United States, racialized bodies are read and recognized as dangerous, always already guilty, and out of place.[1] I contend that to have a life that matters, one must also possess a body that matters, that is, a body that is read as safe, acceptable, and thus potentially free. To be Black in America is to live in the tension of a place and among people

---

1. Though Butler's work focuses on gendered bodies, I argue that racialized bodies also are similarly read and recognized in very particular ways.

who value our Black bodies for their profit while concomitantly seeking to destroy our lives.[2]

In our contemporary moment and in antiquity, bodies serve myriad purposes in discourse. In texts, bodies are deployed to convey messages. In her book *Corporal Knowledge: Early Christian Bodies*, Jennifer Glancy writes: "What stories do these bodies tell? What secrets do they know? How do they give birth to theological discourse—or act as midwife to our birthing of theological discourse?"[3] These are a few of the questions to consider when encountering bodies in ancient texts. Bodies create new understandings. Bodies contain knowledge; they reveal truths, instruct us, and warn us. Following philosopher Mark Johnson's propositions concerning bodily metaphors, Glancy contends that bodies "inevitably structure human knowing." She continues: "Parallel to Johnson's insistence that bodies structure thought, I work from the assumption that bodies structure social exchange and create worlds of meaning."[4] Like Glancy, I believe we should be attuned to the work that bodies do when they are employed in ancient literature, such as the Bible. Encountering bodies in the biblical text requires excavation work. This excavation attempts to recover a world of meaning that may otherwise remain lost. To reduce the body to merely an abstraction or object in ancient texts or our contemporary discourse can result in the loss of meaning and, ultimately, the loss of a revelation of truth.

In this essay, I explore Black bodies in the United States and how they inform American identity. I examine ancient bodies, specifically bodies in Hebrews, and attempt to discern what we can learn from these bodies and what they might teach us about an early Christian community. Finally, I investigate the possibilities of the Bible as both a weapon of oppression and a tool for liberation.

---

2. The perceived value of enslaved peoples in both North America and South America is well documented. I suggest that white supremacist systems continue to value what Black bodies can produce, from athletic performances to artistic contributions, while at the same time negating the worth of Black lives. This is evidenced by the killing of Black people, particularly state-sanctioned violence, with impunity.

3. Glancy, *Corporal Knowledge*, 14.

4. Glancy, *Corporal Knowledge*, 4.

Black Bodies and the Making of American Identity

In his award-winning book *Between the World and Me*, Ta-Nehisi Coates writes to his son: "We are all our beautiful bodies and so must never be prostrate before barbarians, must never submit our original self, our one of one, to defiling and plunder."[5] For Coates, protecting one's body is of the utmost importance. Indeed, our bodies are what matter most; they are everything. Death (or as he describes it, "the loss of the body," particularly through violence) is simply unforgivable because it is essentially the utter end. Concerning the death of his friend, he writes: "I sat there feeling myself a heretic, believing only in this one-shot life and the body."[6] What does it mean to *believe* in the body? This is a question to which we will return. Coates's humanist positioning and belief in the body escalate the stakes of our lives, here and now. This is it. Coates's perspective is instructive. Acknowledging the singularity and distinctiveness of each body, Coates reminds us that Black bodies matter, although perhaps differently for different people. The body is not simply a container; it is inherently valuable; indeed, it is a treasure. And because Black bodies in particular are at risk of being destroyed, they must be protected.

Coates's concerns for the body—his body, his son's body, and Black bodies in America—are informed by one of the ways that African American identity is constructed: through violence. That is, brutality, often bloodshed, is an integral part of constructing African American identity. Coates instructs his son:

> Here is what I would like for you to know: In America, it is traditional to destroy the black body—its heritage. Enslavement was not merely the antiseptic borrowing of labor—it is not so easy to get a human being to commit their body against its own elemental interest. And so, enslavement must be casual wrath and random mangling, the gashing of heads and brains blown out over the river as the body seeks to escape.[7]

This graphic description is our historical reality, and understanding it fully is necessary, especially in a society that insists upon "antiseptic" views of the past. And yet, the violent construction of African American

5. Coates, *Between the World and Me*, 36.
6. Coates, *Between the World and Me*, 36.
7. Coates, *Between the World and Me*, 103.

identity is not simply a historical phenomenon—it is a contemporary ideology as well.

The destruction of Black bodies is often associated with a Black person's own "mistake." Coates advises his son that "the story of a black body's destruction must always begin with his or her error, real or imagined—with Eric Garner's anger, with Trayvon Martin's mythical words ('You gonna die tonight'), with Sean Bell's mistake of running with the wrong crowd, with me standing too close to the small-eyed boy pulling out."[8] The devastating consequence of such errors is all too often death. The result of these and numerous other examples is that Black people are conditioned to live in a continuous state of anxious fear: the fear of committing such an error and the trauma of repeatedly seeing the results of the various forms of punishment inflicted upon Black bodies. Our bodies hold these emotions and move through spaces acutely aware of the potentially dire consequences of making what can be perceived as a minor mistake or, at times, no mistake at all. How we understand various aspects of our identity (national and religious identity, for example) is intricately related to how we understand our bodies, and this understanding informs how we construct our ways of being in this world.

In the United States, Black bodies are a site upon which national identity is negotiated. American identity was constructed in contrast to enslaved African identities. In fact, the denial of the dependence of one upon the other is the basis of America's founding grand narrative. Recognizing the contradiction of a foundational myth that espouses freedom, justice, and liberty while at the same time denying these ideals to its own citizenry (and to those who were already here and those who were pivotal for building the nation) is critically important for identifying similar disjunctions as the harvest of previously planted seeds. Kelly Brown Douglas surmises, "These seeds produced a myth of racial superiority that both determined America's founding and defined its identity. This myth then gave way to America's grand narrative of exceptionalism."[9] The concept of chosenness undergirds this notion of exceptionalism.[10] Thus, religion is

8. Coates, *Between the World and Me*, 96.

9. Douglas, *Stand Your Ground*, 4.

10. The title of God's chosen people has been applied to various groups throughout history, from the ancient Israelites to the Jewish people to ancient persecuted Christians. (See, for example, Deuteronomy 14:2: "For you are a people holy to the Lord your God, and the Lord has chosen you to be a people of his own possession, out of all the nations that are on the face of the earth" and 1 Peter 2:9: "But you are a chosen race,

used to validate this myth. The ideology of manifest destiny is dependent upon the notion of upholding the will of God. Conceptions of superiority are inherent in these ideologies.

To make a people, the foundation narrative insisted on a genealogy that asserted the superiority of Anglo-Saxon identity. As Douglas states, "To be Anglo-Saxon, then, was to be a moral and freedom-loving people. Morality and freedom literally belonged to them. It was in their blood as if it were a genetic marker."[11] If freedom and morality were in their blood, then they were actualized only through the bloodshed of others. Additionally, Douglas notes, "The emphasis on blood was not lost on America's founding fathers. It is behind both Jefferson's and Franklin's fixation on language. A marker of America's exceptionalism, therefore, was the language of the nation."[12] For example, the language of war and battle persists in our national lexicon and has resulted in the perpetual development of an enemy or other. Indeed, language is yet another way through which kinship ties and thus peoplehood are solidified. Language has the power to signify which lives and which bodies matter.[13] In addition, religion binds people together. Religious discourse in America has been used to support the ideology of the inferiority of Black people.[14] Therefore, in this context, white supremacy and religious discourse are entangled. Consequently, the very formation of (North) American identity depends upon the denial and rejection of others, and in many ways, this narrative is written in blood and maintained through bloodshed. To be sure, where there is bodies, there are also bodies.

Violence accompanies the formation of this American identity. Black bodies must be regulated. As property, Black bodies were controllable and disposable. Yet Black bodies remained a constant threat because Black people have always demanded the recognition of their humanity. Although the contemporary moment has birthed the motto that Black lives matter, the truth of this assertion exists beyond time and space. Black bodies' refusal to be contained resulted in the persistent need by

---

a royal priesthood, a holy nation, God's own people, in order that you may proclaim the mighty acts of him who called you out of darkness into his marvelous light").

11. Douglas, *Stand Your Ground,* 21.

12. Douglas, *Stand Your Ground,* 21.

13. I am grateful to Lisa Bowens for this observation.

14. From the myth of the curse of Ham to the ill-conceived notion that suffering is necessary for salvation to an otherworldly focus on justice and retribution at the demise of present realities, the Bible has been used as a tool of oppression.

whites to discipline them. White people's desire for discipline is not simply an assertion of power; it is an integral part of a national discourse rooted in violence and beholden to the production of knowledge that transforms Black bodies from property into always already criminal.[15] In either case, free Black bodies challenge any stable American identity because the ground upon which this identity was built insists upon containing the perceived threat of their mere existence.[16]

Whereas narratives place bodies in particular places, real bodies move through and across spaces. This placement, or more often displacement, results in an opportunity to negotiate one's identity. For example, the Black body that once was marked as chattel now is marked as criminal. Laws to control the movement of Black bodies, historically and currently, demonstrate the continual need to control Black bodies directly and indirectly. Changes in legal status are closely associated with changes in physical locations, whether marching or migrating north or west. Marking Black bodies as already criminal serves the same purpose as the construct of chattel: "It relegates the Black body to an 'unfree' space. It preserves the free space as a white space. This transformation began shortly after emancipation."[17] To be sure, there are still places where Black bodies are neither safe nor free. This knowledge is not simply part of a historical discourse—it is the present reality.

Black bodies tell the story of systemic racism in America. Trauma is carried in these bodies. Black lives remain threatened by disproportionate imprisonment, poverty, and lack of access to appropriate healthcare. These injustices are evidence of power structures intent upon keeping freedom elusive.

Bodies in Hebrews and the Making of Christian Identity

The body and the work that it performs in literature have long been subjects of inquiry. More than a metaphor, the body in ancient discourse provides insight into that social world. However, Dale Martin cautions that modern conceptions of the body should not be applied to bodies

15. Douglas, *Stand Your Ground*, 74.

16. Notably, this ground or "conquered" land was first inhabited by the native people of the Americas, whose histories, bodies, and stories have been erased and/ or suppressed.

17. Douglas, *Stand Your Ground*, 77.

in antiquity. In particular, he critiques a dualistic understanding of the body that biblical scholarship has often implied. Instead, he argues for the acknowledgment of diverse expressions of Romanness, Greekness, and Jewishness in the ancient world that would have resulted in a variety of understandings of the body. This diversity further complicates any overly simplistic perspective concerning our understanding of bodies in antiquity. Martin writes:

> In other words, all the Cartesian oppositions—matter versus nonmatter, physical versus spiritual, corporeal (or physical) versus psychological, nature versus supernature—are misleading when retrojected into ancient language. A "one world" model is much closer to the ancient conception, and, instead of an ontological dualism, we should think of a hierarchy of essence.[18]

To ascertain Paul's use of the body in his letters to the Corinthians, Martin first explores the cultural milieu in which Paul writes and the various ways the body may have been employed in ancient discourses. He reaches two significant conclusions for consideration. First, he argues that "hierarchy was also inscribed on the ancient body in the way sexuality was constructed."[19] That is, the presentation of the body can be read along a spectrum of social status. The higher one moves, the more majestic—even divine—the body becomes. In other words, "In popular Greco-Roman culture, bodies were direct expressions of status."[20] Second, Martin reminds us: "But in the ancient world, the human body was not *like* a microcosm; it *was* a microcosm—a small version of the universe at large."[21] According to Martin, the constant influence of the universe on the body "blurs any boundary between the inner body and the outer body."[22] There are resonances to note here with how Coates describes

18. Martin, *Corinthian Body*, 15.

19. Martin, *Corinthian Body*, 32.

20. Martin, *Corinthian Body*, 34.

21. Martin, *Corinthian Body*, 16. Others have similarly noted this cosmic understanding of the human body. In his essay "The Body in Western Catholic Christianity," Andrew Louth summarizes Origen's presentation of a double or two-stage creation: "Origen, for instance, envisaged a primal state of pure spiritual beings (with, perhaps, spiritual bodies) freely and perfectly contemplating the primal unity of God: but these beings turned away from God and fell; in their fall they became souls and were provided with bodies (or terrestrial bodies) and it is these fallen souls with their bodies that constitute the cosmos." See Louth, "Body in Western Catholic Christianity," 112.

22. Martin, *Corinthian Body*, 17.

bodies in his work, a body that is in and of itself the universe. Though early Christian writers are writing within this context and with these various understandings of the body, in some cases there is an attempt to turn this hierarchical worldview upside down and challenge or reject Roman standards. Glancy observes, "Early Christians relayed paradigmatic stories that implied rejection of Roman norms of bodily interaction and embodied self-understanding."[23] As will be seen in this examination of bodies in Hebrews, to rewrite history, the writer employs bodies to create a new narrative.

Another important consideration concerning bodies in the ancient world is how individual bodies inform what we know about collective identities. Martin suggests that "we must not concentrate so much on the individual human body, however, that we forget that it was but an instance of the social body. The same dynamics and mechanics that were expected to operate within the individual body provided the political rhetoric for the operation of the body politic."[24] In Hebrews, individual bodies often also signify a collective identity. The bodies inform its audience of what the qualifications are for becoming followers of Christ. This group identity is formed with and on bodies.

As I examine the stories these bodies tell, it is important to read these ancient bodies within their cultural context. This context is the first-century Mediterranean world, where the Roman Empire was the political power. In conquering and subduing nations, the Roman Empire used crucifixion to maintain imperial power; dead and dying bodies were displayed publicly as examples of what would happen to those who did not follow its rules. *Pax Romana*, or the peace of Rome, was sustained through violence and intimidation. Conquered people were surveilled and continuously reminded of their status in the Roman apparatus.[25] Even as the words on the pages of Hebrews attempt to create a new reality, the audience being addressed comprises people having their own encounters with imperial powers and influences. The audience of the homily that is Hebrews is experiencing or has experienced suffering.[26]

23. Glancy, *Corporal Knowledge*, 137.

24. Martin, *Corinthian Body*, 37.

25. For more details on the context of the Roman Empire, Hebrews, and the conditions in which the conquered lived, see Johnson, *Hebrews*; deSilva, *Perseverance in Gratitude*; and Koester, *Hebrews*.

26. That the audience is experiencing suffering is evident from the text. There is also consensus among scholars that suffering existed, although the extent of that

These all are important considerations as we turn to the text to examine bodies in early Christian religious discourse.

Hebrews describes itself as a "word of exhortation."[27] This context is significant; the writer encourages his audience to preserve or to keep the faith. Remaining faithful in spite of their circumstances is a theme of this homily. The first bodies we encounter are fallen bodies. Hebrews 3:17 queries: "Was it not those who sinned whose bodies fell in the wilderness?" In the precarious desert location, these "fallen bodies" are dead bodies (*kōla*) or, more precisely, bodies that have fallen apart. These bodies represent those who are apart from God. These are the ones who did not enter the promise of God's rest—that is, they did not persevere in the faith.[28] The audience is reminded of the "good news [that] came to us just as to them; but the message they heard did not benefit them, because they were not united by faith with those who listened" (4:2). These fallen bodies represent the antithesis of what the author wants from the audience. The explicit call in Hebrews 6:11–12 states: "And we want each one of you to show the same diligence so as to realize the full assurance of hope to the very end, so that you may not become sluggish, but imitators of those who through faith and patience inherit the promises." In exchange for unity, patience, and faithfulness, the audience could anticipate the promise of God's rest. To turn away from the faith was to "fall" out of relationship with both God and the community of believers. These fallen bodies teach us the dire consequence of hearing the good news but not remaining faithful to it.

Later in the homily, other ancestors are described as animal skin-clad wanderers who were abused, imprisoned, and even dismembered bodies. The writer describes them thusly: "Others were tortured, refusing to accept release, in order to obtain a better resurrection. Others suffered mocking and flogging, and even chains and imprisonment. They were stoned to death, they were sawn in two, they were killed by the sword; they went about in skins of sheep and goats, destitute, persecuted, tormented—of whom the world was not worthy"(11:35–38). Clearly, these ancestors are portrayed as suffering. These suffering saints in search of

---

suffering is subject to debate. The writer offers words of encouragement while acknowledging their situation. Hebrews 12:4 states: "In your struggle against sin you have not yet resisted to the point of shedding your blood."

27. Heb 13:22.

28. The author makes clear: "Therefore, while the promise of entering his rest is still open, let us take care that none of you should seem to have failed to reach it" (4:1).

a resting place cannot be made perfect apart from the *community*, the audience who should imitate their faithfulness (11:38–39). Even when commended for their faith, these self-identified strangers and aliens remain restless. These bodies did not have clothing, or at least not proper clothing. They had no city, no home, and no resting place. This delayed gratification of rest emphasizes the importance of unity. A (final) resting place—a heavenly Jerusalem, the city of God where they will find an unshakable kingdom—is what awaits those who persevere.[29] And at the same time, there is an understanding that the suffering communities are not simply united in their pain (which will end); they are united in their hopeful expectation of a world that is different from the one they inhabit. The audience learns that the saintly body is often an afflicted body, and they simultaneously are reminded that they are not alone.

The next body in the text can be found in Hebrews 10:5, and this is the body of Christ. Here the author writes of a "prepared body." Placed in the mouth of Jesus, Psalm 40:6–8 is used to elucidate Jesus' purpose. Jesus' prepared body is offered as a sacrifice to sanctify the believer (10:10), enabling the audience to enter the sanctuary (10:19) or the holy place confidently "with hearts sprinkled clean from an evil conscience and our *bodies* washed with pure water" (10:22, italics mine). Christ's prepared body makes it possible for the audience to have clean bodies—purified bodies that can enter the holy place. "For Christ did not enter a sanctuary made by human hands, a mere copy of the true one, but he entered into heaven itself, now to appear in the presence of God on our behalf" (9:24). The audience with clean bodies can penetrate the holy place and approach God. Jesus is an intercessor who continues to act on the behalf of those who follow him. Jesus also makes it possible for all who approach God to receive mercy and compassion. Jesus' prepared body clears the path to God.

The final body we encounter in the text is in chapter 13. Here, there is an admonition to remember those who are in prison and those who are mistreated "as though you yourselves were being tortured" (13:3) or, more precisely, as if one were also being mistreated in the body. Jesus suffered just as the wandering saints suffered. The audience is told to remember the suffering of the ancestors, the suffering of Jesus, and the suffering of the people in their community. They are asked not only to recall past sufferings but also to empathize with those who are suffering in their midst. They are to feel their pain as though they have experienced

29. See Heb 12:22–29.

it in their own bodies. In other words, the writer instructs the audience of Hebrews that these imprisoned and tortured bodies *matter*.

Concluding Thoughts: Is the Bible a Weapon of Oppression or a Tool for Liberation?

In literature, bodies often signify lives. Lived experience reminds us that pain, suffering, and torture are matters of the body—matters that should not be ignored or dismissed. Therefore, to declare that "Black Lives Matter" is at the same time to affirm the significance of the body and to assert the right to lives lived free of the fear of death and destruction. The right to simply live, to matter, does not seem like an outrageous or audacious stance, yet in a country that upholds a foundational myth created by violence and maintained through bloodshed, such a claim has become a point of contention.

To better understand this inflection point, one must question the ways that religion, and specifically Christianity, is implicated in upholding white supremacist systems that undermine the significance of all bodies. I illumine this entanglement with three examples. First, the Bible has been used to justify narratives of racial superiority and inferiority. Biblical texts must be examined within their own cultural contexts, and although these examinations may have implications for our contemporary context, we should not use the texts to justify our personal and political positions. The interpretation of the myth of the curse of Ham (Gen 9:24–27) is an example of such a text. Second, although it is important to recognize and acknowledge the presence of suffering and pain, one need not glorify it. These factors are not necessary components of the Christian experience, and to suggest otherwise is to ignore the gospel's teaching of abundant life (John 10:10). For example, Romans 15:13 instructs: "May the God of hope fill you with all joy and peace in believing, so that you may abound in hope by the power of the Holy Spirit."[30] Finally, by elevating the status of the soul and/or spirit over the body, we risk treating the body as disposable. A more holistic approach recognizes that the lives we have here and now are significant, and the circumstances in which we live also matter. We do not have to wait until the hereafter to experience justice, joy,

---

30. This is but one example. Others include John 10:10; Gal 5:22; Deut 28:12; 1 Kgs 2:3; and Eph 3:20.

or peace. Recognizing our bodies' strength and beauty (reflections of the image of God) can then be extended to recognizing the same in others.

Though the Bible has been used to support systems of oppression, the Bible is also a source of this life-giving and life-changing hope. The bodies encountered in Hebrews tell stories. We learn of an early Christian community trying to form its identity in a complicated cultural milieu. The members' newly formed community struggles to find its place, and so the writer suggests that while they may never feel fully accepted in this world, they can look to the world to come, where they will have full citizenship.[31] Concomitantly, the bodies in Hebrews reveal the importance of being part of an empathetic community. Freedom is not a solo project; liberation is a communal effort. The author encourages this community, united by its circumstances and by faith, to practice patience and perseverance. Violence is not meant to have the final say. There is hope: an essential ingredient for faithful and faith-filled lives. Hope is transformative. Hope reminds us of the potential of the future—a future we can influence. This possibility speaks both to ancient and contemporary audiences. Although often elusive, if hope can be embraced and nurtured, it has the potential to move us beyond what we can see. Hope has the potential to transform matters of the bodies into bodies that matter.

Black bodies, and specifically free Black bodies, challenge a system that would otherwise seek to destroy them. As Coates instructs his son, we too must learn to protect and value our bodies, "our original selves, our one of one."[32] When this happens, when we can see the value of each and every body, we will then begin to realize the value of each and every life.

To return to a query posited at the beginning of this essay, what does it mean to *believe* in the body? I feel this question can be approached in multiple ways. One can believe in one's own body—in its strength and ability to heal, protect, and serve us. From a Christian perspective, one can believe in the redemptive work of Jesus' body and the power of resurrection in the body of Christ. One can also believe in the united body of Christ as a community of believers and the potential for realizing the

---

31. Heb 12:22–23, "But you have come to Mount Zion and to the city of the living God, the heavenly Jerusalem, and to innumerable angels in festal gathering, and to the assembly of the firstborn who are enrolled in heaven to God the judge of all, and to the spirits of the righteous made perfect."

32. Coates, *Between the World and Me*, 36.

kin-dom of God on earth.[33] To believe in the body is to believe in the possibilities of life. Dead and alive, bodies tell stories, if only we would listen.

Discussion Questions

1. When you think of the body of Christ, do you think of the communal/social body of believers or do you think of Jesus' body?

2. How do you think of *your* body in relation to the body of Christ?

3. What story does your body tell?

4. How have different bodies been treated historically and in our contemporary moment?

5. How can a (re)newed understanding of the body help move us toward a more just world?

Works Cited

Butler, Judith. *Bodies that Matter: On the Discursive Limits of "Sex."* New York: Routledge, 1993.

Coates, Ta-Nehisi. *Between the World and Me.* New York: One World, 2015.

DeSilva, David Arthur. *Perseverance in Gratitude: A Socio-Rhetorical Commentary on the Epistle "to the Hebrews."* Grand Rapids: Eerdmans, 2000.

Douglas, Kelly Brown. *Stand Your Ground: Black Bodies and the Justice of God* Maryknoll, NY: Orbis, 2015.

Glancy, Jennifer. *Corporal Knowledge: Early Christian Bodies.* Oxford: Oxford University Press, 2010.

Isasi Diaz, Ada Maria. *Mujerista Theology: A Theology for the Twenty-First Century* Maryknoll, NY: Orbis, 1996

Johnson, Luke Timothy. *Hebrews: A Commentary.* Louisville: Westminster John Knox, 2006.

Koester, Craig. *Hebrews: A New Translation with Introduction and Commentary,* Anchor Yale Bible. New Haven: Yale University Press, 2001.

Louth, Andrew. "The Body in Western Catholic Christianity." In *Religion and the Body,* edited by Sarah Coakley, 111–30. Cambridge: Cambridge University Press, 1997.

Martin, Dale B. *The Corinthian Body.* New Haven: Yale University Press, 1995.

33. Theologian Ada Maria Isasi Diaz coined the term "kin-dom." Isasi Diaz writes: "I use 'kin-dom' to avoid the sexist and elitist kingdom." It also communicates a vision of a world where we are kin or siblings. She further explicates: "The unfolding of the kin-dom of God happens when instead of working to become part of structures of exclusion we struggle to do away with such structures." Isasi Diaz, *Mujerista Theology,* 42–43, 66.

Prophetic Tenacity

Jaime L. Waters

But let justice roll down like waters, and
righteousness like an ever-flowing stream.

(AMOS 5:24)

HUTZPAH. AUDACITY. GALL. DETERMINATION. Resolve. These words typ-
ify *prophetic tenacity*, the spirit, energy, and attitudes that propel growth
and change in society. Prophetic tenacity permeates the literature of the
Old Testament,[1] and it remains invaluable today, especially for people
working for black advancement and empowerment. Biblical prophets
emerged in various contexts over centuries in the history of Israel. Some
prophets, such as Moses, Deborah, Elijah, and Huldah, were remembered and written about because of their abilities to unite communities,
enabling people to foster relationships with God and one another. Several
prophets have biblical books attributed to them that contain oracles, sermons, and occasionally biographical information about their lives and

---

1. The biblical texts discussed in this essay come from the Christian Old Testament. Given the title and interests of this edited volume, the term Old Testament is
used instead of Hebrew Bible to denote content within the first part of the Christian
biblical canon. However, these texts are also in the Jewish Bible, the Tanak. The ideas
and attitudes expressed in this treatment are foundational for Christians and Jews, and
there are many universal ideals that might inspire anyone working for racial justice
and equality.

prophetic careers. The backgrounds of the prophets are varied. Jeremiah and Ezekiel, for instance, came from priestly lineage (Jer 1:1; Ezek 1:3). Amos was an animal herder in addition to his prophetic career (Amos 1:1; 7:14), and Jonah was a reluctant prophet who initially fled his calling (Jonah 1:2–3). There is diversity in the prophetic traditions, and yet one aspect that connects many of the greatest prophets is their tenacity and drive to help people survive and thrive, especially in the midst of difficult circumstances. Although separated by time and place, prophetic texts of old can speak to black empowerment initiatives of today, offering insights and inspiration for addressing injustices and inequalities in society.

Money Matters

Amos and Micah were prophets in the eighth century BCE. The superscription of the book of Amos dates his career to the reigns of Kings Uzziah of Judah (783–42) and Jeroboam II of Israel (786–46). Although Amos was from Judah, he traveled north to Israel to deliver his messages. Micah's prophetic activity was soon after Amos, during the reigns of Kings Jotham (742–35), Ahaz (735–15), and Hezekiah (715–686). Micah's prophecies addressed both the northern and southern kingdoms. Amos and Micah were deeply concerned about social and economic injustices, and they critiqued and warned their communities of forthcoming punishments on account of their oppressive actions.

Wealth, Debt Slavery, and Continued Economic Injustices

Amos's prophetic activity emerged during a time of relative peace and prosperity in Israel, yet his book suggests that there were significant wealth gaps in the land. Amos depicts wealthy people as secure and living at ease, lavishly lounging on ivory beds and couches, feasting on choice meats, and drinking bowls of wine. While the poor people in the land suffered financial hardships, the wealthy are said to live in leisure, enjoying music and anointing themselves with the finest oils (Amos 6:4–6). Amos indicts people with financial means, proclaiming, "they sell the righteous for silver, and the needy for a pair of sandals" (2:6).[2] He accuses them of trampling "the head of the poor into the dust of the earth" (2:7),

---

2. All biblical translations are the author's unless otherwise noted. English Bible verse numbers are followed for ease of locating passages.

graphically depicting the crushing effects of financial injustice. Later in the book, Amos reuses this imagery, accusing the wealthy of "buying the poor for silver and the needy for a pair of sandals" (8:6).

The language of buying and selling people indicates a legal system that enslaved poor people or made them sell themselves into slavery if they were unable to pay their debts. Amos critiques the abuses of such debt slavery, particularly when people were enslaved for inexpensive debts like a pair of shoes. Likewise, Amos highlights victims who are righteous (*ṣaddîq*), which in legal contexts means that they are innocent or in the right. The other victims who are bought and sold are needy ('*ebyôn*) and poor (*dallîm*), terms often used to denote oppressed and powerless peoples.

Biblical legal traditions offer insights into how the system of debt slavery might have developed in ancient Israel. According to the book of the covenant, a collection of laws in Exodus 20–23, there were parameters on how long people could be enslaved: "When you buy a Hebrew slave, he shall serve six years, but in the seventh he shall go out a free person, without debt" (Exod 21:2). This law permits debt slavery, but it requires the release of slaves after a designated period, adding a restriction to slave owners. The six-year enslavement period echoes the account of God creating the world in six days and resting on the seventh day (Gen 1:1–2:4a). This account of creation influenced ideas about resting and relief occurring in intervals of seven.

The book of Deuteronomy also includes parameters on owner-slave relationships. Every seven years, the sabbatical year,[3] debts were to be forgiven to decrease debt slavery, financial hardship, usury, and other financial abuses (Deut 15:1–6). Relatedly, after six years of servitude, slaves were to be freed in the seventh year (15:12).[4] Upon release, slaves

3. Leviticus 25 includes variant legislation regarding debts and manumission. Debts were relieved, and slaves were freed in the jubilee year, which happened every fiftieth year, calculated in intervals of seven (Lev 25:8–12). Leviticus affords more benefits to slave owners and permits longer service for slaves. Deuteronomy offers a more humanitarian approach to debt slavery and relief that is closer in line with the tradition in Exodus. The varied legislation may reflect differing schools of thought or different practices. Assuming Deuteronomy is the latest of the three, it reflects an intentional revision and expansion of debt slavery laws that is more favorable towards slaves.

4. Deuteronomy 15:1 and 15:12 refer to two different seventh years. The forgiveness of debts was set for everyone on a seven-year schedule, but the timing of manumission could vary depending upon when a person became enslaved. However, the prophet Jeremiah reflects a tradition of interpreting these as one combined event of debt forgiveness and manumission that happened at the same time every seven years (Jer 34:8–22).

were not to leave empty-handed: "Provide liberally out of your flock, your threshing floor, and your wine press, thus giving to him some of the bounty with which Yahweh your God has blessed you" (15:14). This law recognizes the difficulties associated with debt slavery and instructs owners to share their divinely given gifts of animals, grain, and wine so that those released from slavery could build their futures.

In "The Case for Reparations,"[5] Ta-Nehisi Coates begins his piece with an epigraph of the text of Deuteronomy 15:12–15, which requires a provision of generosity toward former slaves. By starting with this Deuteronomic passage, Coates frames his discussion of the economic impacts of American slavery in light of principles of corrective and re-storative justice. Coates's article offers compelling interviews, historical and statistical data, and thoughtful insights into the pervasive problem of racism and the ways it has fostered race-based economic disparities. Coates highlights many (il)legal financial and land management prac-tices—sharecropping, home seizures, redlining, segregation, lending schemes—practices that targeted black communities and created wealth gaps that continue to plague the nation.

In antiquity, financial and land manipulation were criticized by the prophet Micah. He critiqued wealthy people who acquired land at the expense of the poor: "They covet fields, and seize them; houses, and take them away; they oppress householder and house, people and their inher-ited property" (Mic 2:2). Micah viewed home seizures as mechanisms that enabled wealthy people to monopolize properties. In some instances, people who were poor would be unable to keep their homes, even in-herited properties, and this would allow the wealthy to accumulate even more land.

According to Micah, financial corruption occurred at the highest offices in society, as he criticizes rulers because they "abhor justice and pervert all equity" (Mic 3:9). Moreover, these rulers, along with priests and prophets, perpetrated and enabled financial crimes, corrupting their offices by taking bribes: "Its rulers give judgment for a bribe, its priests teach for a fee, its prophets practice divination for money" (3:11). Mi-cah paints a picture of systemic financial corruption in which the poor experienced oppression through land and money mismanagement, and political and religious leaders were a part of the problem rather than

---

5. Coates, "Case for Reparations."

the solution. Micah is fearless in speaking truth to power in an effort to change behavior and affirm forthcoming punishments.

By condemning wealth and economic disparities, Amos and Micah show prophetic tenacity as they call out abuses and criticize those with power in order to provoke change and support the disenfranchised poor. For people working for black empowerment, Amos and Micah offer strong reminders that money matters. Economic justice is a necessary aspect of black advancement, particularly when the racial wealth divide is so staggering.

In one of his final addresses, Martin Luther King, Jr. emphasized the importance of economic justice, stating that many of the problems that plague black communities, i.e., shortcomings in housing and education, could be eliminated with the elimination of poverty.[6] Since black people contend with the evils of racism and violence against them, access to money would help to secure resources, as financial security has positive tangible and psychological impacts. Unfortunately, the racial wealth gap has worsened with the typical white family having eight times the wealth of the typical black family.[7] It is necessary to fight for higher wages, opportunities for educational and professional development, and financial investment in black communities as measures to correct the damage of race-based disenfranchisement.

Confront Problematic Histories

The prophet Huldah showed prophetic tenacity when prophesying in the seventh century BCE during the reign of King Josiah (640–609). Although no biblical books bear her name, Huldah was a significant prophet who lived in Jerusalem, and royal officials consulted her for guidance and wisdom.

Huldah played a pivotal role in the story of the finding of the book of the law and the religious reformation described in 2 Kings 22–23. In

6. See King, "Where Do We Go From Here?" See also the Poor People's Campaign of 1968, inspired by King's vision of economic justice and its revival in 2017.

7. This statement is based on the 2019 Survey of Consumer Finances (SCF) and analysis by the Federal Reserve Board. Using the SCF data, the Institute of Policy Studies published a report on the trends, implications of racial wealth gaps, and measures that can be taken to lessen the divide. For data, analysis, and suggestions such as wealth and inheritance taxes and increased minimum wage, see Collins et al., "Dreams Deferred."

the narrative, the high priest Hilkiah uncovers a book within the temple treasury (22:8), which many scholars posit as a version of the book of Deuteronomy, containing laws, blessing, and curses.[8] Realizing the people and leaders had failed in keeping its laws, Josiah laments, seeks prophetic guidance, and begins to reform his community.

Josiah sends Hilkiah with four royal officials to consult Huldah regarding the authenticity and validity of the book. Huldah confirms its content and predicts disaster because the people had forgotten their covenantal obligations. Huldah proclaims a divine message, saying: "I will indeed bring disaster on this place and on its inhabitants—all the words of the book that the king of Judah has read. Because they have abandoned me and have made offerings to other gods, they have offended me with all the work of their hands, therefore my wrath is kindled against this place, and it will not be quenched" (2 Kgs 22:16–17). Huldah's condemnation and ominous warning strongly suggest that people were worshipping images and idols devoted to gods other than the God of Israel, actions forbidden in Deuteronomy and throughout the biblical legal corpora.

Decisive Actions

Inspired by Huldah's word, Josiah took several actions. He read the book to the people of Judah, reminding them of the law. He reaffirmed covenantal loyalty to God, making "a covenant before Yahweh, to follow Yahweh, keeping his commandments, his decrees, and his statutes, with all his heart and all his soul, to perform the words of this covenant that were written in this book. All the people joined the covenant" (2 Kgs 23:3). Josiah then enacted reforms to dismantle unsanctioned religious practices. He tore down and burned altars, pillars, and sacred poles used in worship of gods and goddesses like Baal and Asherah, removed monuments dedicated to other gods, and desecrated vessels and cultic objects. As an extreme measure, Josiah deposed and killed priests who facilitated idolatry in the land. The extent and historicity of Josiah's reforms are not

---

8. "Finding" a long-forgotten book was a popular literary motif in the ancient Near East as a way to remind communities of the past and reinvigorate practices in the present. Some scholars suggest that Hilkiah or authors of the laws and historical traditions influenced by Deuteronomy (Deuteronomistic Historians) wrote the book and created a discovery story to compel people to follow the law. For discussion of the book discovery motif and scholarly perspectives on the book of the law, see Römer, *So-Called Deuteronomistic History*, 45–66.

known, but 2 Kings 23 envisions a robust and decisive reform to implement the laws that were written in the book in order to repair the relationship between the people and their God (23:24).

Although Josiah's reforms were impactful and were deemed necessary to eliminate idolatry, 2 Kings 23 must be read cautiously, as it could inspire intolerance and murder, particularly with the actions against religious leaders. Despite these warranted concerns, Josiah's reform is generally regarded as an important act towards restoration in which the people of Judah were able to reorient themselves back to worship of God. Huldah's compelling prophecy was the impetus for this reform, and Josiah's removal of idols, altars, and monuments shows a willingness to confront and eliminate vestiges of a problematic past.

Remove Symbols of Hate

Reading Huldah and Josiah's reform in light of modern debates about Confederate symbols offers important lessons. Confederate symbols—flags, monuments, building names—have been important topics of discussion for decades, as these public symbols are lingering evidence of racism and race-based discrimination in American history. Since the Confederate States' secession was inextricably linked with white supremacy and represented desires to maintain and expand the enslavement of black people, honoring images and flags of Confederates is problematic, to say the least. It is a tacit endorsement of their principles.

The Southern Poverty Law Center has compiled a list of Confederate monuments, and most originated in the Jim Crow era in order to intimidate black people and promote white supremacy, not simply to commemorate history.[9] Work to remove these monuments has been active since the 1960s. In 2013, urgent calls grew louder and more boisterous, reignited by the #BlackLivesMatter movement and calls for racial justice and police reform. Painful flashpoints have also compelled leaders to strip Confederate symbols from public spaces, especially the 2015 mass shooting of nine black church members at Emanuel African Methodist Episcopal Church in Charleston, South Carolina, by a white supremacist; the 2017 white supremacist rally in Charlottesville, Virginia in protest to the removal of a statue of Confederate general Robert E. Lee; and the 2020 murder of George Floyd by a police officer in Minneapolis, Minnesota. These events

9. Southern Poverty Law Center, "Whose Heritage?"

and other tragedies have inspired actions, such as the removal of the Confederate flag from the South Carolina State House (2015), changing of school names like a Mississippi school named for Confederate president Jefferson Davis becoming the Barack H. Obama Magnet Elementary School (2017); Congress passing a bill calling for the removal of Confederate names from Department of Defense property and equipment within three years (2020).[10] Like Josiah removing altars and cultic items devoted to false gods, the removal of the Confederate statues teaches people not to glorify Confederate insurrectionists or their hateful ideals.

The quest for black advancement and empowerment requires an understanding of the racist practices that dehumanized and marginalized black people in the first place. Those ideas must be remembered in history books, in museums, and in our collective consciousness lest we forget, or worse, repeat the mistakes of the past. The potential to repeat the past was on display in the 2021 storming of the United States Capitol with many would-be insurrectionists waving Confederate flags. Removing visible symbols of hate from positions of honor is a necessary and obvious step towards eliminating racism in America.

Take Time to Mourn

The scars of oppression and inequality are evident, and the prophet Jeremiah offers reminders to mourn for heartache and loss. Often called the weeping prophet, Jeremiah prophesied during the seventh and sixth centuries BCE during the reigns of Kings Josiah (640–609), Jehoiakim (609–598), and Zedekiah (597–86). He witnessed the Babylonian siege on Jerusalem, deportations of Judahites to Babylon, looting and destruction of the temple, and the fall of the kingdom. Jeremiah laments the suffering, death, and destruction around him, the inaction and exile of his people, and the difficulties of being a prophet: "My eyes weep bitterly and run down with tears, because the flock of Yahweh has been taken captive" (Jer 13:17). On an occasion when Jeremiah could not fully comprehend the suffering in his midst, he implores God for help, and the divine instruction was to summon the mourning women who would be able to express the distress of the period.

---

10. The status and precise timeline of this action are still pending. See https://www.politico.com/news/2021/01/05/pentagon-confederate-name-bases-455180.

Jeremiah is told to "Consider, and call for the mourning women to come; send for the wise women to come" (Jer 9:17).[11] The community responds by affirming the importance of the women mourners: "[L]et them quickly raise a dirge over us, so that our eyes may run down with tears, and our eyelids flow with water" (9:18). The mourning women cry, wail, gesticulate, and sing, leading the community in a release of emotions. As the people cry, they become self-reflective, speaking aloud the devastation of attack. They verbalize the pain of invasion, death, and loss of land, and they express shame because of their circumstances, implicitly taking some responsibility for the exile (9:19).

It is likely that many of the people of Judah, Jeremiah included, experienced numbness, blunted emotions, and disbelief, which are common reactions to traumatic events.[12] The community required help in coping with and articulating their trauma, and the mourning women mediated their grief, providing therapy, healing, and guidance on how to react to national tragedy. In addition to providing an emotional outlet, the women receive instruction to listen to the divine word and teach their daughters and neighbors how to lament (Jer 9:20). By teaching their daughters, the women ensure that the next generation also knows how to reflect on disaster.

For communities who suffer, it is important to express pain and anguish. Weeping reveals the painful realities of suffering and is a catharsis that can facilitate understanding in the present and future. Jeremiah and the mourning women weep to acknowledge pain and lead to healing, modeling behaviors that are essential for all who are working to overcome adversity.

Expect Haters, Naysayers, and Counter-Movements

Many of the biblical prophets experienced condemnation, ridicule, and violence from their families, local communities, and leaders. Prophets called for people to shift their consciousness and behavior. They shook up

11. Hebrew *haḥăkāmôt* is translated here as "the wise women" based on the Hebrew root *ḥkm*, "to be wise." Modern translations such as NRSV, NAB, NIV, and NKJV often render *haḥăkāmôt* as skilled or skillful women, which highlights the training and professional nature of women mourners in antiquity. However, calling the women wise is a clearer rendering of the Hebrew, and it fits the context of Jeremiah 9:12–24, which considers wisdom and understanding.

12. See Parkes and Prigerson, *Bereavement*, 73–79.

the status quo in an effort to effect change, and they often faced hostility for it. While biblical kings consulted prophets, they were not all eager to listen, especially if a message was unfavorable. In the ninth century BCE, King Ahab consulted prophets about whether he should go to war. Ahab initially only called prophets whom he thought would agree with him. Regarding the prophet Micaiah, Ahab said, "I hate him, for he does not prophesy anything favorable about me, but only misfortune" (1 Kgs 22:8; 2 Chr 18:7). When he finally invites Micaiah's perspective, Ahab is unsatisfied with his assessment and has Micaiah imprisoned.

In the sixth century BCE, Jeremiah and Ezekiel encountered hostility and counter-narratives especially during such a volatile period. During their careers, the kingdom of Judah faced threats from the Babylonians, including invasion and war, waves of exiles sent to Babylon, abrupt changes in leadership, looting and destruction of the temple, and the conquering of the kingdom. The period was devastating and traumatic, and Jeremiah and Ezekiel often blamed the people for their corrupt religious and social practices, which did not endear the prophets to their communities.

Jeremiah says he was mocked, targeted, and threatened because of his messages, even in his hometown of Anathoth and by a fellow religious leader. "Pashhur struck the prophet Jeremiah, and put him in the stocks" (Jer 20:2). Pashhur was a priest and chief officer in the temple. When he strikes Jeremiah (from the Hebrew root *nkh*, "to strike, smite, injure"), he commits a violent assault, an attack that often leads to death. When Pashhur puts Jeremiah in stocks, he may have been bound by his neck, arms, and legs, or he may have been bound away in prison. In either interpretation, Pashhur committed a hostile act of suppression.

A contemporary of Jeremiah, Ezekiel, prophesied while exiled in Babylon. He encountered false prophets who gave inauthentic or lying visions, creating counter-narratives. God routinely condemns these naysayers, and Ezekiel gives a divine statement against such false prophets: "My hand will be against the prophets who see false visions and utter lying divinations; they shall not be in the council of my people" (Ezek 13:9). The false prophets are condemned for not acknowledging reality: "[T]hey have misled my people, saying 'Peace,' when there is no peace" (Ezek 13:10). The false prophets often gave favorable statements, misrepresenting facts to make them more agreeable to their communities. The true prophets highlighted problems and inequities and called for honesty and accountability.

When there are calls for change and revolution, many in society will resist, especially those who need to change the most or who have the most to lose. Animosity and counter-narratives will likely emerge. The biblical prophets attest to this, and activists of today will likely concur. Look at the #BlackLivesMatter movement and its calls for racial justice and an end to police brutality. The movement has garnered national and international support, sparking conversations, marches, individual and collective reflection and accountability, and some policy changes and oversight. Yet, Black Lives Matter (BLM) activists have been threatened and demonized. BLM signs and murals have been defaced and destroyed. Like clockwork, the counter-movements of All Lives Matter and Blue Lives Matter sprung up to corrupt the message, failing intentionally or unintentionally to recognize BLM's point. People working for black advancement and empowerment must recognize these realities, anticipating opposition but not letting it deter their cause. Haters, naysayers, and counter-movements are to be expected, but they must not stop the fight.

Seek Justice

Prophetic literature offers much inspiration and wisdom, especially on issues of suffering, perseverance, and the importance of justice. Like many of today's activists, the biblical prophets worked to improve their societies. Their prophetic tenacity propelled them to critique wrongdoings, educate their communities, and inspire justice, especially for those who were oppressed and most vulnerable. Isaiah offers an important nuance on justice, especially for people of faith.

When the people of Judah were suffering during political instability and unrest, they performed various religious acts, such as praying, offering sacrifices, and celebrating solemn festivals (Isa 1:11–15). However, God rejected their religiosity because there was injustice in their society. An active faith in God is directly connected to the pursuit of justice, as Isaiah affirms: "[L]earn to do good; seek justice, rescue the oppressed, defend the orphan, plead for the widow" (1:17). Isaiah highlights classes of people who were most likely to suffer and who had the least legal recourse. The prophet proclaims that marginalized groups needed protection, advocacy, and access to resources, among other things. Such is the same today. The pursuit of black advancement and empowerment is a pursuit of justice, and Isaiah affirms that justice and repentance lead to divine blessing and redemption (1:27; 33:15–16; 56:1). For people of faith, the call to action is clear. The prophets condemn injustice in order to correct it. They accuse people of wrongdoings in order to arouse them to change their ways. As the work for justice continues today, the biblical prophets can inform those efforts and inspire individual and collective transformation.

Discussion Questions

1. What resources are needed to support black advancement and empowerment?

2. What can you do to overcome opposition to necessary change?

3. How can you live out prophetic tenacity and inspire your community?

4. What risks are associated with pursuing justice? What risks are there if justice is not pursued?

Works Cited

Bhutta, Neil, Andrew C. Chang, Lisa J. Dettling, Joanne W. Hsu, and Julia Hewitt. "Disparities in Wealth by Race and Ethnicity in the 2019 Survey of Consumer Finances." Division of Research and Statistics, Board of Governors of the Federal Reserve System, September 28, 2020. https://www.federalreserve.gov/econres/notes/feds-notes/disparities-in-wealth-by-race-and-ethnicity-in-the-2019-survey-of-consumer-finances-20200928.htm.

Coates, Ta-Nehisi. "The Case for Reparations." *Atlantic* 313, no. 5 (June 2014) 54–71. https://www.theatlantic.com/magazine/archive/2014/06/the-case-for-reparations/361631/.

Collins, Chuck, Dedrick Asante-Muhammed, Josh Hoxie, and Sabrina Terry. "Dreams Deferred: How Enriching the 1% Widens the Racial Wealth Divide." Institute for Policy Studies, January 15, 2019. https://inequality.org/wp-content/uploads/2019/01/IPS_RWD-Report_FINAL-1.15.19.pdf.

Gunter, Booth, Jamie Kizzire, and Cindy Kent. "Whose Heritage?: Public Symbols of the Confederacy." Southern Poverty Law Center, April 21, 2016. https://www.splcenter.org/sites/default/files/com_whose_heritage.pdf.

King, Martin Luther, Jr. "Where Do We Go From Here?" The Martin Luther King, Jr. Research and Educational Institute. https://kinginstitute.stanford.edu/king-papers/documents/where-do-we-go-here-address-delivered-eleventh-annual-sclc-convention.

O'Brien, Connor. "The Pentagon has 3 years to strip Confederate names from bases. Here's what comes next." *Politico*, January 5, 2021. https://www.politico.com/news/2021/01/05/pentagon-confederate-name-bases-455180.

Parkes, Colin Murray, and Holly G. Prigerson. *Bereavement: Studies of Grief in Adult Life*. London: Routledge, 2010.

"Poor People's Campaign." https://www.poorpeoplescampaign.org/.

Römer, Thomas. *The So-Called Deuteronomistic History: A Sociological, Historical and Literary Introduction*. New York: T & T Clark, 2007.

Southern Poverty Law Center. "Whose Heritage? Public Symbols of the Confederacy." https://www.splcenter.org/20190201/whose-heritage-public-symbols-confederacy.

Protesting Police Brutality and Criminal Injustice with Paul and Silas[1]

Dennis R. Edwards

Introduction

THOSE WHO PROFESS FAITH in Christ ought to lend their voices and energy to transforming law enforcement—including policing—rather than maintaining the status quo. Instead, some of the most vocal supporters of the current system, which disproportionately mistreats dark-skinned people—particularly African Americans and Latinos—profess to be Christians.[2] Recently, some of the protestors denouncing police brutality, especially in the wake of the police shooting of Breonna Taylor in her own home and George Floyd's heinous public execution by Minneapolis police officer Derek Chauvin—both in the spring of 2020—called for defunding the police by redirecting some of the money allocated for policing policies. Rather than some money continuing to be used to maintain a dysfunctional status quo, where police often perceive dark-skinned residents as more dangerous, unruly, and otherwise threatening when compared to whites, dollars can be channeled to different agencies that directly interact with the public. But many people did not take seriously calls for defunding—or even abolishing—the police. Even in Minneapolis, the epicenter of anti-brutality protests in 2020–21, citizens

---

1. This essay builds upon my earlier work, "Raising Our Voices: A Missional Reading of Acts 16:35–40" in *Haymanot Journal* Vol 1 (2021): 11–23

2. See Griffith, *God's Law and Order.*

rejected a measure to reimagine policing in its current form.[3] Ironically, a large segment of our society views protesting police violence as unpatriotic while validating—not merely accepting—police brutality. Earlier, in 2017, the President of the United States, Donald J. Trump, endorsed police brutality while addressing police officers in Brentwood, a community in Long Island, New York. The former president commented on the way police officers guard the heads of suspects when placing them in a squad car after an arrest admonishing the officers, "Please don't be too nice."[4] The president later publicly vilified former NFL player Colin Kaepernick, saying "Get that son of a bitch off the field." Kaepernick knelt during the playing of the National Anthem as a form of protest against police brutality, which President Trump and those in his camp mischaracterized as unpatriotic and anti-military. Even though increasing numbers of athletes have knelt without obvious penalty, and the NFL has made perfunctory overtures of solidarity with African Americans, it seems many in our society are agitated by such acknowledgements of police brutality. With #BlueLivesMatter as a rallying cry, many are not convinced that policing can or should be reimagined. Of course, much more could be said about society's general acceptance of heavy-handed police practices especially in light of the way "law and order" became coded language for targeting Blacks and other ethnic minorities, influencing the passing of the 1994 Crime Bill under President Clinton. This essay, however, is not a detailed analysis of policing as a practice but does constitute a call for Bible-readers to resist the status quo.

We may take a cue from Paul and Silas in Acts 16:35–40 as we consider what challenging policing might mean. The story of Paul and Silas the morning after their imprisonment supports the prophetic role that African Americans and their accomplices often play in confronting police brutality as well as broader injustices related to mass incarceration within our society. What follows is an analysis of Paul's and Silas's run-in with the police in the prominent Roman colony of Philippi. Employing principles of African American biblical interpretation, I explore Acts 16:35–40, a text that frequently gets overlooked or minimized, but as the epilogue to Paul's and Silas's evangelization of Philippi, the passage not only notes how they leveraged their relative privilege, but also demonstrates that the way of Jesus challenges injustice and does not support

3. https://www.npr.org/2021/11/02/1051617581/minneapolis-police-vote.

4. https://apnews.com/article/immigration-police-donald-trump-ap-top-news-crime-64169ad2576b4fc98ae8febc3554155d.

it. Paul's rebuke to the magistrates in Acts 16:37 does not picture him as a compliant, docile citizen of Rome who accepts injustice as merely the cost of policing. Instead, the apostle speaks out to denounce the way power operates in Philippi. Societal power can dehumanize those who cut against the grain, to the point of abusing and imprisoning innocent people. Paul's rage against the Philippian authorities is akin to prophetic cries against injustice that many African American Bible-readers see in Scripture and attempt to practice in society.

African American Biblical Interpretation's Emphasis on Liberation

African American hermeneutics is not monolithic. Perhaps no hermeneutical approach is. Even so, there are some shared assumptions among African American interpreters, as our work has historically rejected readings of the Bible that reinforce the systemic oppression caused by whiteness. *Whiteness* refers not primarily to skin color, but to a perspective that determines access to power and privilege.[5] I note four emphases of African American biblical interpretation as starting points for our analysis of Acts 16:35–40.

First, African American biblical interpretation recognizes the *missio Dei*, the mission of God, as fundamentally a rescue operation. God is the Liberator.[6] Salvation, in a full sense of the term, includes God's work to free humanity—spiritually and physically—from the clutches of sin and Satan.[7] "Since, therefore, the children share flesh and blood, he himself likewise shared the same things, so that through death he might destroy the one who has the power of death, that is, the devil, and free those who all their lives were held in slavery by the fear of death" (Heb 2:14–15). African American hermeneutics highlights God's rescue mission in the world. God, often through the efforts of God's people, performs the work to help deliver creation physically as well as spiritually. The book of Exodus has long served as the quintessential picture of God as deliverer. As James H. Evans, Jr. asserts, "the content of God's *revelation* is *liberation*."[8] Likewise, in the NT, Jesus exclaims, "For the Son of

---

5. See Powery and Sadler, *Genesis of Liberation*, 83–95.

6. E.g., Fields, *Introducing Black Theology*, 15

7. See Middleton and Gorman, "Salvation."

8. Evans, *We Have Been Believers*, 10 (emphasis original).

Man came not to be served but to serve, and to give his life a ransom for many" (Mark 10:45). The language of ransom, to people enmeshed in a world where slavery was commonplace, evokes emancipation—freedom from captivity. Furthermore, the Lord's own job description, or personal mission statement, taken from Isaiah 61:1–2 and found in Luke 4:16–19, rings out with the themes of liberation.

> When he came to Nazareth, where he had been brought up, he went to the synagogue on the sabbath day, as was his custom. He stood up to read, and the scroll of the prophet Isaiah was given to him. He unrolled the scroll and found the place where it was written:

> "The Spirit of the Lord is upon me,
> because he has anointed me
> to bring good news to the poor.
> He has sent me to proclaim release to the captives
> and recovery of sight to the blind,
> to let the oppressed go free,
> to proclaim the year of the Lord's favor."

Second, African American biblical interpretation serves to connect the liberating work of God to our own efforts to free those in captivity— spiritually as well as materially. African American biblical interpretation invites us to question oppressive readings of Scripture. Such interpretive efforts coincide with other postmodern approaches to biblical texts, especially liberation theology and Womanist interpretation, in resisting racist and otherwise oppressive interpretations of Scripture while advancing a "hermeneutic of wholeness."[9] Promoting the wholeness of African Americans and women does not diminish the wholeness of others.

My third point about African American biblical interpretation is the obvious respect it gives to African American readers, demanding we see ourselves as focal points within the biblical text and not ancillary to it. One simple example is the way many in the USA have been conditioned to visualize most biblical characters as white, except for occasional "special" individuals, such as Simon of Cyrene who carried Christ's cross, or the Ethiopian official.[10] When African American eyes peruse the text, we

9. St. Clair, "Womanist Biblical Interpretation," 59.

10. That eunuch is not often pictured as an important African official, but as a lowly lackey. Yet, even the Candace of Ethiopia—an important woman leader that Luke brings to our attention—often gets glossed over in retellings of the Acts 8 encounter with Phillip the evangelist.

see ourselves more clearly and engage the text with questions and commentary that white readers often miss or downplay.

Finally, African American biblical interpretation honors our social condition. When recognizing that the Bible often focuses on and celebrates people pushed to society's periphery, including a Savior who was a marginalized Jew, African American readers find resonance with our status and unique societal situation. We learn to follow the early church's lead in applying Scripture to present conditions under the guidance of the Holy Spirit, even with the obvious differences between the first and twenty-first centuries. For example, mainstream society alienated many of the earliest Christ-followers, such as the recipients of the letter called 1 Peter (e.g., 1 Pet 2:11–12). Yet Christ honors those who suffer unjustly because they reflect Christ's character most visibly (e.g., 1 Pet 2:19). Therefore, African American biblical interpretation sees the ways that our social condition mirrors that of early Christians.

While much more could be said about the liberative aspects of African American hermeneutics, the present issue is how a frequently overlooked passage of Scripture speaks directly to the situation of many Black people in the USA. The story of Paul and Silas in prison (Acts 16:16–40) is well-known to many churchgoing people, but the emphasis is typically placed on the conversion of the jailer and not what happens afterwards.[11] Yet, the words of the agitated apostle Paul in Acts 16:37, along with the response of the magistrates, affirms the godly mission of African Americans particularly regarding police brutality and mass incarceration.

Philippian Hospitality (Acts 16:12–24)

Philippi was a "first" (Luke uses *protos*) or "leading" city within Macedonia and a colony of Rome. As a Roman colony, Philippi enjoyed certain financial and self-governing advantages.[12] The imperial backdrop is important to our understanding of ministry in Philippi, but space prevents detailed discussion. It is sufficient to acknowledge, however, that residents of Philippi well understood the dynamics of social power within the Roman Empire. Upon arriving in Philippi, Paul and Silas find Lydia

---

11. E.g., Shiell, *Acts*, 127–32. This commentary geared toward preaching must be selective but serves as an example of how popular preaching on Acts 16 focuses on the conversion story but not Paul's outrage with the Philippian magistrates.

12. See, for example, Bird and Gupta, *Philippians*, 3–6.

down by the riverside and as this businesswoman receives the apostolic message, she gets baptized, along with her household, and offers the apostles hospitality, inviting them to stay in her home. Paul and Silas, however, briefly lose the comfort of Lydia's home and find themselves overnight guests of a Philippian jailer.

Paul and Silas land in prison after an encounter when they were heading to the place of prayer. Some men had been exploiting an enslaved girl, using her as a fortune-teller. The girl's daily pronouncement that "These men are slaves of the Most High God, who proclaim to you a way of salvation" (v. 17) agitates Paul so intensely that he exorcizes the demon that empowered the girl's utterances.[13] Interestingly, the Philippian businessmen do not seem impressed by Paul's supernatural power over the spirit that possessed the girl, but are furious over a loss of their source of income. The girl's enslavers seize the apostles and bring them before the local authorities. It doesn't take long for other Philippians to join in denouncing Paul and Silas, and soon the pair are tossed into prison.

C. Kavin Rowe helps us appreciate the significance of Paul's and Silas's imprisonment, noting how those who exploited the girl "have witnessed in Paul's exorcism the inherently destabilizing power of Jesus Christ for the pagan way of life."[14] These enslavers lost a source of income as the power of Jesus Christ confronted their business. The businessmen's charge against Paul and Silas, directed to the city officials is, "These men are disturbing our city; they are Jews and are advocating customs that are not lawful for us as Romans to adopt or observe" (Acts 16:20b–21). We ought not miss the point that as Luke tells the story, Paul and Silas are innocent. Rowe notes well that "in a strictly legal sense, the charges are untrue and incapable of substantiation."[15] Furthermore, the accusers exploit anti-Jewish bias, adding to the crowd's animosity toward Paul and Silas.[16]

---

13. Paul seems to be bothered by how the statements, even though accurate, flow from the mouth of a demon-possessed girl, perhaps sending a confusing message to onlookers. See Craig S. Keener, *Acts*, 394–402. Even though Paul is silent regarding the young women's social predicament as an exploited slave who brought her enslavers "a great deal of money" according to Acts 16:16, the exorcism liberates the woman from evil forces (Keener, *Acts*, 402). It is also noteworthy that the enslaved girl refers to Paul and Silas as God's "slaves." Paul's attitude toward Greco-Roman slavery, as well as his own appropriation of the word *doulos* ("slave") is beyond the scope of this essay, but see e.g., Mitzi Smith, "Slavery in the Early Church."

14. Rowe, *World Upside Down*, 26.

15. Rowe, *World Upside Down*, 26.

16. Bird and Gupta, *Philippians*, 11, assert that the enslavers, "used the naming of

Keener highlights the episode's irony in that the enslavers "act by incit-ing xenophobic unrest—meanwhile audaciously accusing the defendants of inciting unrest!"[17] The issue is not strictly one of disobeying the law, but of upsetting the status quo for people possessing societal clout and using ethnic (including religious) difference to discredit Paul and Silas. By way of comparison, consider the interaction between two people with the surname Cooper in Central Park back in 2020.[18] African American bird-watcher Christian Cooper requested white Amy Cooper to leash her dog that was roaming freely. At one point during the interaction, Amy Cooper called emergency number 911, telling the dispatcher to send the police because an African American man was threatening her. Christian Cooper video-recorded Amy Cooper's call to the police. Mr. Cooper was not a threat, according to the recording, but Amy Cooper expected the police to believe her—a white woman frightened of a Black man. The police did respond, but both Coopers had departed by the time the police arrived. It seems clear that Christian Cooper did not commit a crime; he threatened Amy Cooper's sense of entitlement, but not her life. Such is the case with Paul and Silas disrupting the Philippian businessmen by challenging their exploitative practice yet not physically assaulting or otherwise harming them. Law enforcement tends to buttress the claims of those with relative status—which encompasses economic and ethnic factors—and such was the case on that day in Philippi.

Police officers strip, flog, and imprison the apostles (16:22–24). Around midnight, however, the apostles were praying and singing hymns to God with other prisoners listening, when a violent earthquake strikes with enough power to unhinge doors and unloose shackles (16:25–27). The *desmophylax* (keeper of the prison, or "warden"), distressed over the possibility that prisoners had escaped under his watch, draws his sword in order to commit suicide. The warden's actions may be extreme to us, but Roman magistrates, to whom the warden was accountable, wielded significant clout. Christopher J. Fuhrmann stresses that "Magistrates were doubly powerful, first by virtue of their office but also because they were by definition members of the local elite, whose importance to imperial

---

their ethnicity ("Jews") to discredit them. See also Fitzmyer, *Acts*, 587, and Keener, *Acts*, 404, who both explore Roman anti-Jewish sentiment.

17. Keener, *Acts*, 404.

18. https://www.nytimes.com/2020/06/14/nyregion/central-park-amy-cooper-christian-racism.html.

society is hard to exaggerate . . . It was obviously dangerous to run afoul of a town's magistrates, especially when one's status was low."[19]

Paul and Silas guide the warden to faith in Jesus Christ, and as with Lydia, that jailer gets baptized along with his household. Paul and Silas receive hospitality once again from a new convert, as the prison warden feeds the apostles and nurses their wounds (16:34). This climatic episode is often the point where many preachers and teachers conclude the story of Paul and Silas in Philippi. Yet, the interaction Paul has with the warden the next morning is especially relevant for African Americans who, as citizens of the USA, are not often afforded the respect that white citizens are given when engaged by law enforcement.

After Midnight in a Philippian Jail

In the morning, the magistrates dispatch the *rhabdouchoi*, literally "rod-bearers" (Latin: *licotes*) (16:35), the "police" who beat Paul and Silas the previous day (16:22). The rod-bearers bring orders to "release these men," which the warden interprets as good news, reporting to Paul that he and Silas can "go in peace." Paul, however, is outraged by the warden's report. Rather than leaving straightway, Paul protests. He accuses the magistrates of beating Silas and him in public without having been convicted in a trial. The magistrates are afraid (16:38) because the Roman *Lex Porcia de provocation* "forbade under severe penalty the flogging of a Roman citizen."[20] According to Rowe, the aforementioned *Lex Porcia* was strengthened under Emperor Augustus by the *lex Iulia de vi publica*, preventing Roman citizens from being beaten, bound with chains, or having a yoke put around the neck.[21] Fuhrmann recounts an incident of a military policeman within the Roman Empire who was castigated by the governor for torturing a man without the presence of witnesses.[22] While the Romans were certainly not opposed to torture (after all, they perfected the horrible practice of crucifixion), citizenship in the empire offered certain privileges. Paul's protest resonates with African American experiences and should get as much consideration as the conversion narrative that precedes. Yet, as noted, there is a tendency to overlook this

---

19. Fuhrmann, *Policing the Roman Empire*, 58–59.

20. Fitzmyer, *Acts of the Apostles*, 589.

21. Rowe, *World Upside Down*, 67.

22. Fuhrmann, *Policing the Roman Empire*, 87.

epilogue to the narrative. There are at least two ways that demonstrate how many people reading Acts 16 miss what an African American reading might catch.

First, the emphasis on the conversion of the jailer bolsters the idea often touted in especially evangelical circles that we should "just preach the gospel," and not be concerned about issues of justice. This perspective is part of the truncated way that many evangelicals tend to read the Scriptures. While the jailer's conversion is important—even critical—so is the prison context as well as Paul's challenge to the magistrates. Economic interests and xenophobia are the main factors in the arrest of Paul and Silas, but those are often glossed over in contemporary recounting so as to focus on the jail warden's conversion. Such focus creates an unnecessary distinction between spiritual matters and practical matters of justice.

Second, within many—mostly white—evangelical circles, one frequently hears the assertion that Christians should not engage in protests against the state. Those who possess relative privilege in society can make such an assertion.[23] Yet such an assertion is hypocritical because people in power will readily challenge the state when their way of life is threatened, as with the Philippian businessmen. The admonition against protesting is directed toward those oppressed by the system, such as when white clergy in Alabama denounced Dr. Martin Luther King, Jr.'s activism in their state, which prompted King's "Letter from a Birmingham Jail," eloquently refuting the arguments of those white clergy. During the civil rights movement, white Christians—as well as some cautious African Americans—questioned and challenged the appropriateness of public protests. Even today, BLM activists and many others who gather publicly to denounce police brutality are seen as a threat to the common good, when in actuality the activists are often challenging injustice in the present system.

A liberative reading of Acts 16:35–40 provides biblical direction for public protests. Paul's complaint to the magistrates and demand that they personally visit the prison to engage the apostles in person, shifts the power dynamic. Paul and Silas no longer appear as hapless and helpless

---

23. Regarding the notion of privilege, see Gilliard, *Subversive Witness*. On pages 83–96, Gilliard explores our passage, Acts 16:35–40, through the lens of privilege, noting that Paul and Silas leveraged their privilege as Roman citizens "to demand judicial accountability" (89).

victims, but as enlightened citizens, aware of their rights. This serves to "put the magistrates on the defensive."[24]

Liberative Implications of Paul's Response

Oftentimes the police of today function similarly to the "rod-bearers" of the Roman Empire, using physical—and even lethal—force on people who appear to have little social capital.[25] I say "appear," because racial profiling has been a factor causing black and brown bodies to bear disproportional abuse by police.[26] The system often appears impotent to deliver justice. African American biblical interpretation draws us to Paul's assertion of his rights with two key implications for our contemporary context.

First, policing and criminal justice are not clear-cut matters of guilt and innocence. Not all imprisoned people are guilty because sometimes the system gets it wrong. Our society has tended to assume that the "rod-bearers"—the police—apprehend only guilty people and that incarcerated people must have committed the crimes of which they've been accused and tried. People in privilege act as if the criminal justice system always works fairly. Police brutality, false charges, coerced confessions, and sham trials maintain a system that favors the wealthy and high-ranking in society at the expense of those deemed expendable, and such was the case with Paul and Silas. These apostles were innocent even though the powerful Philippian justice system had assumed otherwise. Willie J. Jennings, in making clear that imprisonment and morality are not necessarily connected, highlights the liberative work of God in this Acts episode:

> We have been brought into the space between people and prison systems through the Spirit who guides us into God's liberating work (Luke 4:18–19). The disciples of Jesus cut through the quick and easy alignments of crime and punishment knowing that what constitutes a crime is a complex reality created at the intersection of public policies, government actions or inactions, and concealed private interests. Who gets arrested, charged, tried, and convicted is very often a matter of who has access to resources or who enters judicial processes already profoundly

24. Fitzmyer, *Acts*, 590.

25. See McCaulley, *Reading While Black*, 25–46.

26. https://www.americanbar.org/groups/criminal_justice/publications/criminal-justice-magazine/2020/winter/racial-profiling-past-present-and-future/.

disadvantaged. This means that we resist the collapsing of our moral vision into the moral language that surrounds judicial systems and imprisonment. The question is not can a judicial or prison system be moral, but rather how must a disciple of Jesus give witness to its end and the beginning of a new way of life together?[27]

The entire episode, Acts 16:12–40, points out how guilt and innocence are not always obvious.

Second, injustice needs to be identified and denounced. Paul's plea for the magistrates to acknowledge their unjust treatment echoes the cries of Israel's prophets, such as Isaiah: "Is not this the fast that I choose: to loose the bonds of injustice, to undo the thongs of the yoke, to let the oppressed go free, and to break every yoke?" (Isa 58:6). The prophets, who speak and act for God, often rebuke people in authority because those people have societal power to harm as well as help. The liberating work of God reverberates in the apostle's call for justice. Furthermore, Paul provides a lesson about peace and justice for Lydia and the warden—recent converts—and also for subsequent generations of Christians. God is committed to justice, which includes fair treatment of the vulnerable. The Roman Empire was certainly not a USA-type democracy, but the overarching message that God rebukes injustice is universal.

Our African American lens on the text does not allow us to gloss over it but to linger with the notions of false imprisonment, police brutality, and the demand for justice. The story of Paul and Silas motivates us not to remain silent in the face of injustice, but to make our plea to the powerful to obey their own laws. Willard Swartley suggests that Paul and Silas sought an apology because peace seeks the restoration of relationships—even between citizens and the state—and is possible "only when misdeeds are duly acknowledged."[28] Although there is always the temptation to fight fire with fire, our faith compels us to live at peace with all people as much as possible (Rom 12:18). Within our history is the awareness that there can be no peace without justice ("no justice, no peace"). Yet we also know that retribution is not the way of Christ. Instead, we demand the acknowledgment of wrong—even on the part of the state—and then subsequent acts of reparation designed to right the wrongs.

---

27. Jennings, *Acts*, 168–69.

28. Swartley, *Covenant of Peace*, 168–69. See also my discussion of this incident in *Might from the Margins*, 100–103.

Conclusion

Paul's sense of justice was a product of his engagement with Israel's Scriptures. His Hellenistic background and status gave him confidence to bring his passion for justice to the secular Roman authorities. Rowe observes a "reversal" motif in Acts 16:35–40, "With officials fearfully kowtowing before a pair of stubborn missionaries, the reversal in Philippi alerts the reader to the social and legal power of Paul's Roman citizenship and its significance for any conflict he might have with the state."[29] Paul's conflicts with the state did not arise because he was immoral or a lawbreaker. He was a victim of injustice. African Americans can read the narrative of Acts 16:35–40 and see that when we are victims of injustice, one course of action that God sanctions is our calling secular authorities to abide by their own laws, intervene positively in the situation, acknowledge the injustice, and do whatever justice demands. Our reading demonstrates that African American demands for justice, especially regarding the mass incarceration and police brutality that disproportionately affect us, find robust support in the apostle Paul's demands to Philippian magistrates. Christians who protest against injustice have the apostle Paul setting a precedent.

Discussion Questions

1. Do you think that Christians should engage in public protest?

2. In what ways might there be a parallel between the *rod-bearers* in the Acts 16 episode and contemporary law enforcement?

3. Do contemporary government officials respond to unjust treatment of black citizens the way that the magistrates responded to Paul and Silas (with fear; Acts 16:38)?

4. How might black citizens leverage that status to combat injustice?

Works Cited

Bird, Michael F., and Nijay K. Gupta. *Philippians*. NCBC. Cambridge: Cambridge University Press, 2020.

Edwards, Dennis R. *Might from the Margins: The Gospel's Power to Turn the Tables on Injustice*. Harrisburg, PA: Herald, 2020.

29. Rowe, *World Upside Down*, 68.

Evans, James H., Jr. *We Have Been Believers: An African American Systematic Theology.* 2nd ed. Minneapolis: Fortress, 2012.

Fields, Bruce. *Introducing Black Theology: Three Crucial Questions for the Evangelical Church.* Grand Rapids: Baker Academic, 2001.

Fitzmyer, Joseph A. *The Acts of the Apostles: A New Translation with Introduction and Commentary.* AB 31. New York: Doubleday, 1998.

Fuhrmann, Christopher J. *Policing the Roman Empire: Soldiers, Administration, and Public Order.* New York: Oxford University Press, 2012.

Gilliard, Dominique DuBois. *Subversive Witness: Scripture's Call to Leverage Privilege.* Grand Rapids: Zondervan, 2021.

Griffith, Aaron. *God's Law and Order: The Politics of Punishment in Evangelical America.* Cambridge: Harvard University Press, 2020.

Jennings, Willie James. *Acts.* Belief: A Theological Commentary on the Bible. Louisville: Westminster John Knox, 2017.

Keener, Craig S. *Acts.* NCBC. Cambridge: Cambridge University Press, 2020.

McCaulley, Esau. *Reading While Black: African American Biblical Interpretation as an Exercise in Hope.* Downers Grove, IL: IVP Academic, 2020.

Middleton, J. Richard, and Michael J. Gorman. "Salvation." In *New Interpreter's Dictionary of the Bible* vol. 5, edited by Katherine Doob Sakenfeld, 45–61. Nashville: Abingdon, 2009.

Rowe, C. Kavin. *World Upside Down: Reading Acts in the Graeco-Roman Age.* New York: Oxford University Press, 2009.

Shiell, William D. *Acts: Preaching the Word.* Macon, GA: Smyth & Helwys, 2017.

Smith, Mitzi. "Slavery in the Early Church." In *True to Our Native Land: An African American New Testament Commentary*, edited by Brian K. Blount, Cain Hope Felder, Clarice J. Martin, and Emerson B. Powery, 11–22. Minneapolis: Fortress, 2007.

St. Clair, Raquel. "Womanist Biblical Interpretation." In *True to Our Native Land: An African American New Testament Commentary*, edited by Brian K. Blount, Cain Hope Felder, Clarice J. Martin, and Emerson B. Powery, 54–62. Minneapolis: Fortress, 2007.

Swartley, Willard M. *Covenant of Peace: The Missing Peace in New Testament Theology and Ethics.* Grand Rapids: Eerdmans, 2006.

Powery, Emerson B., and Rodney Sadler. *The Genesis of Liberation: Biblical interpretation in the Antebellum Narratives of the Enslaved.* Louisville: Westminster John Knox, 2016.

Biblical Accounts of Racial Profiling and the Social Death of Black Lives

JAMAL-DOMINIQUE HOPKINS

Introduction

I WAS STANDING IN the family room of my parents' California home on January 27, 2023, when CNN announced that police body camera footage of the Tyre Nichols police beating would be aired live across various cable news channels.[1] The footage involved the beating of yet another Black man, but this time by Black police officers. I thought, do I really want to witness another incidence of brutality against a Black-bodied individual who had been profiled and killed by law enforcement? Nonetheless, I resolved to watch.

Ethnic profiling is not new or even a modern-day phenomenon. Within the biblical account, due to a host of reasons, sanctioned profiling by respective officials existed from the Egyptians oppressing the Israelites in Egypt (Exod 1:8–17 and 2–12) to the Babylonian oppression of Israel, which included Babylonian King Nebuchadnezzar targeting three young Hebrew boys (Shadrach, Meshach, and Abednego) for not worshiping Babylonian idols (Daniel 3). In the New Testament, King Herod profiled and killed the male toddlers and infants of Bethlehem in an attempt to root out Jesus, the newborn Messiah (Matt 2:16–18). Considering these varying accounts, this essay explores similarities between experiences from the biblical texts, Matthew 2 in particular, and contemporary experiences

---

1. Hammond et al., "January 27, 2023 News on the Death of Tyre Nichols."

of police brutality against Black people, most recently witnessed from the murder of Tyre Nichols. Utilizing aspects of poststructural intertextuality and reader response criticism, these experiences are also explored by recognizing that a historical-critical analysis of the biblical text shows that historical realities illuminate our contemporary experiences and demonstrates that these texts have profound embedded meaning.

Racial Profiling in the Days of King Herod

In Matthew 2:1–18, the visitation of magi from the east to worship the newborn King of the Jews precipitates King Herod's indignation. Matthew 2:1–9 describes the magi's arrival in Jerusalem. Upon following the star of Bethlehem, the magi inquire regarding the whereabouts of the child who has been born King of the Jews. A fearful and paranoid King Herod learns from his counsel that the prophesied Messiah was to be born in Bethlehem of Judea. Upon learning the vicinity, and now threatened by the prospect that a prophesied king had been born who would possibly overtake his reign, Herod requests that the magi return to him to make known the exact location of the child. Matthew 2:12 states, "And having been warned in a dream not to return to Herod, they [the magi] left for their own country by another road."[2] These same magi, who were familiar with and open to following astrological phenomena (here, the star), are also responsive and open to following the phenomena of the Judean deity.[3] Matthew 2:13–15 similarly describes Joseph, the stepfather of the newborn king, being instructed in a dream to flee Bethlehem for Northern Africa to escape preemptively Herod's imposed infanticide.

Police body cameras, cell phone video cameras, social media live streams, and close-captioned video cameras that can convey tragedies like the Nichols beating provide graphic visual depictions of the brutality that took place in Matthew 2:16–18. The divine warning to only one family escaping Herod's murderous campaign does not negate the physical death of so many. Yet the warning to and the fleeing of Jesus' family does enable God to establish sovereign grace, which implements hope and

---

2. All verses are taken from the New Revised Standard Version unless otherwise indicated.

3. Tannehill et al., eds., *New Interpreters Bible Commentary*, 77–78, similarly notes this.

salvation from a societal structured system that perpetuates social death and natal alienation.

Racial Profiling in America

Over the span of nearly a decade, since the 2014 televised killing of Eric Garner, who was choked to death by New York City police officers on suspicion of selling cigarettes, subsequent police inflicted deaths of un-armed Black victims occurred: Michael Brown (Ferguson, Missouri); Ezell Ford (Los Angeles, California, who suffered from mental health issues); twelve-year-old Tamir Rice (Cleveland, Ohio, shot and killed by police officers while playing with a toy gun in a public park); Walter Scott (North Charleston, South Carolina, who was shot in the back while attempting to flee officer Michael Slager, who pulled him over for a non-functioning brake light); Freddie Gray (Baltimore, Maryland); Philando Castile (Falcon Heights, Minnesota); Stephon Clark (Sacramento, California, who was shot while on the ground in the yard of his grandmoth-er's residence); Botham Jean (Dallas, Texas, fatally shot by officer Amber Guyger while he was sitting in his living room eating ice cream); Breonna Taylor (Louisville, Kentucky, an emergency medical technician who was shot and killed in her home after officers, who without a search warrant failed to knock or announce themselves, breached her front door with a battering ram); George Floyd (Minneapolis, Minnesota, who died after officer Derek Chauvin kneeled on Floyd's neck, while he was handcuffed on the ground, for nearly nine minutes). The murders of other Black people have, in some form, also been publicly broadcast in the media, which has only reinforced trauma within Black communities.

Recurring instances of such deaths evoke shock, horror, anger, sad-ness, and a sense of hopelessness. The public beating and death of Tyre Nichols was different, though. The nation witnessed a Black man being murdered by the hands of five Black police officers. Aside from a mix of emotions, a deep sense of grief gripped the nation with what appeared to be a profound expression of self-loathing that extended beyond injustice and an egregious abuse of police power and moral responsibility. The na-tion witnessed the disregard of life, dignity, and humanity of the Black self.

Black Police Officers Not Exempt
from Being Racially Profiled

The ironic tragedy is that this very encounter could have happened to any one of the five Black Memphis cops who violently carried out the execution of Nichols. Like police profiling of Black civilians, instances of Black law enforcement officers themselves being racially profiled and suffering abuse by police is equally common. Such encounters, which have occurred across the nation, include Herb Robinson, a sergeant with the Kansas City Police Department, who was profiled while in uniform;[4] David Conners, a Clayton County, Georgia detention center officer who was profiled and handcuffed while shopping at Walmart;[5] Michael McQueen, a retired and disabled military veteran and recent police academy graduate in Texas, who was profiled while in uniform;[6] Herschel Smith, a police constable of Waller County, Texas who was profiled while in uniform;[7] Christopher Williams, an officer with the Detroit Police Department who was profiled and assaulted while at the department's training center;[8] four black parole officers in New York who were held at gunpoint while on official business;[9] and countless others. The four parole officers, who subsequently filed a lawsuit against the Suffern, New York Police Department, claimed that they were traumatized. Such encounters evoke memories of the opening scenes of the 1967 film *In the Heat of the Night*, featuring Sidney Poitier and Rod Steiger. While this film's narrative unfolds with a seemingly calm racial resolve, the impact of racially motivated policing has affected the mental health of Black communities and individuals,[10] even leading to diagnoses of post-traumatic stress syndrome, according to the American Psychological Association: "being bullied at school for being 'different,' racial profiling by police, and workplace racial harassment can all be DSM-5

---

4. Roberts, "Black Kansas City, Mo. Cop Sues." Also, see Rice and Nozicka, "He Was a Detective with the KDPD."

5. Berlin, "Officer Sues Walmart."

6. Grio Staff, "Recent Black Police Academy Grad Says."

7. Langford, "Black Texas Cop Accuses Fellow Officers of Racial Profiling."

8. Wimbley and Komer, "White Detroit Cop Found Guilty."

9. Higgins, "Video Shows 4 Black Officers Held at Gunpoint."

10. Pieterse, "Perceived Racism May Impact Black Americans' Mental Health." Also see Cho, "How Trauma Impacts Black Communities."

Criterion A events, but these are rarely included in conventional check-lists and batteries for trauma."[11]

In 2017, John Paul and Michael Birzer completed a study that ex-plored Black police officers who were racially profiled.[12] In this study, they noted, "racial profiling has been an institutionalized and systemic part of law enforcement culture."[13] Paul and Birzer highlight additional studies, which conclude that such practices are a matter of policy for "curtail-ing crime and criminal behavior."[14] Paul and Birzer go on to highlight a number of factors behind Black officers who have been racially profiled by other police, including:

1. Black officers driving in the wrong neighborhoods;

2. White officers' upbringing and their perceptions of media's biased depictions of Blacks as criminals;

3. The anomaly of Black officers and a perception that Black cops oc-cupy white spaces;

4. Stereotyping of Blacks as less intelligent and beneficiaries of affirma-tive action programs;

5. White officers not viewing Black officers as real cops due to a sus-picion that Black officers have an allegiance to Black communities.

Studies noting policing policies and behavior reveal that officers feel justified in using excessive force, even violence, illegally, if a citizen showed disrespect, talked back, or was hostile, uncooperative, or im-polite.[15] Despite some of this data dating back to the mid-twentieth century and considering the fact that new laws affecting changes in law enforcement policy and police behavior have been put in place, William Westley, in a 1958 study, reveals some yet held views baked into twenty-first-century police culture. His study reveals that some officers feel le-gitimized in roughing up a citizen, legally or illegally, to coerce respect: "The individual who lacks respect for the police, the 'wise guy' who talks back, or any individual who acts or talks in a disrespectful way, deserves

11. See Williams, "Uncovering the Trauma of Racism."

12. Paul and Birzer, "Experiences of Black Police Officers."

13. Paul and Birzer, "Experiences of Black Police Officers," 568.

14. Paul and Birzer, "Experiences of Black Police Officers," 568.

15. Westley, "Violence and the Police." Also see Paul and Birzer, "Experiences of Black Police Officers," 579, and Schenwar, Macaré, and Price, eds., *Who Do You Serve, Who Do You Protect?*

brutality. This idea is epitomized in admonitions of rookies such as 'You gotta make them respect you' and 'You gotta act tough.'"[16]

Excessive Force Baked into Police Culture

Westley's study reveals that some police feel that although justified in using excessive force, they may limit it to situations where they feel they can get away with it or cover it up in cases where they recognize that a person is guilty of a serious crime. These officers are quick to accuse a suspect of resisting arrest, "and the extent to which they believe a man guilty tends to act as a precondition to the use of violence."[17] The Memphis city police officers who fatally beat Nichols provided such a narrative while their body cameras were recording the incident. As seen from the recorded footage, Memphis officers can be heard repeatedly shouting "get on the ground," while Nichols was already on the ground, and "give me your hands," while body camera footage clearly shows officers holding Nichols' arms and hands.[18] The initial police report, according to *The New York Times*, states that officers wrote that Nichols was "an irate suspect who had 'started to fight' with Memphis police officers, even reaching for one of their guns."[19] The *Times* reports that officers claim that Nichols was stopped on January 7 after quickly driving into oncoming traffic. Officers reported that Nichols "had been 'refusing a lawful detention' and fought detectives on the scene."[20] Videos of the incident, however, show the opposite. After approaching Nichols's car with guns drawn and yanking him out of the vehicle, Nichols can be seen on the ground complying with officers as they aggressively curse at him, barking contradictory commands as if to create a narrative to justify their seemingly premeditated excessive use of force. In the video footage, officers are heard threatening to blow Nichols away, to break his arms, to knock him out, and to tase him. They eventually pepper-spray him while he is on the ground with his hands behind his back. It is then that Nichols makes it up onto his feet and flees from multiple officers as they seemingly watch. This odd spectacle appears staged, as if the officers planned and anticipated his fleeing.

---

16. Westley, "Violence and the Police," 39.

17. Westley, "Violence and the Police," 40.

18. See embedded videos at Helsel, Madani, and Lenthang, "Harrowing Videos."

19. Jaglois, Bogel-Burroughs, and Smith, "Initial Police Report."

20. Jaglois, Bogel-Burroughs, and Smith, "Initial Police Report."

After Nichols flees from officers and is subsequently captured within a few feet from his home, a subsequent video shows the Black Memphis cops brutally beating him while his hands are being held behind his back and eventually lying on the ground crying out for his mother. The initial police report does not mention officer aggression or the brutal beating. Towards the end of the footage, while officers are standing around, one Black officer can be heard saying that Nichols is on something, that he is high. Officers can be heard rehearsing the narrative that Nichols reached for and grabbed one of the officer's guns. Officers also paint Nichols as aggressively fighting them during the initial stop.

The way the Nichols incident unfolds coheres with policing policies and police culture described in the above studies. The most telling part of Westley's study relates to how police view and respond to Black people. According to Westley, police culture teaches that Blacks only respond to fear and rough treatment, whereas "In the good districts you appeal to people's judgment and explain the law to them."[21] A Henry J. Kaiser Family Foundation (KFF) Health Tracking Poll reports, as of 2020, that 63 percent of Black adults say they have experienced racial profiling during a twelve-month period. Forty-one percent reported being stopped or detained by the police and 21 percent reported that they have been the victim of police violence.[22]

What Is Social Death?

The Tyre Nichols fatal beating is akin to the encounter of Matthew 2:16–18. Like the five Black Memphis cops, King Herod shared ethnic affiliation with those whom he brutalized: the male toddlers and infants of Bethlehem. Herod was Idumaean, from Edom, and, thus, a descendant of Isaac, who was the father of Esau and Jacob. As such, Idumeans shared ethnic heritage and religious affiliation (Judaism) with the descendants of Jacob, who was the brother of Esau. In consideration of this, Herod was no different. Matthew 2:1–3 notes that King Herod's act of infanticide was motivated by his fear of losing political and social power sanctioned under Roman authority. Another factor motivated Herod, though: self-hatred! As such, Herod's act not only led to physical death, but it was also

---

21. Westley, "Violence and the Police," 40.

22. KFF, "Poll." Also see Schwartz and Jahn, "Mapping Fatal Police Violence." Finally, see Bor, Venkataramani, and Tsai, "Police Killings and Their Spillover Effect."

an act of natal alienation and self-natal alienation. Herod's act of killing these particular children was psychotically an act of separating children from their parents, which essentially was a second type of death: a social death whereby his objectification of these ethnic-born Judean children was self-reflected. The idea of social death comes from the thought of Orlando Patterson and is reoriented in Frank Wilderson III's work on Afro-pessimism. According to Wilderson,

> Social death has three constituent elements: One is gratuitous violence, which means that the body of the slave is open to the violence of all others. Whether he or she receives that violence or not, he or she exists in a state of structural or open vulnerability. This vulnerability is not contingent upon his or her transgressing some type of law, as in going on strike with the worker . . . Because you exist in a regime of violence which is gratuitous, open, and you are openly vulnerable to everyone else, [it is] not a regime of violence that is contingent upon you being a transgressing worker or transgressing woman or someone like that. And the third point is general dishonor, which is to say, you are dishonored in your very being—and I think that this is the nature of Blackness with everyone else. You're dishonored prior to your performance of dishonored actions.[23]

It is significant to highlight what Wilderson notes in this excerpt, that is, Blackness is dishonored in its very being. Such dishonoring can take place even among those who share the same state or space of "dishonored Blackness" as demonstrated by the five Memphis police officers. King Herod was, like the children he was killing, also Judean, which meant that his action was self-reflected and self-objectifying, for he engaged in the murder of those who looked like him. Perhaps wrestling with an unresolved warring of what W. E. B. DuBois called the double consciousness of Black folks,[24] the Memphis officers' actions led not only to the physical death of a Black man, but their actions were also self-reflecting and self-objectifying, which actualized and furthered the notion of the social death of Black people. Such Black objectification and social death have a history in this nation, particularly in the socially enforced family separations highlighted in the treatment of enslaved Black families during America's antebellum period. Remarking on a 1774 freedom petition,

23. Wilderson, "Blacks and the Master/Slave Relation," 18. Also see Paterson, *Slavery and Social Death*.

24. See DuBois, *Souls of Black Folk*.

where enslaved Africans wrote to government officials of Massachusetts, Lisa Bowens notes:

> while slaveholders often begin and end their scriptural exegesis with Ephesians 6:5–6, Colossians 3:22–24, or 1 Timothy 6:1–2, these enslaved Africans maintain that true scriptural exegesis begins in Ephesians 5:22 [and Colossians 3:18–20] with instructions to fathers. The practice of slavery, which separates family members from one another, violates all the household admonitions set forth by the apostle.[25]

Bowens's examination demonstrates that agents of oppression reinterpreted Scripture to validate violence and the social death of Black people but black people resisted such interpretations. This experience of separation is saliently recounted in the autobiography of Henry Box Brown, an enslaved Virginian during the nineteenth century, who describes watching helplessly as his wife and children were being taken away in chains.[26] The reader of this episode senses his struggle with a resolve that he would one day see them again in heaven. Brown writes:

> I received a message, that if I wished to see my wife and children, and bid them the last farewell, I could do so, by taking my stand on the street where they were all to pass on their way for North Carolina. I quickly availed myself of this information, and placed myself by the side of a street, and soon had the melancholy satisfaction of witnessing the approach of a gang of slaves, amounting to three hundred and fifty in number, marching under the direction of a Methodist minister, by whom they were purchased, and amongst which slaves were my wife and children . . . These beings were marched with ropes about their necks, and staples on their arms, and, although in that respect the scene was no very novel one to me, yet the peculiarity of my own circumstances made it assume the appearance of unusual horror. This train of beings was accompanied by a number of wagons loaded with little children of many different families, which as they appeared rent the air with their shrieks and cries and vain endeavours to resist the separation which was thus forced upon them, and the cords with which they were bound; but what should I now see in the very foremost wagon but a little child looking towards me and pitifully calling, father! father!

---

25. Bowens, *African American Readings of Paul*, 23.
26. Bowens, *African American Readings of Paul*, 23–25.

> This was my eldest child, and I was obliged to look upon it for
> the last time that I should, perhaps, ever see it again in life.[27]

The violent actions of the five Black Memphis police officers mimic the abhorrent acts of separation witnessed and experienced during the enslavement of Africans in antebellum America, and their actions recapitulate the horrors of Matthew 2:16–18, particularly recounted in this passage's appropriation of the prophet Jeremiah's words: "A voice was heard in Ramah, wailing and loud lamentation, Rachel weeping for her children; she refused to be consoled, because they are no more" (Jer 31:15). This Jeremiah passage describes the matriarch, Rachel, lamenting the capture and deportation of Israel to Babylon.

As with George Floyd, the television viewing public witnessed the wailing of Nichols as he cried out for his mother, whose house was a mere sixty yards from his fatal beating. In the Matthean text, the killing of infants and toddlers in Bethlehem probably took place a short distance from the families of these children and the communities in which they lived. The mothers of these children probably witnessed the massacre of their children in the Matthean account. This seems apparent considering Matthew's appropriation of Jeremiah 31:15, "lamentation and bitter weeping. Rachel is weeping for her children . . . ," which interpretatively describes Genesis 37. Echoes of Rachael's weeping can be analyzed and understood through a poststructural intertextual reading of Jeremiah 31:15 and Matthew 2:1–18 in relation to the Nichols's murder. Sébastien Doane and Nathan Robert Mastnjak remark:

> In contrast to traditional critical practices in biblical studies, poststructural intertextuality opens both text and readers to outside influences and to the extra-textual world. Poststructural intertextuality drives readers from their social worlds towards other texts, contexts, and other social worlds in a transformative way. From this perspective, post structural intertextual readings opens Jeremiah's poem and its readers to a plethora of narratives, art forms, and even to real mothers who cry inconsolably for children who are no more.[28]

---

27. Bowens, *African American Readings of Paul*, 24. Also see Brown, *Narrative of the Life of Henry Box Brown*, 80–81.

28. Doane and Mastnjak, "Echoes of Rachel's Weeping," 415–16.

Two weeks after Nichols's beating and death, his mother, RowVaughn Wells, spoke out during a press conference.[29] She bemoaned a feeling of emptiness and being numb to the reality that she would never see her son or hear his voice again. Wells said, "I don't know anything right now. All I know is my son Tyre is not here with me anymore. He will never walk through that door again. He will never come in and say 'hello parents' . . . I will never hear that again."[30] Nichols's mother articulated the dichotomy between the narrative told about her son by the five Black officers and her son's daily life, which was spent with her and his family. Tyre Nichols was a human being with a family who cared for and loved him, yet he was objectified and murdered by Memphis police officials who perpetuated a narrative that portrayed him as a deserving candidate for social death.

While Nichols's mother did not hear her son crying out to her during the attack, she later heard it virtually and thus experienced what the mothers in Matthew 2:16–18 experienced. Nichols's mother shared in the same pain, grief, and trauma that was experienced by the mothers in the Matthean account. Those in power (Herod and the Memphis officers) destroyed the lives of those they should have protected. Despite sharing similar racial backgrounds, the powerful used their power to perpetuate the social death of fellow human beings. Moreover, like Henry Box Brown, Nichols's mother was unable to do anything for her son, which likely compounded her sense of hopelessness and trauma. She experienced and participated in deep lament and weeping. Nichols's mother stated that "she loved him to death!" Her words moved beyond mere symbolic platitudes echoed in daily casual conversations. She embodied a lived, experiential expression of trauma. She literally loved him to death and she loves him in death. She has not only experienced his death—she, too, has experienced a type of death, which inhabits her grief and trauma.

Collective Lament

Nichols's death brings about a collective lament among Black people. Black mothers lament because they know all too well that this could have been their son. Black community members echo a collective cry because they know that this continues to be the reality for Black males. Black men echo a collective cry because they know it could have been any one of

29. "Tyre Nichols' Mother Speaks Out."
30. "Tyre Nichols' Mother Speaks Out."

them. In a White House press conference, then President Barack Obama expressed this very sentiment when Trayvon Martin was killed at the hands of a community vigilante:

> You know, when Trayvon Martin was first shot I said that this could have been my son. Another way of saying that is Trayvon Martin could have been me 35 years ago. And when you think about why, in the African American community at least, there's a lot of pain around what happened here, I think it's important to recognize that the African American community is looking at this issue through a set of experiences and a history that doesn't go away.[31]

This author echoes the same collective cry via his own personal experience of being racially profiled by police officers at the age of ten. I remember this encounter when I was in elementary school. Growing up in Southern California afforded me the opportunity to attend integrated public schools. I sat in class and participated in various extracurricular activities with an ethnically diverse group of my peers. Such activities included playing sports, joining after-school clubs, and playing the saxophone in the school band. Attending integrated schools at this time meant traveling to school on public district school buses. One afternoon while I was walking home from the bus stop, two Los Angeles County Deputy officers drove up beside me in their patrol car. As I walked along the sidewalk, they began interrogating me about my whereabouts and my possessions: "Where are you heading?" "Where do you live?" "What's in your backpack?" and "What are you carrying in your hand?" Attempting to address each question, as a ten-year-old I was overwhelmed with fear and confusion as to why I was being singled out for such treatment. These were not the friendly officer types that I watched on television shows like the *Andy Griffith Show* or *Leave It to Beaver*. I was profiled for being Black, walking while Black, and living in a Black neighborhood. As the patrol car came to a stop, one of the officers jumped out and forced me to sit on the sidewalk. The other carelessly rummaged through my backpack and saxophone case before the pair abruptly hopped back into their squad car and sped off. Without any clarification or explanation, I was left sitting on the sidewalk with my instrument and books lying haphazardly on the pavement. Still a bit shaken, I got up, repacked my things, and

---

31. White House Office of the Press Secretary, "Remarks by the President on Trayvon Martin."

headed home traumatized by that experience. Despite experiencing this incident many decades ago, its impact, alongside other profiling encounters, including being stopped and held at gunpoint by two Los Angeles city (LAPD) police officers by the time I was seventeen years old, have left an undeniable traumatic effect on me. This latter encounter seemed to be for no other apparent reason than driving while Black. Yet in spite of all of these experiences, I share in a hope that comes from exploring my story alongside and read within the biblical text. In Matthew 2:13–15, the Messiah escapes Herod's murderous campaign in order to establish his sovereign grace of hope and salvation from a societal structured system that perpetuates social death and natal alienation. Like Psalm 30:5b, I look forward to a joy that follows a night of weeping.

Discussion Questions

1. Can traumatic experiences optimistically be shared alongside and read within the biblical text? If so, how?

2. How can Scripture share in the telling of one's experiences?

3. What are positive ways to cope with the idea that Blackness (one who identifies as Black or being part of the Black experience) has been equated with social death?

4. How might one who is non-Black empathize, sympathize, and even stand in solidarity with one who is Black?

Works Cited

Berlin, Samantha. "Officer Sues Walmart, Claims He Was Racially Profiled and Handcuffed Inside Store." *Newsweek*, January 25, 2022. https://www.newsweek.com/officer-sues-walmart-claims-he-was-racially-profiled-handcuffed-inside-store-1672854.

Bor, Jacob, Atheendar S. Venkataramani, and Alexander C. Tsai. "Police Killings and Their Spillover Effect on The Mental Health of Black Americans: A Population-Based, Quasi-Experimental Study." *The Lancet* 392, July 28, 2018. https://www.thelancet.com/journals/lancet/article/PIIS0140-6736 (18)31130-9/fulltext.

Bowens, Lisa. *African American Readings of Paul: Reception, Resistance & Transformation*. Grand Rapids: Eerdmans, 2020.

Brown, Henry. *Narrative of the Life of Henry Box Brown, Written by Himself*. Edited by John Ernest. Chapel Hill: University of North Carolina Press, 2008. Originally published 1831.

Cho, Jeena. "How Trauma Impacts Black Communities and Police Officers Psychologically." *Forbes*, July 13, 2016. https://www.forbes.com/sites/jeenacho/2016/07/13/how-trauma-impacts-black-communities-and-police-officers-psychologically/?sh=748e9a313e26.

Doane, Sébastien and Nathan Robert Mastnjak "Echoes of Rachel's Weeping: Intertextuality and Trauma in Jer. 31:15." *Biblical Interpretation* 27 (2019) 413–35.

DuBois, W. E. B. *The Souls of Black Folk*. Chicago: A. C. McClurg & Co., 1903.

The Grio Staff, "Recent Black Police Academy Grad Says Texas Officers Racially Profiled Him." *Yahoo! News*, June 28, 2022. https://thegrio.com/2022/06/28/texas-officers-racially-profiled-grad/.

Hammond, Elise, et al. "January 27, 2023 News on the Death of Tyre Nichols." CNN, January 28, 2023. https://www.cnn.com/us/live-news/tyre-nichols-memphis-news-1-27-23/index.html.

Helsel, Phil, Doha Madani, and Marlene Lenthang. "Harrowing Videos Show Police Fatally Beat Tyre Nichols, Who Cries Out For His Mother." NBC News, January 27, 2023. https://www.nbcnews.com/news/nbcblk/memphis-police-set-release-video-showing-fatal-beating-tyre-nichols-rcna67710.

Higgins, Lee. "Video Shows 4 Black Officers Held at Gunpoint by Police." *USA Today*, May 3, 2015. https://www.usatoday.com/story/news/nation/2015/05/03/black-parole-officers-police/26843733/.

Jaglois, Jessica, Nicholas Bogel-Burroughs, and Mitch Smith. "Initial Police Report on Tyre Nichols Arrest is Contradicted by Videos." *New York Times*, January 30, 2023. https://www.nytimes.com/2023/01/30/us/tyre-nichols-arrest-videos.html.

KFF. "Poll: 7 in 10 Black Americans Say They Have Experienced Incidents of Discrimination or Police Mistreatment in Their Lifetime, Including Nearly Half Who Felt Their Lives Were in Danger." June 18, 2020. https://www.kff.org/racial-equity-and-health-policy/press-release/poll-7-in-10-black-americans-say-they-have-experienced-incidents-of-discrimination-or-police-mistreatment-in-lifetime-including-nearly-half-who-felt-lives-were-in-danger/.

Langford, Cameron. "Black Texas Cop Accuses Fellow Officers of Racial Profiling." Courthouse News Service, October 20, 2020. https://www.courthousenews.com/black-texas-cop-claims-racial-profiling-in-traffic-stop/

Palosky, Craig. "Poll: 7 in 10 Black Americans Say They Have Experienced Incidents of Discrimination or Police Mistreatment in Their Lifetime, Including Nearly Half Who Felt Their Lives Were in Danger." KFF. June 18, 2020. Accessed February 17, 2023. https://www.kff.org/racial-equity-and-health-policy/press-release/poll-7-in-10-black-americans-say-they-have-experienced-incidents-of-discrimination-or-police-mistreatment-in-lifetime-including-nearly-half-who-felt-lives-were-in-danger/.

Paterson, Orlando. *Slavery and Social Death: A Comparative Study*. Cambridge: Harvard University Press, 1982.

Paul, John, and Michael Birzer. "The Experiences of Black Police Officers Who Have Been Racially Profiled: An Exploratory Research Note." *Journal of African American Studies* 21 (2017) 567–84.

Pieterse, Alex L. "Perceived Racism May Impact Black Americans' Mental Health." American Psychological Association, 2011. https://www.apa.org/news/press/releases/2011/11/racism.

Rice, Glenn E., and Luke Nozicka. "He Was a Detective with the KDPD and He Still Got Pulled Over for Driving While Black." *Kansas City Star*, April 18, 2022. https://www.kansascity.com/news/local/article259626234.html.

Roberts, Nigel. "Black Kansas City, Mo. Cop Sues Police for Racially Profiling Him in Traffic Stop." Bet.com, April 22, 2022. https://www.bet.com/article/si9coi/black-kansas-city-cop-sues-department-over-racial-profiling-traffic-stop.

Schenwar, Maya, Joe Macaré, and Alana Yu-lan Price, eds. *Who Do You Serve, Who Do You Protect? Police Violence and Resistance in The United States.* Chicago: Haymarket, 2016.

Schwartz, Gabriel L., and Jaquelyn L. Jahn. "Mapping Fatal Police Violence Across U.S. Metropolitan Areas: Overall Rates and Racial/Ethnic Inequities, 2013–2017." Plos One. June 24, 2020. https://journals.plos.org/plosone/article?id=10.1371/journal.pone.0229686.

Tannehill, Robert C., et al., eds. *The New Interpreters Bible Commentary.* The Gospels and Narrative Literature, Jesus and the Gospels, Matthew, Mark 7. Nashville: Abingdon, 2015.

"Tyre Nichols' Mother Speaks Out After Seeing MPD Footage Related to His Death." *Commercial Appeal,* January 23, 2023. https://www.commercialappeal.com/videos/news/2023/01/23/tyre-nichols-mother-speaks-out-after-seeing-mpd-footage-related-his-death/11108278002/.

Westley, William A. "Violence and the Police." *American Journal of Sociology* 59 (1953) 38–41.

The White House Office of the Press Secretary. "Remarks by the President on Trayvon Marti." July 19, 2013. https://obamawhitehouse.archives.gov/the-press-office/2013/07/19/remarks-president-trayvon-martin.

Wilderson, Frank B., III. "Blacks and the Master/Slave Relation." In *Afro-Pessimism: An Introduction*, edited by Frank B. Wilderson III. Minneapolis: Racked & Dispatched, 2017.

Williams, Monnica T. "Uncovering the Trauma of Racism." *APA Journals Article Spotlight,* February 13, 2019. https://www.apa.org/pubs/highlights/spotlight/issue-128.

Wimbley, Randy, and David Komer. "White Detroit Cop Found Guilty of Assault of Black Police Officer." Fox2 Detroit News, December 5, 2022. https://www.fox2detroit.com/news/white-detroit-cop-found-guilty-in-racial-profiling-assault-of-black-police-officer.

Section Two

Theological Reflections and Expressions of Black Empowerment

Black Lives Moved by the Bible

Moving from the Love of Power to the Power of Love

Danjuma Gibson

They bind heavy burdens, and grievous to be borne, and lay them on men's shoulders, but they themselves will not move them with one of their fingers. All their works they do for to be seen of men . . . Woe unto you, scribes and Pharisees, hypocrites! For ye are like unto whited sepulchers, which indeed appear beautiful outward, but are within full of dead men's bones, and of all uncleanness. Even so ye also outwardly appear righteous unto men, but within ye are full of hypocrisy and iniquity.

Dark and terrible as is this picture, I hold it to be strictly true of the overwhelming mass of professed Christians in America. They strain at a gnat, and swallow a camel. Could any thing be more true of our churches? They would be shocked at the proposition of fellowshipping a sheep-stealer; and at the same time they hug to their communion a man-stealer, **and brand me with being an infidel, if I find fault with them for it.** They attend with Pharisaical strictness to the outward forms of religion, and at the same time neglect the weightier matters of the law, judgment, mercy, and faith. They are always ready to sacrifice, but seldom to show mercy.

They are they who are represented as professing to love God whom they
have not seen, whilst they hate their brother whom they have seen.

—FREDERICK DOUGLASS[1]

Sixty Million and more
I will call them my people, which were not my people;
and her beloved, which was not beloved.

—TONI MORRISON[2]

There is never time in the future in which we will work out our
salvation. The challenge is in the moment, the time is always now.

—JAMES BALDWIN[3]

Black Lives Moved by the Bible: Expanding
Our Christian Imagination

THE INTRODUCTORY PASSAGES FROM Frederick Douglass, Toni Morrison,
and James Baldwin are but a few examples of black personalities in the
nineteenth and twentieth centuries who, in their own way, were involved
in the fight for black and brown freedom and used the biblical text—in
varying degrees—to catalyze the thrust of their message, and to illuminate
the self-evident truth of black humanity, value, and self-worth. Douglass
references Matthew 23 in order to accentuate the hypocrisy of white slave
owners, who were card-carrying Christians with church membership,
that trafficked in the brutalization, raping, and murdering of black lives
and bodies, all while justifying the slavocracy system through the use of
Scripture and a variety of other Christian symbols and practices. Douglass's
observation that he was demonized for exposing the hypocrisy of a system
of oppression (when he asserted they "brand me with being an infidel, if
I find fault with them for it") remains a common cultural response even
today when freedom lovers dare challenge structures of oppression that
have been normalized in Western civilization. Toni Morrison's genius is

1. Douglass, *Narrative of the Life of Frederick Douglass*, 121–22.
2. Morrison, *Beloved*, ix.
3. Baldwin, "Nobody Knows My Name," 214.

captured decisively in the epigraph of her masterpiece *Beloved,* when she uses Romans 9:25 to characterize the impassioned Divine love and affection for black bodies and black life—an irrefutable truth that the history of Western Christianity conveniently overlooks or outright denies. For James Baldwin, in a demonstration of artistic creativity, a portion of Philippians 2:12 is used to counter William Faulkner's suggestion to those in the fight for equality that they should go slow, be patient, and that there is a right time in the future where all of their aspirations would be realized.[4] In essence, Baldwin cautions his readers that there is no such thing as the right time, and that the effectuation of their salvation must be intentional, deliberate, and always in the present.

I begin with these three black personalities being moved by the Bible to demonstrate examples of biblical imagination beyond the confines of the institutional church and pulpit. For these black thinkers, the final arbitrator to determine the appropriate use of the Bible was not delimited to a sophisticated set of hermeneutical tools that hold the promise of uncovering an ultimate or single truth (as if the Bible were a book of hieroglyphs to be deciphered), nor was it some variation of a historical critical methodology deemed to be infallible. Instead, for Frederick Douglass, James Baldwin, and Toni Morrison, their determination of the appropriate use of the Bible was not limited to their cognitive faculties alone, but to the entirety of their being, which included affect, body, and cognition—each of which contained elements of human intellection. Their use of Scripture was connected to the instantiation of life-giving human experience whereby black life, black bodies, and the human spirit were radically affirmed and invested with value and dignity. From a practical theological perspective, I suggest that Douglass, Baldwin, and Morrison endeavored to make the word become flesh to dwell among humanity. It is when the words of the biblical text are enfleshed that we can truly evaluate their veracity and vitality. It is when the words of the Bible become flesh and dwell among humanity that they have their greatest potential to affect and move the human spirit, lives, and bodies in a way that signifies healing, liberation, and freedom. When the spoken words of the Bible instigate the destruction of black lives and black bodies, or when biblical interpretation vanquishes the human spirit, such does not reflect the power of the Divine Spirit. Instead, it reflects the religious abuse of power. Moreover, the risk of using the Bible to abuse power and destroy

4. Baldwin, "Nobody Knows My Name."

lives increases exponentially when the understanding and expression of Scripture is limited to cognitive faculties alone.

In his final book before his assassination, Martin Luther King, Jr. reflected on the long history of how the Bible and other religious symbols were co-opted to justify, and even sacralize, the brutalization and oppression of black people.[5] He offers up a forceful critique of this abuse of power in the history of American Christianity when he observes:

> Religion and the Bible were cited and distorted to support the status quo. It was argued that the Negro was inferior by nature because of Noah's curse upon the children of Ham. The Apostle Paul's dictum became a watchword: "Servant, be obedient to your master." In this strange way theology became a ready ally of commerce. The great Puritan divine Cotton Mather culled the Bible for passages to give comfort to the plantation owners and merchants. He went so far as to set up some "Rules for the Society of Negroes," in which, among other things, Negroes disobedient to their masters were to be rebuked and denied attendance at church meetings, and runaway slaves were to be brought back and severely punished. All of this, he reasoned, was in line with the Apostle Paul's injunction that servants should be obedient to their masters.
>
> Logic was manipulated to give intellectual credence to the system of slavery. Someone formulated the argument for the inferiority of the Negro in the shape of a syllogism: "All men are made in the image of God; God, as everybody knows, is not a Negro; Therefore the Negro is not a man."[6]

Notice how King observes that the perversion of Scripture occurred in the isolation of cognition. While the distorting and corrupting of various theological and biblical themes used to justify oppression can vary over time, to be certain, each instance reflects the religious abuse of power by a Christian power structure that seeks to dominate and control people. This essay offers a cursory practical theological reflection on the religious abuse of power and the Bible and how the internalization of this abuse can lead to self-hate and self-flagellation for individuals and groups. It concludes by offering examples and reflections on how engaging the biblical text with the entirety of our human experience—that is to say, on how making the word become flesh and dwell with humanity—can lead

---

5. King, *Where Do We Go From Here.*
6. King, *Where Do We Go From Here,* 77.

to healing and redemptive sensibilities that affirm the intrinsic worth and value of black life, even in a world that constantly suggests that black life does not matter. Indeed, the biblical witness is clear: black life does matter.

Practical Theological Reflection on Religious Abuse of Power

In a reflection on intimate partner violence and domestic abuse, I defined such abuse as "the oppression that occurs in any intimate relationship where one person, in order to get their needs met or enhance their sense of self-worth and identity, seeks to subjugate and control their partner/lover through the use of violence and domination . . . [Consequently] domestic violence is not about arguments that have gone bad . . . [but it] is about control and subjugation through the use of violence and domination."[7] Likewise, the same goals of subjugation and domination can also be applied to the abuse of power and the Bible. Let us be clear then that the religious abuse of power that leads to the misappropriation of Scripture is also intended for the purpose of control and domination.

The love of power is the beginning of the abuse of power. It necessarily leads to the abuse and violation of human beings. The apostle Paul, in the second chapter of his Letter to the Philippians, refers to how Jesus utilizes power. In this passage, the power of Jesus is revealed in his equality with God (i.e., "who being in very nature God, did not consider equality with God something to be used to his own advantage"). That is to say, through the lens of the Trinity, Jesus is God. Nevertheless, this power was not deployed in a coercive manner to gain an unfair advantage in the relationship with humanity—the people he was sent to love and redeem. This is precisely what occurs when Scripture is distorted and corrupted to control and dominate another person or group. Instead, Paul argues that Jesus became like them—that is to say, human likeness—in order to serve us. This raises an important question: how can we serve people if we are not willing to become like them? Or how can the word of God serve people if it is not located in the context and social location of the community it seeks to serve? Through this example, power could be understood to reflect the deployment of any resource a person or group possesses that can be used to advance its personal well-being, the well-being of others, or the well-being of a community, organization, institution, or nation.

7. Gibson, "From Harmful to Helpful," 26.

Such resources (to name only a few) can include physical force, reputation, time, prestige, tradition and pedigree, political and social influence, or financial assets. In a very profound way, then, Jesus demonstrated his use of power—à la love—by becoming human like us. The love of power destroys people and communities. The power of love builds and restores people and communities. The important point to be made here is that power is not simply coercive or militaristic (as it is most commonly perceived). For our purposes here, we must understand that the explication and expounding of the Bible reflects a source of power as well.

Power tends to be more clearly seen when a person or group possesses resources that another does not possess (whether it be in terms of potency or quantity). Power, understood as relational human capital, can be used to the benefit of the possessor, to do for another what they cannot do for themselves, or to do for others what they might have great difficulty doing by themselves. Jesus did for us what we could not do for ourselves. At some point in life, because of the inevitability of loss or human suffering, coupled with the pervasiveness of sin and evil, all of us will be in need of the assistance and power of another human being in order to sustain our own life and well-being. Power in and of itself is innocuous. It is the use of power that will prove to be either life-giving, life-limiting, or death-dealing. The biblical witness is clear in its intention of power: it should be used in service to the other, not for "selfish ambition or vain conceit." Power is most safely employed when, in humility, we value others above ourselves.

Theologian William David Spencer makes a compelling case that in the United States, we have a long history of misappropriating the love of God and have instead projected into our God-image (i.e., how we unconsciously or implicitly experience and view God), and biblical hermeneutics, the perverse content of our own insatiable desires.[8] That is to say, we mistake our need for prestige and recognition, or our lust for possessions and conspicuous consumption, as God's will for our lives, God's affirmation of our lives, or that to which our constructed Christian identity entitles us—all of which is based on an ill-constructed theological anthropology propped up by abusive power. Spencer uses the parable of the rich owner found in Luke 12, where instead of sharing his resources (i.e., using his power) to benefit others, the magnate used his power to allocate greater resources to himself in an abundance that one

---

8. Spencer, "God of Power versus God of Love."

individual could not possibly consume over a lifetime. Instead of trusting God, the rich owner could not conquer the overwhelming temptation to trust (or believe) in himself (and his power) for life, fulfillment, and self-preservation. Indeed, it is easier for a camel to go through the eye of a needle than for someone who is rich to [truly] enter the kingdom of God (Matt 19:24 NIV)—not because of the money itself—but because of the illusion of control, invincibility, and immortality that wealth (achieved through abusive power) creates. When Scripture is used to condone this lifestyle, especially on the backs of others—à la oppression—it reflects a religious abuse of power.

Alternatively, power must be propelled by the Christian love ethic. Propositional statements, religious platitudes, or Sunday-morning worship practices that declare our love and trust of God are insufficient for Christian praxis. Engaging in a power analysis must become a part of our daily bread. Using personal and communal power to serve the other (the most vulnerable or the least of these among us) is consistent with—and demonstrative of—loving and trusting God. The synoptic witnesses are clear that our love of God is inseparably connected to how we treat other people.[9] Spencer is very sound on this:

> When one examines the arrival of Europeans to establish the Americas, one sees graphically a choice between greed or trust presented to them . . . Therefore, for the majority, rather than seeing God as one who believes wealth should be distributed evenly, a God of love, most of these earliest explorers and settlers projected God in the image of Jesus' greedy landowner. The primary attribute of God in their perspective was that of God's power, God's omnipotence. Eventually, their imperial theology would turn the Americas from a vestige of Eden's garden to a grinding sweatshop of greed, enslavement, pollution, and degradation in the service, not of God, but of money. Had the majority choice for God's primary attribute from the beginning been that of love, rather than of power, the history of the Americas and of the United States would have been very different, as would the United States' present national state, its role in the world, and the requirement before it to ensure its place in the future. But, as the operating view of God of so many was through the characteristic of power, those who saw themselves called by such a God also saw themselves as invested with a portion of

9. See Matthew 22:35–40 and Mark 12:28–34.

that absolute power to subdue the land and its inhabitants as "Providence" so willed.[10]

Abstract theological reflections on the abuse of power that do not take into consideration the material effect abuse has on the lives and bodies of those victimized by deleterious power relations is in effect disembodied theology. That is to say, it is theological reflection that has not taken seriously how the word became flesh and dwelled among humanity.[11] Whether it be conversation(s) on church polity and abuse, theological reflection as it relates to power and its abuse in the church and community, or strategic planning at the local church level, any such discussion that subordinates the experiences of those whose lives, spirits, and bodies have been broken by abusive power runs the risk of becoming an exercise in futility, capable of yielding only ecclesial policies that depict the letter of the law, but fail to fulfill the spirit of the law—policies that only project a form of Godliness, but denies the power of God.[12] Consequently, anytime we come into contact with a human being whose body, personhood, and spirit has been broken by another person, group, or institution (whether it be physical abuse, psychological abuse, emotional abuse, sexual abuse, intimate partner violence, etc.), a prima facia case of an abuse of power within the prevailing power structure has been inherently established. If the abuse occurs within the church, the Christian response should include taking responsibility in recognizing the abuse, holding the perpetrator(s) and enabler(s) of the abuse accountable, and notifying and using the appropriate authorities and resources within and outside of the church. Care for the victim(s) is paramount. Working to redeem the perpetrator of abuse is secondary. While this may seem obvious, the church—through counterproductive cycles of religious meandering and bankrupt theological rhetoric—has the long and painful history of suppressing, or outright ignoring, the voices of those who have been victimized and marginalized by the abuse of power. Among the most powerful examples of this is epitomized in the public testimony of Rachael Denhollander, one of the sexual abuse victims of Larry Nassaer, the USA Gymnastics team doctor. In her article "My Larry Nassar Testimony Went Viral," she states:

---

10. Spencer, "God of Power versus God of Love," 38–39.

11. See John 1:14.

12. See 2 Cor 3:4–6, 2 Tim 3:1–5.

Church is one of the least safe places to acknowledge abuse because the way it is counseled is, more often than not, damaging to the victim. There is an abhorrent lack of knowledge for the damage and devastation that sexual assault brings. It is with deep regret that I say the church is one of the worst places to go for help. That's a hard thing to say, because I am a very conservative evangelical, but that is the truth. There are very, very few who have ever found true help in the church.

She goes on to lament:

I have found it very interesting, to be honest, that every single Christian publication or speaker that has mentioned my statement has only ever focused on the aspect of forgiveness. Very few, if any, of them, have recognized what else came with that statement, which was a swift and intentional pursuit of God's justice. Both of those are biblical concepts. Both of those represent Christ. We do not do well when we focus on only one of them.[13]

From a practical theological perspective, then, the point of departure for all conversation about power abuse are the voices and experiences of those who have been injured by abusive power. This includes those who have been injured by the precarious use of the Bible. In any remedial action, the stories of those who have been injured by abusive power should be prioritized. Abstract rules of biblical interpretation that are limited to cognitive faculties alone are insufficient for determining the heart of God, as such hermeneutics lack sufficient depth to move those who have been subjected to generations and systems of abusive power. The interpretations of bystanders, onlookers, or enablers are secondary at best. Rhetoric pontificated from this latter group (towards the victim)—along the lines of "do you want to be a victim forever?" or "when will you move on?" or "choose whether you want to be a victim or a conqueror" or "when will you forgive?"—are immoral, misguided, precipitous of secondary trauma, biblically and theologically bankrupt, and indicative of the ongoing abuse of power perpetrated by the larger community. Pastoral theologian James Poling captures this dilemma persuasively when he defines evil in the context of the abuse of power:

Genuine evil is the abuse of power that destroys bodies and spirits; evil is produced by personal actions and intentions which are denied and dissociated by individuals; evil is organized by

13. Lee, "My Larry Nassar Testimony."

economic forces, institutions and ideologies, but mystified by
appeals to necessity and truth; evil is sanctioned by religion, but
masked by claims to virtue, love, and justice.[14]

French philosopher Michel Foucault's perspective on the essence of
power is useful in imagining a redemptive praxis for the church, community, and victims of power abuse. While acknowledging the reality of institutional structures of power, and the potency of violence and
coercive forms of power, Foucault believes that these do not represent
the fundamental nature of power. For Foucault, power is fundamentally
expressed in interpersonal relations between everyday people. According to him, "The exercise of power is not simply a relationship between
partners, individual or collective; it is a way in which certain actions
modify others. Which is to say, of course, that something called Power,
with or without a capital letter, which is assumed to exist universally in a
concentrated or diffused form, does not exist. Power exists only when it
is put into action."[15] Simply put, Foucault argues that all of us have power,
not just an elite few. To deny one's power is to live in an illusion. Furthermore, it is sinful, as denying one's power reflects an attempt to abdicate
one's responsibility to God and neighbor. The power abuses that we see
in institutional, social, cultural, or governmental structures or systems
represent the fruition and culmination of power abuses at the communal
and interpersonal level. We all play a role. This point cannot be over-
emphasized, especially in a contemporary Western church community
that demonstrates a pathological need to be innocent of sexism, racism,
xenophobia, sexual assault, and other manifestations of power abuse. It
is as if protecting a façade of innocence and righteousness in church has
been mistaken for spreading the gospel. Obeying God and the divine
mandate for love has been replaced with defending our narcissistic God-
images. For the purposes of this essay, such interpersonal relations necessarily include those who have been gifted with the privilege of preaching
and teaching the Bible to others, whether that is at an individual level or
a group level. Preaching the Bible is an act of power, and where this is
power being used, there exists the potential to abuse such power.

    In his interpretation of Foucault, Joseph Rouse posits that "power is
not possessed by a dominant agent, nor located in that agent's relations
to those dominated, but is instead distributed throughout complex social

14. Poling, *Deliver Us From Evil*, 110.

15. Foucault, "Subject and Power," 788.

networks . . . actions of the peripheral agents in these networks are often what establish or enforce the connections between what a dominant agent does and the . . . frustration of a subordinate agent's desires."[16] Moreover, womanist theologian Kelly Brown Douglas forcefully captures the communal implications of a Foucauldian paradigm of power when she states, "Foucault has judiciously placed the responsibility for the kind of society in which we live back in the hands of those who have shaped and formed that society. He has held people—not impersonal or sometimes elusive structures of domination—accountable for the sexism, racism, classism, and heterosexism that terrorize much of our world."[17] Self-examination then forces the church to consider how many followers of Christ have witnessed acts of sexual harassment and misconduct, racism, sexism, or any other form of power abuse, have witnessed how Scripture has been used to either ignore or appease criminal behavior, and have remained silent out of fear of being expelled from the in-group or running afoul of the status-quo master narrative. Choosing to do nothing or to say nothing is a manifestation of interpersonal and relational power: it is a move for self-preservation and preservation of the system. In the second chapter of Philippians, Jesus used his power to become like us, not to distance himself from us!

Preaching or teaching the Bible reflects an exercise of power. As such, the risk of abusing that power is present. For those who have been entrusted to expound on and explicate the biblical witness, to deny that you have power is implicitly an abuse of power. Such abuse occurs most easily when the biblical witness is delimited to cognitive faculties, and when the hermeneutical process is what I term here as phenomenologically unidirectional. With this term, I argue that when biblical interpretation is proffered and concretized by cognition alone—without the benefit of human experience or the material impact of the interpretation being able to interrogate what was originally proffered or interpreted—it opens the door to the abuse of power that produces death-dealing results.[18] Such

16. Rouse, "Power/Knowledge," 109.

17. Douglass, *Sexuality and the Black Church,* 21.

18. It will be observed that I am intentionally using the term *cognition* as opposed to *intellection.* It is the fruit of the enlightenment era that privileged cognitive faculties, while subordinating human faculties related to affect and body—faculties that were deemed to be either barbaric or feminine. A postcolonial corrective to this sort of Cartesian thinking is to recognize that cognition and intellect are not the same. For the purposes of this essay, cognition simply refers to the conscious and intentional discernment and awareness of self, others, and the outside world through human

interpretations run the risk of producing the kind of religious corruption and ecclesiological depravity that Martin Luther King, Jr. alluded to when he observed how theology and the Bible fueled the system of slavery. This is when the word has not become flesh and dwelled among humanity.

Anecdotal Examples of Religious Abuse of Power

In my experience of over twenty years as clergyman, senior pastor, and trained psychotherapist on the South Side of Chicago, I offer up two anecdotal examples from a macro perspective of what can materialize when the biblical witness is not enfleshed: (1) the war on drugs epidemic that ravished black and brown neighborhoods and, (2) the HIV/AIDS epidemic that traumatized thousands of black and brown people who were alienated from families and communities. First, the alleged war on drugs essentially reflected the proliferation of the prison industrial complex on the backs of black and brown persons who became chemically dependent in the final decades of the twentieth century. To be clear, the argument being made here is not to rationalize away or minimize the violence related to the crack cocaine epidemic of the 1980s and 1990s that cost many lives. The point here is that the overarching social intervention was to moralize drug addiction in black and brown communities—which ultimately led to draconian drug laws being enacted and enforced as a way to punish those who had become addicted. The same approach was not taken in richer white neighborhoods where more expensive and pure forms of cocaine were being used. The infamous "say no to drugs" slogan from the Reagan administration brutalized and flattened the lived experiences of thousands of people who suffered from chemical dependency. Federal mandatory minimum sentences destroyed communities and families.

But what is not often talked about is how urban clergy used the Bible to moralize drug addiction in black and brown communities. Taking its cue from "just say no to drugs," coupled with the humiliation that black communities had become the face of the war on drugs, the biblical text was used (by clergy, communities, and even families) in countless ways to suggest that the lack of faith in Jesus, poor Christian character, and

---

faculties that do not include affect, emotion, or the physical body. Intellect, on the other hand, reflects the capacity to learn, make meaning, and produce knowledge. Intellect can stem from body, affect, and emotion, and cognition or brain functions. Moreover, it must be stressed that the belief we can cleanly distinguish between cognition, body, and affect or emotion, is a strenuous belief at best.

sin were the cause of drug abuse. On countless occasions I encountered families who communicated sentiments along the lines of "if my loved-one would just give their life over to Christ" or "if my loved one would just stand on the word of God . . . they could beat these drugs." In these instances, biblical interpretation was phenomenologically unidirectional. Biblical interpretation was not enfleshed and put into conversation with the instantiation of actual human experience. Families and communities were destroyed, in part, from a lack of social and cultural empathy and compassion. This represents the failure of the Enlightenment's privileging of cognition, and modernity's move to flatten and commoditize all of human experience, both of which reflects components of the growing *evangelicalization* of America. Understood in this manner, drug addiction and chemical dependency could only be understood as a moral failure, and never understood through the lens of a medical model where biology, neurology, and psychology could be allowed to provide interpretive power. Biblical interpretation must be phenomenologically bidirectional in order to move the lives of those forced to exist on the underside of modernity. Otherwise, we end up with death-dealing propositional statements where the letter kills, and the Spirit gives no life. Compare this approach in the 1980s and 1990s to the current opioid epidemic (from 2010 to the present) where the vast majority of the victims seem to be white. Here, the interpretive power of the medical model for addiction is in full effect. The opioid pandemic is not being moralized against its victims (or nowhere near the degree that drug addiction was moralized in black and brown communities). Blame, for the most part, is being levied against the pharmaceutical companies, as evidenced in class action lawsuits yielding multibillion-dollar settlements to aid victims. Where there is love, aid, resources, and assistance to those who are chemically dependent, there is less violence to contend with. That is to say, big pharmaceutical companies have become the face of the opioid addiction crisis, not the victims of drug addiction. Again, expounding on the biblical text in a reckless manner can yield destructive material results.

Lastly, in the HIV/AIDS crisis of the 1980s through the turn of the twenty-first century, a common religious motif in many minority communities was that the virus reflected the wrath of God against sexual immorality and that for those who contracted the virus, it reflected God's judgment against their sins. Such irresponsible use of the biblical witness by many clergypersons only served to impose secondary trauma on the victims of HIV/AIDS. Again, this biblical interpretation was phenomenologically unidirectional and as such, was death-dealing in the material results it yielded. In my experience as a psychotherapist at an infectious disease clinic on the South Side of Chicago, I discovered that in what could be deemed as the most traumatic season of a person's life (i.e., people who were diagnosed with HIV), many were harshly judged, and in some cases exiled from their families and churches, because of what was viewed in their communities as sinful living and God's corresponding judgement. Once again, this biblical interpretation was phenomenologically unidirectional. The psychological and emotional trauma being imposed on victims of HIV/AIDS should have necessarily required an interrogation of how the Bible was being used to understand and interpret the spread of HIV. But during the same period in which the rate of infection was skyrocketing in black and brown communities, the rate of infection was plummeting in white male gay communities, communities which according to certain conservative clergypersons and churches, should be judged by God for their sinful behavior. So why was God being so hard on black and brown communities, but being so forgiving on white male gay communities? Again, it is obvious we are dealing with erroneous biblical interpretation that was fueled by unidirectional phenomenology. Such biblical interpretations blinded communities to the importance of appropriate healthcare measures and HIV/AIDS awareness. Indeed, expounding on the biblical text in a reckless manner reflects the abuse of power that contributes to the destruction of people and communities.

Conclusion: The "Call and Response" Allows Lives to be Moved by the Bible

As a black professor, whether teaching in a predominantly white institution, or inhabiting the spaces of theological education, I am inevitably confronted with questions or observations about black religious experience. One of the most common observations is in regard to the call-and-response phenomenon that can be observed in African American worship and homiletical encounters. Most outsiders tend to simply view call and response as an aesthetic. But here, I suggest that it is more of a hermeneutical posture, where the preacher does not maintain sole authority of what is preached or biblical interpretation. Instead, the homiletical authority is in the space between the preacher and the listeners. Homiletical authority is shared and is communal. Call and response is reflective of phenomenology being bidirectional. It reflects the intersubjective and psychosocial beginnings of the word becoming flesh and dwelling among humanity.

I suggest the most compelling practical examples of the word becoming flesh, or phenomenology being bidirectional, is in the historical personality of Frederick Douglass, and the biblical personalities of Peter and Cornelius in Acts 10. In his third autobiography, Frederick Douglass describes his irritation with fellow black people who believed in the divine sanctioning of their enslavement. He often referred to such beliefs as a kind of enchantment that was fueled by the slavocracy's perversion of the biblical text. In a bit of irritation, he asserts, "I have met many good religious colored people at the south, who were under the delusion that God required them to submit to slavery and to wear their chains with meekness and humility . . . and I quite lost my patience when I found a colored man weak enough to believe such stuff."[19] However, Douglass did not always possess such emotional and spiritual strength. In his second autobiography, he describes when his biblical view on the divine sanctioning of enslavement shifted. It occurred in a moment when he was beaten and traumatized by the plantation overseer and the plantation owner:

> My religious views on the subject of resisting my master, had suffered a serious shock, by the savage persecution to which I had been subjected, and my hands were no longer tied by my religion. Master Thomas's indifference had severed the last link. I had now to this extent "backslidden" from this point in the slave's religious creed; and I soon had occasion to make my fallen state known to my Sunday-pious brother, Covey.[20]

In this example, Douglass's biblical views on the enslaved fighting their masters did not shift because of cognitive reflections that challenged the religious sanctioning of the slavocracy. Instead, his views shifted as the perverse biblical interpretation interacted with both his body (i.e., the savage persecution to which he had been subjected) and his affective state (i.e., Master Thomas's indifference had severed the last link). Douglass's views about the Bible shifted because he now engaged the biblical text with the entirety of his being. For him, the word had now become enfleshed and dwelled with him.

Lastly, in the biblical story of Peter visiting the house of Cornelius after God had commanded him to go in a vision, Peter was clear in communicating to Cornelius that "you are well aware that it is against our law for

19. Douglass, *Life and Times of Frederick Douglass*, 77.

20. Douglass, *My Bondage and My Freedom*, 241.

a Jew to associate with or visit a Gentile."[21] Nevertheless, the shift in how Peter understood the law was already in place after he had experienced the vision from God, and after the men sent by Cornelius to connect with Peter had verified (enough for Peter) that his vision was authentic. But the genius of the Spirit was fully revealed when Cornelius and his entire house were filled with the Spirit as Peter was speaking to them. If the law of the Jews prohibited Peter from even visiting with Gentiles, to baptize them would represent an outright assault on Jewish culture and the status quo. Yet, Peter's decision to baptize Cornelius and his house was not the result of cognitive reflections on the law to discover the heart of God. Instead, Peter's limited understanding of the law was phenomenologically bilateral in his encounter with Cornelius. Peter's understanding of the law turned upside down by what he saw with his physical body (i.e., his eyes) and by what he emotionally experienced when he saw the Spirit fall on Cornelius in the same way it had fallen on Peter himself. Peter and all who were with him "were astonished" (Acts 10:45).

The beginning of 2021 witnessed the biblical text being used to justify white dominance, the January 6th assault on the nation's capital, racism, xenophobia, and other forms of hatred and violence. Such abuse of Scripture to justify the violence of America is nothing new. The democratic experiment is on life support. The distinction between nationalism and Christianity is becoming indistinguishable in the public sphere. But there is hope. The fight for freedom is tried and true. Black lives that have been moved by the Bible, like those of Frederick Douglass, James Baldwin, and Toni Morrison, bear witness to the time-tested veracity of freedom fighting and the power of love. We cannot allow those who would sanction hate and violence to have a monopoly on using Scripture. When the biblical witness is allowed to become flesh and dwell among humanity, it has the potential to heal, liberate, and revolutionize. But such a move takes courage. Biblical interpretation that is limited to cognition and the institutional confines of what we already know or are comfortable with, runs the risk of perverting Christian praxis and misrepresenting the heart of God. Divine prerogative is distorted. But when the preaching of the Bible is phenomenologically bidirectional, when homiletical authority is shared between the speaker and the listener, when the text is allowed to become flesh and dwell with those who are oppressed, an entire nation can be prepped to be moved by divine justice, divine Love, and divine freedom.

21. See Acts 10 for the entire encounter between Peter and Cornelius; quote is verse 28.

Discussion Questions

1. What are other historical examples you can think of where the Bible was erroneously used to justify the abuse and oppression of people?

2. In the present day, or in your own personal context, where are you seeing evidence that the Bible is potentially being used as an abuse of power to mistreat or oppress individuals and groups?

3. What lessons can be learned and applied from history to keep the Bible from being used as an abuse of power in our present-day lives?

Works Cited

Baldwin, James. "Nobody Knows My Name." In *James Baldwin: Collected Essays*, 197–287. New York: Literary Classics of the United States, 1998.

Douglass, Frederick. *Life and Times of Frederick Douglass: His Early Life as a Slave, His Escape from Bondage, and His Complete History to the Present Time*. Hartford: Park Publishing Company, 1881.

———. *My Bondage and My Freedom*. New York: Miller, Orton & Mulligan, 1855.

———. *Narrative of the Life of Frederick Douglass, an American Slave: Written by Himself*. Boston: Published at the Anti-Slavery Office, 1845.

Douglass, Kelly Brown. *Sexuality and the Black Church: A Womanist Perspective*. Maryknoll, NY: Orbis, 1999.

Foucault, Michel. "The Subject and Power." *Critical Inquiry* 8, no. 4 (1982) 777–95.

Gibson, Danjuma G. "From Harmful to Helpful: Religion and Masculinity." In *Healing the Healers Series 2: Domestic Violence, Encouraging and Preparing Faith Leaders to Respond, Expert Resource Guide*, 26–29. New York: Odyssey Impact, 2021.

King, Martin Luther, Jr. *Where Do We Go From Here: Chaos or Community?* Boston: Beacon, 1968.

Lee, Morgan. "My Larry Nassar Testimony Went Viral. But There's More to the Gospel Than Forgiveness." *Christianity Today*, January 31, 2018. https://www.christianitytoday.com/ct/2018/january-web-only/rachael-denhollander-larry-nassar-forgiveness-gospel.html.

Morrison, Toni. *Beloved*. New York: Vintage, 1987.

Poling, James Newton. *Deliver Us From Evil: Resisting Racial and Gender Oppression*. Minneapolis: Fortress, 1996.

Rouse, Joseph. "Power/Knowledge." In *The Cambridge Companion to Foucault*, 2nd Edition, edited by Gary Gutting, 95–122. New York: Cambridge University Press, 2003.

Spencer, William David. "God of Power versus God of Love: The United States of America." In *The Global God: Multicultural Evangelical Views of God*, edited by Aída Besançon Spencer and William David Spencer, 37–62. Grand Rapids: Baker, 1998.

Hagar's Lament

Affirming Black Lives Matter through Resilience, Interconnectedness, Spirituality, and Expectancy

VALERIE RANEE LANDFAIR

I'm a mother.
I have black boys
who wear hoodies,
and from the time they were old enough
to go outside and play
alone,
I've given them "the speech."
The Speech
THE SPEECH
more times than I can remember.
You know the speech,
don't you?
Of course you know
the speech.
ALL black mothers
HAVE to tell their
black children,
especially,
their little black boys

when they leave the house
for any reason.
The Speech: Don't get out of line. Don't make too
much noise. If you see a cop be respectful.
Do what he says. Don't raise your voice. Don't argue. Keep your hands visible.
You know—the speech!
Sometimes.
many times,
often times,
the speech doesn't matter
when it comes to black and brown
boys and girls.[1]

Introduction

To be a Black person in the United States is to be a person who has had moments of wordless groans under the weight of racialized, institutionalized dehumanization and violence. The groaning in the Spirit by African Americans harmonizes with the groaning of creation because the blood of enslaved Africans cries out from the ground, the same ground that is soaked with the blood from the slain bodies of Breonna Taylor, Trayvon Martin, Botham Jean, and Atatiana Jefferson. The Spirit testifies to those who have an ear to hear that Black Lives Matter, Asian Lives Matter, Native American Lives Matter, and Latinx Lives Matter.

In this chapter, a Pentecostal Womanist hermeneutic is employed to critique the ways in which many white Pentecostal, white evangelical, and white Catholic theologians have failed to hear the inward groanings of the Black community in waiting for adoption and redemption (Rom 8:22–23).[2] These wordless groans find expression in the lament, "Black lives matter." This chapter explores a Pentecostal Womanist rereading of the Hagar narratives in Genesis and Galatians. Thus, this chapter is written for the following communities of readers: African Americans, Womanists, and Pentecostals, to provide a sample of how Scripture informs

1. Denyse, "Women Gather," 4–5.

2. For a helpful discussion of Womanist theology, see Townes, "Womanist Theology."

African American prayers broadly, with a particular focus on African American Pentecostal prayers. Hagar's narrative is a biblical example of the transformation of despair to hope.

Pneumatological Orientation

The descendants of enslaved Africans had, and some might argue still have, a complicated relationship with some of the prescribed writings of the apostle Paul. It was not the compilations of Jesus' sayings, but rather Paul's words that were used to establish the theological foundation that Black lives do not matter. The enslaved were baffled that certain Scriptures could and would have a different interpretation based on the color of one's skin. For example, who were the children of God? The enslaved thought that their humanity was inherent and that Scripture affirmed that they also were God's children. So, imagine their trauma when they realized that their testimony that Jesus is Lord did not make them welcome into the communities of faith occupied by white women and men.[3]

Vincent L. Wimbush concludes that for the majority of African Americans, the Bible has "historically functioned not merely to reflect or legitimize piety (narrowly understood), but as a language-world full of stories—of heroes and heroines, of heroic peoples and their pathos and victory, sorrow and joy, sojourn and fulfillment."[4] Therefore, enslaved Africans in the New World adopted a hermeneutic of suspicion regarding European justification for the necessity of enslavement. It is a historical and contemporary paradox that "white man's religion permits him to hate his brother because he is black," when, for a Black Christian, "religion teaches him to love his white brother not because he is white, yellow, or black, but because Christ has taught him to love his neighbor as he loves himself."[5] How can one profess a love for God and remain silent while enslaved Africans' descendants are dying on the streets? How can Christians retain their deafening silence in the face of African Americans', Native Americans', and Hispanics' unequal and inequitable educational services, wages, and healthcare? How can faithful Bible-reading communities overtly or passively embrace a white supremacy ideology?

---

3. See Marbury, *Pillars of Cloud and Fire*; Martin, "Eyes Have It."

4. Wimbush, *Bible and African Americans*.

5. Mathews, *Doctrine and Race*, 153.

Enslaved Africans interpreted the Bible through their collective experiences as a virtual language-world under the guidance of the Spirit.[6] The retained African spirituality of groaning in the Spirit provides the prayerful religious expressions of this virtual language-world. African Americans use verbalized and non-verbalized expressions of prayer as a coping mechanism establishing that private prayer or asking someone to pray on their behalf helped them navigate and respond to situations including "health issues, caregiving burdens, chronic poverty, poor neighborhood conditions, structural exclusion," and structural racism.[7] The pneumatological orientation of prayerful expressions of an inward groaning of anguish and distress that are rooted in the very soul of Black communities are transformed into a belief that God will take actions on their behalf. African Americans' prayer legacy is rooted in remembering what God has done and what God can do.

Hagar: Pneumatological Transformation of Pathos

A Pentecostal Womanist methodology utilizes a pneumatological transformation of pathos as a theological framework to examine the ways African Americans and other marginalized people deal with oppression.[8] Hagar reflects pneumatological transformation in that she was able to sustain her unbearable suffering. Hagar's silent prayers of lament, and God's response to her, prophetically remind Black women that just as God sought Hagar, God seeks Black women today. God did not seek Hagar because she was Abram and Sarai's slave; God sought and cared for Hagar because she was the object of God's love. In the same way, God sees, seeks, and cares for Hagar's sisters and daughters amid the multicausality of racism. The Spirit empowers and effects change in the act of prayers by turning the expressions of grief, anguish, and trauma into hope, awe, and joy. The Spirit is continually crying, Abba! Father! (Gal 4:6). Pneumatological transformation of pathos empowers believers through love to serve one another (Gal 4:13).

6. Wimbush, *Bible and African Americans*, 86.

7. Chatters et al., "Religious Coping Among African Americans, Caribbean Blacks and Non-Hispanic Whites."

8. Solivan, *Spirit, Pathos and Liberation*, 146. Pneumatological transformation of pathos builds on Samuel Solivan's appropriation of pathos. See Landfair, "'Trouble In My Way, I Have To Cry Sometimes.'"

In reflecting on the plight of Black women, Delores Williams appropriated the Hagar narrative in Genesis as an articulation of the struggles of African American women.[9] In the European context, theology produced by people of color and particularly Black people are assumed heretical and heterodox.[10] Renita Weems writes, "Each community has its own ideas about what the reader should be reading for in a text, and each one is governed by its own vested interests."[11] Voiceless, powerless, oppressed, and marginalized communities have appropriated Scripture as validating that they are also created in God's image (Gen 1:27). In short, the Bible stories affirm a triune God who declares and decrees the triune God's image on Africans and their descendants (Gen 1:31). This hermeneutic is a countercultural movement against the dominant authoritative readings, which sought to minimize enslaved Africans and their descendants' experience and scoff at their interpretations as they sought to control the visions of their identities. African American communities—in prayers, songs, dances, tears, sermons, and shouts—have an embodied protest of resistance and celebration affirming that Black Lives Matter. Weems argues that the consequences of the "dominant reading conventions within a society often reinforce the dominant class's interest in that society."[12]

Similarly, Jacqueline Grant argues that a God-consciousness resides within the reality of Black women's religious experiences. The reality of the sacred is in part due to the pneumatological orientation of our foremothers and forefathers, where historical and contemporary African American women first received revelations directly from God and secondly received revelation as read and heard in their community that helped them to understand, navigate, and interrogate their experiences.[13] Phillis Sheppard asserts, "Reading Scripture through the lens of experience—and reading experience through the lenses of Scripture—can be a means of reclaiming the language, and re-forming our sense of self, of black embodiment."[14] Sheppard claims the formation and malformation of Black women's embodiment are "relational, historical, psychological, and cultural" and therefore requires the "transformation of

9. Williams, *Sister in the Wilderness.*

10. Tisby, *Color of Compromise,* 202.

11. Weems, "Reading Her Way through the Struggle," 67–68.

12. Weems, "Reading Her Way through the Struggle," 72.

13. Grant, *White Women's Christ and Black Women's Jesus,* 211.

14. Sheppard, "Dark Goodness Created in the Image of God," 25.

heart, mind, and imagination," which I contend can be experienced by a pneumatological orientation in praying and reading Scripture.[15]

Valerie C. Cooper classifies Maria Stewart's writings simultaneously as glossolalia and heteroglossia. Cooper appropriates Mae Gwendolyn Henderson's biblical framework of glossolalia, speaking in tongues in her rereading of Stewart's literary expressions. For Henderson, speaking in tongues includes glossolalia, the ability to utter divine mystery (1 Cor 14), and heteroglossia, speaking in multiple languages (Acts 2), otherwise known as code-switching. Speaking in tongues are Black women's tools to disrupt the dominant white and male discourses and the Black male subdominant discourses. Black women writers and speakers are also encouraged to interpret the tongues, the multiplicity, and simultaneity of discourses used by Black women writers and speakers.

> While glossolalia refers to the ability to "utter the mysteries of the spirit," heteroglossia describes the ability to speak in the multiple languages of public discourse. If glossolalia suggests private, non-mediated, nondifferentiated univocality, heteroglossia connotes public, differentiated, social, mediated, dialogic discourse.[16]

Therefore, Stewart's speaking in tongues, the orality of her public prayers, requires the hermeneutical task of interpreting the tongues of her writings. Stewart, a free Black woman, was the first woman of any race to speak in public to a racially and gender diverse audience in 1832. Stewart's writing as God's mystical "language spoken only in heaven and known only to God" reaffirms how Scriptures are used to interrogate the Black woman's identity as coping and conquering racism, sexism, and classism. Cooper suggests that African American women employed the Bible as a Rosetta Stone, thereby learning to speak in tongues and interpret tongues intuitively.

Hagar in Genesis

Hagar's narrative provides a brief sample of how African American Pentecostal women read the Bible to give expression to their grief. One can argue that Hagar's prayers model lament, growth, and hope for transformation. Due to Deloris Williams's landmark parallel treatment of Hagar's

15. Sheppard, "Dark Goodness Created in the Image of God," 25.
16. Henderson, "Speaking in Tongues," 22.

and Black women's wilderness spirituality, African American women regard themselves as Hagar's sisters and daughters.[17] Sheppard recognizes that Hagar and Ishmael's plight mirrors Black women's historical and contemporary realities of enslavement, lack of control over reproductive rights, single parenting, concern for survival, and "forced homelessness at the hands of a more powerful woman and man of a different culture."[18]

Ancient and modern readers and hearers are drawn into a dilemma regarding the Genesis storyteller's inclusion of Hagar. Paul and Augustine are examples of ancient readers. Their views reaffirm Sarah as blessed by God. Thus, her treatment of Hagar is rationalized. A subtle modern example is the overemphasis on the exodus exile motif over Hagar's survival motif. Complicating this text further, biblical scholars have examined this text with a bias towards maintaining an image of Abraham as the father of faith and minimizing or erasing any of his blemishes. The inconsistencies of Abraham's faith are often minimized (Gen 15:6; 7–21).[19] In order to maintain a more favorable picture of Abraham, Hagar is identified by a political identity imposed upon her: slave, concubine, and surrogate.[20] According to Nahum Sarna, Yahweh did not specify Sarai as the mother of Abram's offspring.[21] The narrator, in order to preserve the righteousness of Abram, minimizes his sin of doubting the word of the Lord; however, Hagar's uppity attitude towards her mistress, Sarai, is remembered. Sarna charges Hagar for her and Ishmael's near-death experiences because, Sarna argues, if Hagar had "not lost her way . . . the original supplies would have been adequate."[22] Similarly, Skinner contends that Abram loves Ishmael, but has no "particular affection" for Hagar.[23] As these examples indicate, some biblical commentators favor Abraham in their readings but either blame Hagar for her situation or disregard her painful plight.

Significantly, however, this Egyptian is the first woman to receive a promise from the Lord Yahweh, who addresses her directly.[24] Hagar is

17. Sheppard, "Dark Goodness Created in the Image of God," 9.

18. Sheppard, "Dark Goodness Created in the Image of God," 9.

19. Mathews, *Genesis 11:27–50:26*, 179.

20. Frymer-Kensky, "Hagar," 86.

21. Sarna, *Genesis*, 118.

22. Sarna, *Genesis*, 147.

23. Skinner, *Critical and Exegetical Commentary on Genesis*, 322.

24. Hagar, Hannah, and Mary are addressed personally concerning their children's destinies.

the first person to receive a birth annunciation and the first woman to receive promises from the Lord to bless her within a covenantal framework (Gen 16:10–12). Hagar is the only person to bestow a name upon God (16:13)[25] and Gen 16:7 is the first reference to the angel of the Lord. Therefore, Hagar is the first person in the Bible whom the angel of the Lord visits.[26]

Hagar is the only person in the Bible, outside of Jesus, honored by God as the recipient of so many firsts mentioned within the Old and New Testament. However, Hagar's theophanies are attributed by many scholars to her relationship with Abram and God's covenant with Abram, rather than to her own relationship with God (Gen 16:10; 21:13, 18). In the patriarchal narrative, apart from the patriarchs themselves, the only woman who is the object of a theophanic experience is Hagar.[27]

Hagar realizes that sex and pregnancy would not curry favors for herself and her unborn child. Nevertheless, one can hear the moans and groans of Hagar and God lamenting over Abram and Sarai's exploitation of Hagar's lower social status in relation to Sarai. Much like Black women's asymmetrical relationship to white women, patriarchy affects Hagar negatively in relation to men and women who have social standing and privileges. Hagar is traumatized just like enslaved Africans (starting in the seventeenth century) and their descendants. God cares enough to initiate a relationship amid her dehumanizing treatments, calls her by name, and blesses her and her seed. Hagar's narrative is the parallel story of African American women, mothers, grandmothers, Big Mama, church mothers, evangelists, preachers, teachers, prayer warriors, and community organizers. Hagar is a prototype of countless Black women who are often an afterthought in social, physical, and economic justice. Diana L. Hayes contends that African American women are Hagar's daughters because our circumstances dictate a daily struggle to survive, to provide for our children, and to have ongoing concerns for the systematic inequality in the Black community.[28] Hagar, like her sisters and daughters, was unknown, unrecognized, and unimportant by society's stilted constructs. God responds to their laments of grief and brooding over their individual

25. Thompson, *Writing the Wrongs*, 18. Note that Samson's mother, Hannah, and Mary were also recipients of divine annunciations.

26. Mathews, *Genesis 11:27–50:26*, 188. The "angel of the Lord" occurs forty-eight times throughout the Old Testament.

27. Noble, *Place for Hagar's Son*, 35.

28. Hayes, *Hagar's Daughter*, 76.

and communal brokenness. For enslaved Africans and their descendants, the afterthought becomes the *beloved*.

One is challenged by God's apparent failure to provide an "escape" from Sarai and Abram. The historical context of Hagar's narrative affords her no rights to complain of her abuse to anyone. Sarai's role in the narrative does not depict her as an example of a biblical ally in the fight against the sins of sexism. The political identity of Black women must include conversations regarding the historical and contemporary control of reproductive rights of forced sexual encounters. Stephanie E. Jones-Rogers concludes that from 1850 to 1860 Southern white women, who made up about 40 percent of slave owners, "personally orchestrated acts of sexual violence against enslaved women and men in hopes that the women would produce children who would augment their wealth."[29] According to Thomas A. Foster, Europeans' sexual assault of enslaved Black men took a "variety of forms, including outright physical penetrative assault, forced reproduction, sexual coercion, and manipulation and psychic abuse."[30] The historical data counters the narratives that European women had no knowledge of or minimal involvement regarding the rape of enslaved African women and men.[31] Nevertheless, Genesis does not record Hagar coming to God, offering a sacrifice, or seeking after God for her freedom. However, God recognizes Hagar's affliction and destitution. Black Lives Matter is a lament that gives voice and power to Hagar's daughters who live in a hostile community of whiteness.

Hagar's Purpose in Galatians

Hagar is mentioned only in passing in Galatians. She is mentioned by name while Sarah is nameless. A Pentecostal Womanist rereading of Paul's rereading of Hagar's narrative leads one to ask, "Why did Paul choose this text (Gal 5:1) to encourage the Galatians that they are free in Christ?" Readers and hearers encounter a dilemma in Paul's Hagar. Paul, the apostle to the Gentiles (Rom 11:13–14) was entrusted with the gospel to the uncircumcised (Gal 2:7). A Pentecostal Womanist reading of Galatians concurs with Bruce Longenecker's observation that one of the dominant themes in the "development of Christian character through the

---

29. Jones-Rogers, *They Were Her Property*, 149.

30. Foster, "Sexual Abuse of Black Men under American Slavery," 447.

31. Foster, "Sexual Abuse of Black Men under American Slavery," 20.

power of the Spirit is the prerequisite for the proper reading of Scripture," which is central to the good news of liberation in Christ from inner and social oppression.[32]

However, while Paul's writing is clear regarding liberation from sin—which for him is understood as the ultimate source of all injustice and oppression—Paul does not challenge the more enormous societal sins. Paul does not challenge the societal sins that birthed the Black Lives Matter movement. Juan M. Floyd-Thomas argues that freedom is the power or right to choose one's "beliefs, actions, and perspectives without external constraints or coercion."[33] Liberation is the "release from all forms of captivity—political, economic, sociocultural, and spiritual."[34] The Galatian Gentiles were free in Christ with their Jewish Christian sisters and brothers; yet a closer reading of Galatians reveals that Paul is not encouraging a commitment to the primacy of praxis of equality for the Christian Jews and Galatian Gentiles.

Rather, in Galatians 4:21–31, Paul is using Hagar and Sarah in a binary allegorical formula. He describes Hagar as a slave woman, who had a son according to the flesh (4:23). He connects this Egyptian woman, a Gentile, with God, the God who gave Moses the commandments and new laws at Mount Sinai—corresponding to the earthly Jerusalem. Paul argues that the Gentiles are children of the free woman who had children through God's promises at an old age. This unnamed woman is assumed to be Sarah, mother of the Gentiles, who is connected to the new heavenly Jerusalem. Paul concludes that Hagar and Ishmael were cast out, for the son of the slave woman shall not inherit with the son of the free woman (4:30). One can interpret Paul's rereading to mean that the Gentiles in Galatia are not to be enslaved by the law of circumcision; instead, they are the children of the free woman, for Christ has set them free (5:1) and they are no longer tied to a yoke of slavery.

If this is the case, the lament of Black Lives Matter would suggest that the majority of white Pentecostal and Charismatics, white evangelicals, and white Catholics are not in Christ nor are they in the Spirit because of their conscious and unconscious refusal to embrace the full humanity of African Americans specifically and communities of color generally.[35]

---

32. Longenecker, *Triumph of Abraham's God*, 170.

33. Floyd-Thomas, "Liberation in African American Theology," 201.

34. Floyd-Thomas, "Liberation in African American Theology," 201.

35. See Jones, *White Too Long*; Marshall, *Christianity Corrupted*.

Pentecostal Womanist's Hermeneutics of R.I.S.E.

African Americans' collective grief is often the catalyst that calls the community together to name, resist, and fight against gun violence, wealth disparity, inequality, and structural racism. Black women are accustomed to lamenting, Black Lives Matter. Hagar and Ishmael's Lives Matter! The tension of Hagar's suffering, which includes enslavement, forced sexual accessibility, teen pregnancy, mental abuse, and abandonment, resonates with examples of modern slavery in the ongoing exploitation of Black people. Modern slavery takes many forms of race-based allocations of resources and the double standards in education, housing, healthcare, and the judicial systems. However, the paradox of hope is a central theme in Hagar's narrative. In spite of her suffering, God actively sought her out, called her by name, and blessed her and her son. Hagar and Ishmael realized that their lives matter because they were recipients of the transforming experiences of the love of God. The Black religious culture affirms that God's transforming love is made real in our daily lives by our mere existence. The paradox of hope of a people through slavery to our present day who continues to confess and believe that through God, all things are possible. Jeanne Porter-King's appropriates Maya Angelou's poem, "Still I Rise," within her Pentecostal rereading of 2 Corinthians 4:7–9 for her sermon by the same name: **R**esilience, **I**nterconnectedness, **S**pirituality, and **E**xpectancy.[36] In what follows, I appropriate Porter-King's hermeneutic of R.I.S.E. to Galatians.

Resilience

Angela D. Sims defines an ethic of resilient resistance as the "ability to name and respond to evil in a manner that challenges practices that are neither just nor fair."[37] Hagar recognizes that her predicament in Genesis 16 is neither just nor fair. She responds to the injustice by fleeing with her child, thus her ability to name and respond to evil is embodied. In Paul's rereading of Hagar's situation, he neither names, responds to, or challenges the evil perpetrated against her. Nevertheless, it would appear that Paul appropriates her abuse and reinterprets it as an example to support the impossibility for Hagar and her descendants to participate in the

---

36. Porter-King, "And Still We Rise."
37. Sims, *Lynched*, 124.

covenantal blessings promised to Abraham and his descendants. "Black lives matter" is one example of how the African American communities have named and responded to the evil of their historical and contemporary predicaments. Like Hagar, contemporary Black communities continue to practice resilient resistance.

Interconnectedness

Paul concludes that Hagar and Ishmael were slaves and therefore will not inherit with the son of the free woman, rereading Genesis 16:11. In reality the descendants of Abraham experienced the same evil predicament in Egypt as Hagar and Ishmael has experienced in the wilderness. The same word used in Exodus 3:16 to refer to the abuse of Abraham's descendants at the hands of the Egyptians was used in Genesis 16:11 to refer to Hagar's abuse at the hand of Sarah.[38] This demonstrated that the writers of the Hebrew Scripture clearly understood that there was an interconnectedness between the descendants of Hagar, the bond woman, and the descendants of the unnamed free woman. If one asserts that all Gentiles are grafted into the body of Christ, then our skin pigmentations should not be used to divide the descendants of Abraham but we should instead affirm that our inheritance is tied to the blood of Christ. Longenecker asserts that the "issue at Galatia, then, is not simply about matters of circumcisions and nomistic observance, but fundamentally about the way one reads Scripture in accordance with Christian character."[39] If we read Scripture through a lens of interconnectedness then we have to acknowledge that Hagar and her descendants' lives are equally as important as the lives of the enslaved Israelites.

"Black lives matter" forces the modern church to wrestle with the interconnectedness of the body of Christ.

Spirituality

If Hagar was a contemporary of Paul, he would have reassured her that she was indeed a child of God and grafted into the family of Abraham. It is the Spirit, not the Law, who gives us our identity as children of the triune God (Gal 4:6). We are no longer under the Law that divides us for

38. Gafney, *Womanist Midrash*, 35.
39. Longenecker, *Triumph of Abraham's God*, 170.

we are called to freedom by the extent to which we love one another and this validates that Christ has set us free (Gal 5:13). True spirituality is one that cries out in prayer that the fruit of the Spirit is love, joy, peace, patience, kindness, goodness, faithfulness, gentleness, self-control: against such thing there is no law (Gal 5:22–23). What results is the power of the Black community and church to develop a unique style of prayer, worship, dance, and songs in the creation of their invisible and visible church. The "Black lives matter" movement is a lived experience of freedom and liberation in the Spirit.

Expectancy

Jesus was crucified to set all, including Hagar and her descendants, free from the curse of the Law so that the Spirit enables all Christians to receive the truth of the gospel that " Black lives matter." The Spirit fills us with the love of God, desire to love God, and our ability to love the other (Gal 2:4.). Whoever has ears, let them hear what the Spirit says to white Pentecostals and Charismatics, white evangelicals, and white Catholics who fail to engage in the dismantling processes of racism embedded in religious institutions, scholarship, and societies. Those who fail to actively seek to dismantle these systems have forsaken the love of Christ by embracing in deeds or by silent affirmation the notions of racism and white supremacy.

Conclusion

Hagar's daughters are groaning in their spirits at the daily onslaught of "Karen's tears" and white male patriarchy's perversion of ethical issues to maintain white supremacy and the comforts of whiteness. The creation groans at the laments "Say Her Name" because while George Floyd's video is cemented on our hearts, nearly 250 women, including forty-eight Black women, have been killed by the police since 2015, and their innocent blood is crying out to God from the streets for justice.[40] Meanwhile, mainstream media, instead of seeking to be a tool for these invisible victims in critiquing state-sanctioned violence, give white victimhood a platform to promote the myth of reverse racism. Martin Luther King, Jr. prophetically speaks to the notion of this nonsensical

40. Owens, "#SayHerName."

idea that white people can experience racism from African Americans: "now they often call this the white backlash . . . It's just a new name for an old phenomenon. The fact is that there has never been any single, solid, determined commitment on the part of the vast majority of white Americans to genuine equality for Negroes."[41] The fact is that white women and men are the benefactors of individual, communal, and systematic racism. Racism is a sin. The mistreatment of Black bodies underscores the necessity for daily engaging in the dismantling and transformation of all dogma, doxa, praxis, and pathos in racism.

If Sheppard is correct, then blasphemy and defilement are words, actions, and thoughts that are sinful acts against God and deny the *imago Dei*. This writer contends that the *imago Dei* is an embodiment of God's love. Blasphemy is the action or offense of speaking sacrilegiously about God or sacred things.[42] Therefore, the triple oppression of Black women by racism, sexism, and classism "run counter to God's proclamation that humans were created in the image of the divine, and require the respect as ones emerging from the Holy's own hands."[43] Defilement is to make something or someone defiled or unclean. The sin of defilement represents the perpetual spoken and unspoken discourses of racial exclusion and racial trauma by white women and men. The perpetual reinforced racial hierarchies of "others" endorse unequal pay, unfair working conditions, along with sexual fetishes. The sins of defilement are "not just considered in terms of what is done to someone but is also accessed by the impact it makes on how the recipient comes to view" oneself.[44] Therefore, the internalized oppression of "white space" finds expressions in Black women's negative self-image and believing the lie of the mainstream media, political leaders, and former President Trump that blackness is a curse.[45]

A Pentecostal Womanist interpretation of Hagar serves as a mirror to proclaim Black Lives Matter, Arab Lives Matter, Hispanic Lives Matter, and Native American Lives Matter. A Pentecostal Womanist interpretation of Hagar's narrative calls Christians to name their sins, repent, lament, and actively engage in the dismantling of systematic oppression. It also calls for a rejection of passive acceptance of internal and external

---

41. King, and Visalli, "Martin Luther King Jr Saw Three Evils in the World."

42. *Oxford English Dictionary*, "Blasphemy."

43. Sheppard, "Mourning the Loss of Cultural Selfobjects," 236.

44. Sheppard, "Mourning the Loss of Cultural Selfobjects," 236.

45. See Sheppard, "Dark Goodness Created in the Image of God."

suffering and trauma in communities of color. The inward groaning of the Spirit and the inward groaning of African American women serve as an invitation to lament and engage in meaningful conversations regarding the many ways—Black Lives Matter!

> God, help us to love Hagar and her children like we love You,
> teach us to cry out with her when she calls upon Your name,
> to believe that You are listening when it seems we sing in vain, God,
> teach us to see, and to know that we are seen.[46]

Discussion Questions:

1. How does the pneumatological transformation of pathos function as a liberative hermeneutic in the interpretation of Scripture?

2. How does the oppression and abuse of Hagar in the Genesis narrative and Paul's portrayal of Hagar in Galatians reflect the power of lament for people of color suffering due to the reality of systematic racism?

3. How does the Pentecostal Womanist hermeneutic of R.I.S.E. affirm that Black Lives Matter and foster the dismantling of white supremacy and white privilege to ensure affirmation of the full humanity and full freedom for all people of color?

Works Cited

Chatters, Linda M., Robert Joseph Taylor, James S. Jackson, and Karen D. Lincoln. "Religious Coping Among African Americans, Caribbean Blacks and Non-Hispanic Whites." *Journal of Community Psychology* 36, no. 3 (April 2008) 371–86. https://www.ncbi.nlm.nih.gov/pmc/articles/PMC2967036/.

Denyse, Tammie. "The Women Gather." *Review and Expositor* 114, no. 3 (2017) 4–5.

Floyd-Thomas, Juan M. "Liberation in African American Theology." In *The Oxford Handbook of African American Theology*, edited by Katie G. Cannon and Anthony B. Pinn, 200–211. Oxford: Oxford University Press, 2014.

Foster, Thomas A. "The Sexual Abuse of Black Men under American Slavery." *Journal of the History of Sexuality* 20, no. 3 (September 2011) 445–64.

Frymer-Kensky, Tikva. "Hagar." In *Women in Scripture: A Dictionary of Named and Unnamed Women in the Hebrew Bible, the Apocryphal/Deuterocanonical Books,*

---

46. Watson, "Hagar Poem."

and the New Testament, edited by Carol Meyers, 86–87. New York: Houghton Mifflin, 2000.

Gafney, Wilda C. *Womanist Midrash: A Reintroduction to the Women of the Torah.* Louisville: Westminster John Knox Press, 2017.

Grant, Jacquelyn. *White Women's Christ and Black Women's Jesus: Feminist Christology and Womanist Response.* American Academy of Religion Academy Series 64. Atlanta: Scholars, 1989.

Hayes, Diana L. *Hagar's Daughter: Womanist Ways of Being in the World.* Notre Dame, IN: Saint Mary College, 1995.

Henderson, Mae Gwendolyn. "Speaking in Tongues: Dialogics, Dialectics, and the Black Woman's Literary Tradition." In *Changing Our Own Words: Essays on Criticism, Theory, and Writing by Black Women*, edited by Cheryl A. Wall, 16–37. New Brunswick, NJ: Rutgers University Press, 1989.

Jones, Robert P. *White Too Long: The Legacy of White Supremacy in American Christianity.* New York: Simon & Schuster, 2021.

Jones-Rogers, Stephanie E. *They Were Her Property: White Women as Slave Owners in the American South.* New Haven: Yale University Press, 2019.

King, Martin Luther, Jr., and Santi Visalli. "Martin Luther King Jr Saw Three Evils in the World." *Atlantic* (MLK Special Edition). https://www.theatlantic.com/magazine/archive/2018/02/martin-luther-king-hungry-club-forum/552533/.

Landfair, Valerie Ranee. "'Trouble In My Way, I Have To Cry Sometimes': Silent Prayers of Sorrow & Lament." PhD diss., Regent University, 2017.

Longenecker, Bruce W. *The Triumph of Abraham's God: The Transformation of Identity in Galatians.* Nashville: Abingdon, 1998.

Longenecker, Richard N. *Galatians.* Nashville: Thomas Nelson, 1990.

Marbury, Herbert. *Pillars of Cloud and Fire: The Politics of Exodus in African American Biblical Interpretation.* New York: New York University Press, 2015.

Marshall, Jermaine J. *Christianity Corrupted: The Scandal of White Supremacy.* Maryknoll, NY: Orbis, 2021.

Martin, Clarice. "The Eyes Have It: Slaves in the Communities of Christ-Believers." In *Christian Origins*, People's History of Christianity Vol. 1A, edited by Richard A. Horsley and Denis R. Janz, 221–39 Minneapolis: Fortress, 2005.

Mathews, Kenneth A. *Genesis 11:27–50:26: An Exegetical and Theological Exposition of Holy Scripture.* New American Commentary 1. Nashville: Broadman & Holman, 2005.

Mathews, Mary Beth Swetnam. *Doctrine and Race: African American Evangelicals and Fundamentalism Between the Wars.* Tuscaloosa: University of Alabama Press, 2017.

Noble, John T. *A Place for Hagar's Son: Ishmael as a Case Study in the Priestly Tradition.* Minneapolis: Fortress, 2016.

Owens, Donna M. "#SayHerName." *USA Today News*, March 11, 2021. https://www.usatoday.com/in-depth/news/investigations/2021/03/11/sayhername-movement-black-women-police-violence/6921197002/.

The Oxford English Dictionary. "Blasphemy." 13 vols. Edited by James Murray, Henry Bradley, William Craigie, and C. T. Onions. Oxford: Oxford University Press, 1961.

Porter-King, Jeanne. "And Still We Rise." Christ Community Church of South Holland. March 11, 2019. 52:49. https://www.youtube.com/watch?v=dvEbLqqanIY&t=1736s.

Sarna, Nahum M. *Genesis: The Traditional Hebrew Text with the New JPS Translation.* JPS Torah Commentary. Philadelphia: Jewish Publication Society, 1989.

Sheppard, Phillis I. "A Dark Goodness Created in the Image of God: Womanist Notes Toward a Practical Theology of Black Women's Embodiment." *The Covenant Quarterly* 61, no. 3 (August 2003) 5–28.

———. "Mourning the Loss of Cultural Selfobjects: Black Embodiment and Religious Experience After Trauma." *Practical Theology* 1, no. 2 (August 2008) 233–57.

Sims, Angela D. *Lynched: The Power of Memory in a Culture of Terror.* Waco, TX: Baylor University Press, 2017.

Skinner, John. *A Critical and Exegetical Commentary on Genesis.* Edinburgh: T & T Clark, 1980.

Solivan, Samuel. *Spirit, Pathos and Liberation: Toward an Hispanic Pentecostal Theology.* Journal of Pentecostal Theology Supplement Series 14. Sheffield: Sheffield Academic Press, 1998.

Thompson, John L. *Writing the Wrongs: Women of the Old Testament among Biblical Commentators from Philo through the Reformation.* Oxford: Oxford University Press, 2001.

Tisby, Jemar. *The Color of Compromise: The Truth about the American Church's Complicity in Racism.* Grand Rapids: Zondervan, 2019.

Townes, Emilie M. "Womanist Theology." https://ir.vanderbilt.edu/bitstream/handle/1803/8226/TownesWomanistTheology.pdf?sequence=1&isAllowed=y.

Watson, Hanna. "Hagar's Poem." *The Poet.* https://open.spotify.com/track/1XrTVsP7IJRpp6Onvew5Y4.

Weems, Renita J. "Reading *Her Way* through the Struggle: African American Women and the Bible." In *Stony the Road We Trod: African American Biblical Interpretation*, edited by Cain Hope Felder, 57–77 Minneapolis: Fortress, 1991.

Williams, Deloris. *Sister in the Wilderness: The Challenge of Womanist God-Talk.* Maryknoll, NY: Orbis, 1993.

Wimbush, Vincent L. *The Bible and African Americans: A Brief History.* Minneapolis: Fortress, 2009.

Toward a Theology of Revolutionary Protest

ANTONIA MICHELLE DAYMOND

All travelers to my city should ride the elevated trains that race along
the back ways of Chicago. The lives you can look into! I think you
could find the tempo of my people on their back porches. The honesty
of their living is there in the shabbiness, scrubbed porches that sag
and look their danger. Dirty gray wood steps. And always a line of
white and pink clothes . . . Waving in the dirty wind of the city. My
people are poor. And they are tired. And they are determined to live.
Our Southside is a place apart: each piece of our living is a protest.

—LORRAINE HANSBERRY[1]

Introduction

IN AN ARRESTING PASSAGE in her 1963 autobiographical work, *To Be
Young, Gifted and Black*, Lorraine Hansberry recounts her early years
of growing up in a black neighborhood on the South Side of the (still)
segregated city of Chicago.[2] In closely observing Hansberry's passionate
account in the above epigraph, we can identify a dialectical tension in

1. Nemiroff, *To Be Young, Gifted and Black*, 17.
2. Nemiroff, *To Be Young, Gifted and Black*.

her description of the status of black life in the American nation. On one hand, she portrays black folk as living at a "place apart" from whites, socially sequestered and beholden to poor and hazardous material conditions that left her people "tired," thereby spotlighting the rigid racial and economic lines that existed during this time, and, for that matter, continue to exist between blacks and whites in American society. On the other hand, despite carrying the weight of economic constraints as well as bearing the coercions of white social/political power and cultural capital, all aimed to sever their human core, Hansberry's remarks exemplify a "nostalgic valorization" that rivals Nietzsche's more popular portrayal of the Greeks' ability to overcome "death, disease, and despair" in the ways that black people have confronted their reality with a determination to live, to continue to inhale and exhale in a world that designates their being as one of suffering.[3]

However, beyond admirable determination, Hansberry attributes black living as one of "protest." That the very essence of living, a vital human function, is an act of protest itself, suggests that Hansberry's merger of protest with living signals the always-already impending threat of extermination, disposability, and expendability against blackness, that which disallows black people to live—that is, black people are left to die. Hansberry's description of black life is existential in nature in that it encapsulates the dire status of black human existence as one that hinges on society's clinging to black subjugation; hence, we hear the chants, cries, and yells of protestors proclaiming that "Black Lives Matter."

I have argued elsewhere, along with others, that racism, in all of its cultural, social, and political nuances, is undergirded by the power to dictate who may/should live and die in this necropolitical era.[4] This menacing, death-dealing reign of racism has yet to be dethroned in the United States; rather, it has flourished like a bed of poisonous flowers. We need only refer to the epidemiological malaise incited by COVID-19, which disproportionately impacted black people in harrowing ways, the stunning forms/compositions of state-allowed violence against black

3. See Gordon, "Of Tragedy and the Blues," 78. My reference to Nietzsche is in no way an attempt to validate the inimitable will of black people through his observation and theory; rather, it is to expose always the irony and the absence of the black subject in the European canon in that its underlying scholarship like Nietzsche's, which had racist tendencies, considers black people as inferior, when in all actuality black people are the prime subjects for their analyses, especially as it pertains to examining exemplars of resilient and sound human subjectivity.

4. See Daymond, "Can These Black Bones Live?"

lives, like that of George Floyd, whose asphyxiation was caused by a state representee's knee stamped upon his neck, uncannily reminding us of James Baldwin's forewarning that "It demands great spiritual resilience not to hate the hater whose foot is on your neck."[5] Further, the white mob uprising that created insurgent, civil unrest, which erupted in the last days of Donald Trump's presidency, displays the ongoing state of emergency concerning white rage and fear of losing a sense of fascist control. Ultimately, while historically blacks have been forcefully distanced from the nation's democratic ideals of freedom, justice, and equality, we have not had the privilege of distancing from the ceaseless conditions of poverty, dehumanization, bigotry, and bias undermining black life.[6] In other words, black bodies have not been historically quarantined from zones of racist danger.

Rather, the pandemonium incited by these supremacist terrors is naturally consistent with an empire bolstered by the economic and social power of whiteness, that is, white supremacy, which is harvested in "racialized social systems."[7] Philosopher Charles Mills categorizes white supremacy as an unnamed political system, a basic one, which has shaped the world for several centuries and that "not only privileges whites but is run by whites, for white benefit."[8] For Mills, deploying the term "white supremacy" moves our thinking from primarily attending to the interpersonal dynamics of race or defining racism as a purely ideological phenomenon to its relation to systems and power, the inhibited capacity for whiteness to push its agenda and interests in relation to other races as well as its capacity to refashion and reorient the system, in a sense pivot, to preserve white advantage even amid society's shifting legal and social dynamics and realities.[9] This systemic racism, dynamized by white supremacy and anti-blackness, infiltrates everyday American living and manifests disparities and disadvantages for blacks, establishing what Eddie S. Glaude calls the value gap, the notion that society values white people over black people, resulting in a distorted American democracy.[10]

5. Baldwin, *Fire Next Time*, 99.

6. Hill carefully assesses this point, especially as it relates to black vulnerability to the COVID-19 crisis. See Hill, *We Still Here*.

7. Bonilla-Silva, *Racism without Racists*, 9. See also Bonilla-Silva, "Rethinking Racism."

8. Mills, "Racial Exploitation and the Wages of Whiteness," 31.

9. Robinson, *Race and Theology*, 23.

10. Glaude, *Democracy in Black*, 29–50. See also Hill, *We Still Here*, 22.

Indeed, the long-standing zeitgeist of racism in the American nation, where white lives are valued more than black lives, has been produced and maintained by systems, institutions, and structures. Processes, policies, and procedures, which are powered by white dominance, entitlement, and privilege, aim to sustain a racial hierarchy created to exclude black bodies from attaining God-ordained livelihoods that fully flourish. From the dawn of the American nation, black people were never included in its fictional dream.

Within this context, the root of this essay grapples with the theological significance and relevance of Christianity to confront the tragedy of the nation's ongoing racial pandemonium and the systems and structures that support its repressive apparatuses of human alienation. Systemic racism has created unnatural communities, that is communities that God did not ordain, which are designed to exclude black people from the necessary resources to maintain human well-being. To maintain this politics of exemption necessitates the violation of racialized bodies in every way possible—dehumanizing conditions, violence, inequitable policies and structures, which excludes black people from the *imago Dei* and further grotesquely compromises and mars black people for the upkeep of white supremacy. The practice and discipline of theology must consider whether or not it should base its protest on inclusion into a highly racialized system—an unnatural system distorted by sin—that is designed to be exclusive. This is to say, we must measure the sharp differences between a protest that advocates for inclusion versus a protest that confronts the core problem of power and thus protests for abolition in the service of creating something revolutionary and new that represents a just society.[11]

In what follows, I briefly discuss the merger of Enlightenment philosophy and Christianity, which helped to advance and solidify a universal white identity, providing the setting for imperialist systems of racism and exclusion. Second, I contrast the message of liberation in the Scriptures and the ways that the earthly ministry of Jesus protested against empire and advocated for life-affirming principles established by the kingdom of God with the modern West's conception of Christianity, in both thought and practice. In doing so, I aim to lay bare the ways that the notion of protest against systemic racism, especially as it pertains to theology, becomes a bit muddied given the ways that the Western

---

11. I am grateful to my colleague and friend, cultural historian Johari Jabir, for pushing me on this point.

Christian enterprise has been blemished and vexed by racist logics in order to establish specific forms of white power and white normativity, namely, American normativity. Finally, I examine the notion of protest stemming from the Protestant Reformation to underscore a principle that might assist adherents to the Christian faith to reconcile its history with racial injustice, which necessitates advocating for something entirely new, something revolutionary, since the life-affirming principles of the kingdom of God may not be fully attained, maintained, or sustained in the present systems as they are wrought by racial currents.

The Tragedy of an "Enlightened" Christianity and the System It Helped to Produce

In *La Pensée Sauvage* (*The Savage Mind*), French anthropologist Claude Levi-Strauss coined the term *bricolage* to refer to the ways a society reinvents itself by retrieving old sources and redeploying them in new ways.[12] Metaphorically, bricolage refers to the process of bricklayers making do with whatever resources are available around them to advance new stock. To be sure, the resources used could have nothing to do with the bricklayer's project in the sense that they aren't necessarily meant to be used in the way the bricklayer uses them, "but is the contingent result of all the occasions there have been to renew or enrich the stock or maintain it with the remains of previous constructions or destructions."[13] However, maintaining the stability or purity of truth of the resources is not the bricklayer's concern; rather, they use whatever they need to accomplish a specific goal.[14]

The concept of bricolage serves a certain usefulness in naming the ways the European colonial project of conquest and domination used whatever available resources to define "whiteness" and resolve the problems of white angst, insecurity, and the desire for superior power. More specifically, "scientific" theories of race along with Christianity, were among the primary resources used to secure whiteness by establishing a project of "othering." This project involved distinguishing whiteness by both physical and mental traits as well as utilizing sacred practices in

12. Lévi-Stauss, *Savage Mind*.

13. Hauerwas and Kenneson, "Flight from Foundationalism, Or, Things Aren't As Bad As They Seem," 684.

14. Mambrol, "Claude Lévi-Strauss' Concept of Bricolage."

order to fabricate others that were not identified as white.[15] On one hand, Enlightenment philosophies, which put forward a deep emphasis on humanism marked by claims to universal truth in the name of sovereign reason, positioned the rational human creature as separate from the savage one, resulting in binary oppositions of those deemed as rational (i.e., white) and those that were not (i.e., inferior, savage, primitive, non-white, or black). On the other hand, placing a premium on rationality gave rise to the creation of a "rational God" for those crowned as "rational." As such, while other religions were marked as pagan, whiteness became the sole proprietor of Christianity, exalting its pieties and practices as rightly "religious."[16] The justification of whiteness, then, through the tools of "science" and "religion" contributed to an ethos of exclusion. This set into motion subordinate notions about blackness while whiteness became attached to a divinized imperialism, which was anchored by racist systems of empire across the globe.

The American nation, specifically as a child of European colonialism, can be viewed as a society that has engaged in bricolage. The invention of the New World required a particular version of Christianity—which does not represent Christian history in its entirety—in order to justify colonization. With the Bible in one hand and a weapon in the other, the Puritan nation became a dedicated disciple of whiteness, shepherding the Enlightenment's illusion with rationality, while at the same time being involved in the very irrational acts of colonial domination and violence in order to secure economic wealth and sociopolitical privilege. Like the bricklayer who melds whatever he needs, and, while in the process, often loses the potency of his source to achieve the outcome of his desire, the nation melded the truth of the gospel by conflating Christian concepts, metaphors, and ideas with colonial logics of race. This conflation turned into a new world ideology resulting in detrimental social consequences for African Americans in its exclusionary practices and systems. What enslaved Africans encounter in America, then, is a colonial Christianity that is specifically nurtured in America, a settler colonial nation, which relies on occupation, annihilation, and brutal exclusion. Hence, we can more readily understand the American project as continuing the practice of these tenets as the elements of Puritan theology remain embedded in the vision of the American experiment and have never disappeared. Put

---

15. Willis, "Impact of David Hume's Thoughts," 214.
16. Willis, "Impact of David Hume's Thoughts."

another way, under the guise of "Manifest Destiny" this religious ethos steadily sustained the American nation at the expense of otherized, raced populations, and functioned as a creed of social unity for whiteness and anti-blackness, which politically indexed physical and psychiatric residues of white superiority and black inferiority that became baked into the racialized systems of the American democratic experiment through the eighteenth century and beyond. Needless to say, this set ablaze a distorted social order in American society that was incompatible with the gospel the nation proclaimed. Naming the settler colonial truth of America helps us to understand why the nation responds to Black Lives Matter with such violence.

"Faith Seeking Understanding?"

Drawing from the scholastic theologian Anselm of Canterbury, this essay is ignited by faith seeking understanding (*fides quaerens intellectum*), an enlivened faith that pursues an in-depth understanding of the ways that theology protests the persisting distorted social order in America, which is sustained by systemic racism.[17] Admittedly, this theological task of understanding is simultaneously simple and complex. On one hand, the message of the Scriptures is clear as it reflects a God on the side of those that are plagued by various empires from Egypt to Babylon to Rome. Christianity's central figure, Jesus, who as the Son of God was robed in his Jewishness, critiqued and rejected the domineering forces of the Roman Empire and protested for the poor and the dispossessed, seeking to empower them from the inexorable assault of oppression, exploitation, and violence. We need only refer to the liberation pronouncement of Luke 4:18–21: "The Spirit of the Lord is upon me, because God has anointed me, to preach the gospel to the poor; God has sent me to heal the brokenhearted, to proclaim liberty to the captives, and recovery of sight to the blind, to set at liberty those who are oppressed, to proclaim the year of the Lord's favor." In Mark's Gospel, Jesus also declared: "You know that among the Gentiles those whom they recognize as their rulers lord it over them, and their great ones are tyrants over them. But it is not so among you" (Mark 10:42). Jesus, who can (and should) be labeled a

---

17. I am grateful to Christian ethicist James S. Logan's influence here, whose public lectures have at times led from this starting point as one of faith as seeking understanding.

political figure, puts forward the kingdom of God as running in deep opposition to the kingdom of Caesar and provides an alternative vision for humans to properly order their social world. The politics of Jesus, which were rooted in a dynamic praxis of protest, fatally resulted in his execution endorsed by the rulers of both the synagogue and the state. In this regard, the Scriptures illumine the tragic yet miraculous nature of the Gospels in the way we humans might reconcile the relationship among God choosing a Jew and planting him in a hegemonic empire that resulted in the blood-drenched scene at the cross and the ways of racist empire in our modern context that result in punitive and ruthless conditions for the raced, poor, and oppressed. The Scriptures signify theological notions of the kingdom of God that disavow all such systems that malign and oppress—which frees humans from the wages of human estrangement and death through the power of the gospel's full revelation of truth, justice, love, and peace.

Nevertheless, despite the obvious messaging of the Scriptures as seen in the example texts cited above, Western Christianity, in its task of "faith seeking understanding" has produced its own canon composed of racist/racial logics, myths, imaginations, ideologies, institutions, and practices, that is tainted by its intimate ties to whiteness. This canon is preserved by a system of empire that performs dominance and violence, especially against those racialized in the modern West. To be sure, the functions of whiteness cannot just be associated with extreme segments of the Christian faith. Western Christianity is a canopy of various historical movements, orientations, and styles of thought, with an assemblage of diverse and often opposing agendas; nevertheless, these articulations all share an offending history of brutal racism. In other words, although there exists white evangelicalism, white Catholicism, and white mainline Protestantism—liberal and conservative Christian traditions—and many other accompanying discursive frameworks, all of them encompass, to borrow J. G. A. Pocock's term, a "family resemblance" to one another; that is, they are all wedded to a religion that was contoured to be compatible with white supremacy.[18] Some of the most egregious offenses against humanity have occurred in the name of the one crucified on Calvary's cross.

Further, in the American Protestant context, Christian theological thought in particular, that is, the Christian desire for seeking a deeper

18. Pocock, "Re-Description of Enlightenment." See also Grote, "Religion and Enlightenment," 145.

knowledge of the transcendent, hidden God as self-revealed in the person of Jesus Christ (Barth)[19] has understood itself in this context of supreme power. This theological framework has held an allegiance to white normativity and modern racist scholarship insofar as its discourses sidelines the subjectivities of those who are gendered, classed, and sexualized and those who are constantly scathed by the processes of racialization. This allows their theological provinces/discourses to form oversimplified judgments (in part due to its preoccupation with human reason and rationality) about social and political matters anterior to race and the ways black subjects have been misused to shape white identity as supreme within the order of things in society. Such misuse weakens theology's attempts to propose the way towards just and egalitarian communities fused with love, radical inclusivity, and nonviolence.

In addition, like Christian religion, the discipline of Western Christian theology concomitantly encompasses multiple differences to which there have been variegated interpretations of the Scriptures and the Christian faith. Nevertheless, those theologies that critically center white supremacy and systemic racism as the reality by which humans conduct their social ontology have been positioned as outliers or, in my own words, "othered."[20] These othered theologies need not only be viewed as interventions or correctives but as protests against the ideological superstructure of whiteness steeped in the tenets of white theology and white Christianity in general. Through concrete engagements with Scripture, these theologies displace the white Western subject and center the experiences of those who have been systemically abused. In making judgements about social and political matters, they deploy the doctrine of humanity to throw light on the ways in which racial/racist tides overflow the nation's sinful systems and structures and how it has functioned to disrupt the God-human relationship as well as human-to-human relationships for both the oppressed and oppressor, in at least two ways. On one hand, the dictatorial workings of systemic racism lodge barriers against humans from thriving as whole persons, and God's will for their wholeness, to be "wholly holy." On the other hand, systemic

19. See Barth, *Epistle to the Romans*.

20. Although this list is definitely not exhaustive, I am referring to theologies such as Womanist theology, which, in addition to interrogating the issue of race and theology, brings to fore the intersections of gender, class, sex, and so on as it pertains to power; Black Liberation theology, Latin-American theology, *Mujerista* and Asian theology, and other theologies that center raced subjectivities and populations.

racism does not reflect the profound interrelatedness displayed in the character of Jesus's human relationships as that which is reconciling and life-giving with those in his midst. Ultimately, these othered theologies underscore the nature of how human societies should be organized via a radical socio-political power for the liberation and agency of the poor and oppressed, and vitalized by a Christian praxis that is based on racial justice and economic equity, such that humans can live in harmonious communion with one another.

Nevertheless, at best, trivial nods to these protest theologies are found within white Western theological discourses as its commitment to engaging the white Western theological tradition, and the experiences of its normed subjects run rampant and supreme. What is at issue here is that Christianity has exhibited a religion about the person of Jesus instead of, to borrow from Howard Thurman, a "religion of Jesus."[21] The question becomes, then, how is one to proclaim that theology protests racism when there is a perpetual marriage between the two entities? Is there a way to revolutionize theology so that it is released from such racist historical trappings and reflect the Jesus tradition that protested empire in a revolutionary way?

Every Period Stands under the Protestant Protest

I'd like to turn our attention to the Protestant tradition, especially with regard to the ways its intellectual and institutional genesis was birthed out of exercising protest (the nomenclature *Protestant* is formed from the root word *protest*). To be sure, it was the writings of Martin Luther, a sixteenth-century German monk and theologian, that sparked a protest against medieval Catholicism that eventually led to the formation of Protestant Christianity, which cultivated the modern West's understanding of religion and culture. As it pertains to the American context, Protestantism arguably remains the most influential religious tradition in the sociopolitical processes within the overall American body politic—regardless of the American citizen's racial makeup. This is to say that the Protestant legacy has an inescapable ideological tension embedded in its theology where the immanent remains of bourgeois liberalism[22] peak at

---

21. See Thurman, *Jesus and the Disinherited*, xix. For the most part, the entirety of this text makes the distinction between the religion of Jesus and Christianity.

22. Bourgeois liberalism usually refers to the emergence of the bourgeois subject

every social, political, and theological corner and maintain perpetual ties to the god of the bourgeoise, whose will justifies the web of capital and exclusion, which can simply be folded into Protestant or even American citizenship. Even the theologies that attempt to retrieve a black Christian subject are at risk of proceeding from vast assumptions about God and personhood preeminently etched by the domineering Protestant discourse and canon.[23]

I have no space to unpack that tension; nevertheless, my turn here is not to make a compelling argument that within the dominant canonical aura there belies an articulation for a total rejection of systemic racism. Rather, I do find that there is an ironic tinge within the Protestant protest. The Protestant Reformation was inaugurated by critiquing the injustices of a system that authoritatively excluded, which, in doing so obscured the divine in the service of justifying exclusionary practices. Yet, the Protestant tradition has historically proceeded to not protest, or even worse, participate in systems that exclude, which have often relied on misconstrued notions about God in the service of arrogantly divinizing its discriminatory tactics.

In his essay "A Theology of Protest: The Reformation and Paul Tillich's 'Protestant Principle,'" historical theologian Paul Capetz seeks to retrieve a principle within the Protestant tradition through the work of Luther, and, even moreso, Paul Tillich.[24] Capetz admits that summoning theological propositions from the medieval era may appear disconnected from modern sensibilities. Capetz also admits the tension with utilizing the work of "dead straight white male theologians" like Luther, or even Tillich levied from the "left" while contending that the "right's" ideology has misrepresented or even distorted the tradition in order to defend conservatism. I am in no way attempting to unpack or reconcile the challenges/critiques of the liberal or conservative stances raised in Capetz's work; however, I do desire to think about the possible sources that are

---

during the rise of capitalism in the eighteenth century in Western society, which sought to accumulate wealth and capital (usually by any means necessary) based on its claim to have liberal rights. The problem, however, is that these rights, although they were claimed to be universally applied to all, were not, which resulted in tremendous economic inequality that exists to this day.

23. Long, *Significations*, esp. chapters 10–12. Undoubtedly, there are black epistemologies not regularly discussed in Western theology, especially if we take seriously Long's use of musical metaphors, "a people's religion is more than thought, it's their rhythms, gestures . . ."

24. Capetz, "Theology of Protest."

illumined in his proposition. Capetz aims to account for a principle of protest within the tradition that streams and strands the manifold dimensions in Protestantism, contending "that there is something in Protestantism that must protest its historical manifestations and forms."[25] For Capetz, despite Luther's anti-Semitic, elitist, and patriarchal positions, he espouses that there is something yet redemptive about the protest that came out of Luther's writings, which eventually led to the Protestant Reformation, and that could prove useful to church and society today. However, to make Luther's case relevant to our times, Capetz turns to Tillich, who is inspired by Luther, and is able to advance and offer an insight into the fundamental character of the Reformation that was grounded in protest:

> In the late medieval context Luther formulated the Protestant principle as the doctrine of justification by faith alone, but Tillich understood that it can be formulated in other ways . . . For Tillich, the Protestant principle is the recognition of what he calls "the boundary situation" of the human being that we are finite, not infinite; mortals not immortal; fallible, not infallible; sinners, not saints; relative, not absolute; creatures, not gods. This means that we are limited in power, our knowledge and perspectives on reality are always partials, the claims on behalf of our own moral goodness and righteousness are dubious, and we are far from what it means to be authentically human whether individually or collectively.[26]

Capetz would go on to directly cite Tillich:

> The Protestant principle implies judgment about the human situation, namely, that it is basically distorted . . . The first word . . . to be spoken by religion to the people of our time must be spoken against religion. It is the word the old Jewish prophets spoke against the priestly and royal and pseudo-prophetic guardians of their national religion, who consecrated distorted institutions and distorted politics without judging them. The same word must be spoken today about our religious institutions and politics.[27]

Tillich's emphasis on the ways that humanity is bound by sin does a certain kind of political work, in that this claim immediately suggests that what

25. Capetz, "Theology of Protest," 65.

26. Capetz, "Theology of Protest," 65.

27. Capetz, "Theology of Protest," 65.

humans concoct and order via human cultures, institutions, systems, and structures are consequently bound to be sinful. There are two takeaways here. First, it's the effort to make visible a form of Protestant identification, as that which recognizes the distortion of human institutional arrangements due to the nature of human fallibility. Second, it is to mine the Protestant tradition's historical incapacity to critically turn inward by recognizing the ways it has—and often with appeals to divine justification—aligned with these political distortions, embodying the vicissitudes of human sin. This is to say, to draw upon Capetz's claim by way of Tillich, "there is something inherent in the nature of genuine Protestantism that makes it not only critical but *self-critical.*" This should lead to a spirit of protest that does not solely reside with those that are subordinated or victimized by the system; rather, the beneficiaries of whiteness, which includes those who, regardless of their racial makeup/social and political identity, have subscribed to, benefited from, and appropriated its imperial tenets. This spirit of protest should lead them to protest against their own stable hand in the maintenance of systemic racism and diagnose its institutional and social arrangements as regulatory regimes that exclude black people and racialized subjects from the benefits of its polity.

Yet, beyond Tillich and Capetz, we may further read the Protestant principle through an even more revolutionary lens (albeit this was unintentional).[28] What is compelling is that Luther and his followers eventually split from the Catholic Church and created something new in that their declarations of faith could not be included within the systemic cadences of Catholicism. The takeaway here is that the Protestant break helps us to ask deeper social and politically textured questions in our own context regarding arguments about creating new systems and so forth. It has to do with inquiring whether or not we can protest for inclusion into a system that is fixed and fated to be exclusive. Or, how can one protest inclusion into a system whose "episodic crises in racism are so socially engineered that it forces black people to participate in a social order" that is so diseased and parasitic "that it cannot deliver to them any of which it promises"?[29] Can we authentically achieve the abundant life that

28. It is important to note that the split from the Roman Catholic Church was not intentional. The intent was to purify and reform the basic tenets of Christian belief within the Christian church and to protest the corruption within it. The leaders of the church rejected the reforms, which resulted in a split in Western Christendom, what we now know as Roman Catholicism and Protestantism.

29. I am indebted to Johari Jabir for expressing this point poignantly in a series of

Jesus proclaimed in the limited systems as they are designed? It's an eye towards problematizing notions of protest that situate inclusion as the primary aim, which inadvertently accepts the dominance that generated the exclusions and erasures that the protest demands inclusion into.[30] This does not imply that our protest becomes divested from anything political. Never. However, it does mean that obtaining inclusion into the state, which remains occupied and framed by white supremacy, cannot be our barometer for achievement; we must go beyond it, reject and refuse it, and demand something entirely new.

To assist with this process, Western theology must properly recover histories that have been discredited and enclosed, whereby "new subjectivities and social relationships" emerge that, by extension, ignite "new political imaginaries and ways of being" and communing.[31] In so doing, it can no longer rely on its normative ways of knowing enunciated and politicized from the white scholarly pulpit but draw upon the freedom, thought, and imaginations of the underside, which cannot be contained or defined by the social frames within which they are expressed. This means that the discourse unsettles its colonial projects of exclusion/erasure through an iconoclastic engagement with them and does complex cultural work. Such complex cultural work brings to the forefront and learns from the othered voices outside of white normativity. For example, the enslaved forged resistance and a politics of refusal in the slave ships, slave quarters, and brush harbors, unearthing a repertoire of signs, rhythms, and gestures, which is a different modality outside of the narratives currently ingested by Western Christian religion.[32]

Indeed, there has been a paradoxical yet synergistic relationship between the American democratic experiment, Christianity, and systemic racism that's left an ongoing affliction yet to be healed. In order to grapple with the grave force of that relationship is to, in fact, unapologetically challenge not only the nation's social and political foundations but also

---

conversations that we've had on this topic.

30. Cohen, Forbis, and Misri, "Protest," 16. See also Wilson, *Golden Gulag*.

31. Cohen, Forbis, and Misri, "Protest." See also Simpson, *As We Have Always Done*.

32. The Black Radical Tradition stands on the fact that Africans were already a people before being forced to the New World. As such, they were not trying to prove their humanity through theology. Rather, the Africans had "critical mixes and admixtures of language and thought, of cosmology and metaphysics, of habits, beliefs, and morality. *These were the actual terms of their humanity.*" Cedric Robinson, *Black Marxism*, 221.

the legitimacy of America's religious history—that is, American history. In other words, it is to locate whiteness and its religious dimensions as that which has utilized exclusionary politics and violent exploitation in order to benefit from the resulting distorted order of things—and contest it. Contesting this history that has orchestrated such white power and entitlement opens up "a broader politics that refuses to accept the legitimacy of the state—to grant rights, services, to "represent."[33] To be sure, this might seem lofty to some or maybe even hallucinatory to others, given the ways that white ideologies are so ingrained in the American psyche, which are not only continuously manifested in social and political spheres but also most certainly religious and theological ones. But maybe that's theology's answer. For Western theology to protest systemic racism, it must protest itself. In doing so, it must intentionally decenter the white normativity that streams through the corpus of Western theological discourse and carefully center the lived experiences of the marginalized like those portrayed in Hansberry's account of black living, whose lived existences are closely shadowed by death.

Ultimately, despite the nation's setbacks and gains, the United States remains marred by the malignant tremors of racism[34] that continue to quake the depths of the nation. This tragic reality beckons that anyone who professes the gospel of Jesus Christ must live out the faith in a revolutionary way, which involves protesting against a despotic American empire that nurtures white supremacies in the service of realizing the ultimate justice of things. As discussed, the very essence of protest resides in the sacred, revolutionary politics and ministry of Jesus. However, a faulty, domineering Christianity has historically infected the churches, the academy, society, and the world. But this infection need not make the Christian religion irredeemable by any means—despite the ways the faith has been battered and bruised. Rather, by way of the cross, we perhaps must envision and protest for something radically new, which encompasses the vision of God's life-giving love, freedom, and justice.

---

33. Robinson, *Black Marxism*. See also Simpson, *Mohawk Interrupts*.

34. To be sure, racism is accompanied by sexism, classism, heterosexism, indifference, xenophobia, hate, vengeance, and so on.

Discussion Questions

1. Jesus purposefully intervened, acted, and was present in various situations in order to protest, dissent, demonstrate, object, question, defend, revolt, and challenge. Can you name some other Scripture passages that give evidence of this protesting tradition?

2. Why is historical context and social location important in the reading and interpretation of Scripture? How can ignoring these factors lead to a distortion of Scripture such that, in the spirit of Howard Thurman, we consciously or subconsciously practice a religion about the person of Jesus instead of a religion of Jesus?

3. This chapter argues that the Protestant principle has been unevenly and selectively applied throughout the history of the Protestant church, particularly as it pertains to racialized social and political issues. How can Scripture be used to protest this uneven and selective application?

Works Cited

Baldwin, James. *The Fire Next Time*. New York: Vintage, 1992.

Barth, Karl. *The Epistle to the Romans*. Translated by Edwyn C. Hoskyns. Oxford: Oxford University Press, 1968.

Bonilla-Silva, Eduardo. *Racism without Racists: Color-Blind Racism and the Persistence of Racial Inequality in the United States*. Lanham, MD: Rowan and Littlefield, 2006.

———. "Rethinking Racism: Toward a Structural Interpretation." *American Sociological Review* 62, no. 3 (1997) 465–80.

Capetz, Paul. "A Theology of Protest: The Reformation and Paul Tillich's 'Protestant Principle.'" *Currents in Theology and Mission* 45, no. 4 (2018) 63–70.

Cohen, Elena L., Melissa M. Forbis, and Deepti Misri. "Protest." *Women's Studies Quarterly* 46, no. 3 (Fall 2018) 14–28.

Daymond, Antonia Michelle. "Can These Black Bones Live?: Addressing the Necrotic in US Theo-Politics" *CrossCurrents* 68, no. 1 (2018) 135–58.

Glaude Eddie S., Jr. *Democracy in Black: How Race Still Enslaves the American Soul*. New York: Crown, 2016.

Gordon, Lewis. "Of Tragedy and the Blues in an Age of Decadence: Thoughts on Nietzsche and African America." In *Critical Affinities: Nietzsche and the African American Experience*, edited by Jacqueline Renee Scott and Todd Franklin, 75–97. Albany: State University of New York Press, 2006.

Grote, Simon. "Religion and Enlightenment." *Journal of the History of Ideas* 75, no. 1 (January 2014) 137–60.

Hauerwas, Stanley, and Philip D. Kenneson. "Flight from Foundationalism, Or, Things Aren't As Bad As They Seem." *Soundings: An Interdisciplinary Journal* 71, no. 4 (1988) 683–99.

Hill, Marc Lamont. *We Still Here: Pandemic, Policing, Protest, and Possibility*. Chicago: Haymarket, 2020.

Lévi-Strauss, Claude. *The Savage Mind*. Chicago: University of Chicago Press, 1968.

Long, Charles. *Significations: Signs, Symbols, and Images in the Interpretation of Religion*. Philadelphia: Fortress, 1986.

Mambrol, Nasrullah. "Claude Lévi-Strauss' Concept of Bricolage." *Literary Theory and Criticism Notes*, March 21, 2016. https://literariness.org/2016/03/21/claude-levi-strauss-concept-of-bricolage.

Mills, Charles W. "Racial Exploitation and the Wages of Whiteness." In *What White Looks Like*, edited by George Yancy, 25–54. New York: Routledge, 2004.

Nemiroff, Robert. *To Be Young, Gifted and Black: Lorraine Hansberry in Her Own Words*. New York: Vintage, 1995.

Pocock, J. G. A. "The Re-Description of Enlightenment." *Proceedings of the British Academy* 125 (2006) 101–17.

Robinson, Cedric. *Black Marxism: The Making of The Black Radical Tradition*. Chapel Hill: The University of North Carolina Press, 2000.

Robinson, Elaine. *Race and Theology*. Nashville: Abingdon, 2012.

Simpson, Audra. *Mohawk Interrupts: Political Life Across the Borders of Settler States*. Durham, NC: Duke University Press, 2014.

Simpson, Leanne B. *As We Have Always Done: Indigenous Freedom through Radical Resistance*. Minneapolis: University of Minnesota Press, 2017.

Thurman, Howard. *Jesus and the Disinherited*. Boston: Beacon, 1976.

Willis, Andre C. "The Impact of David Hume's Thoughts about Race for His Stance on Slavery and His Concept of Religion." *Hume Studies* 42, nos. 1–2 (April/November 2016) 213–39.

Wilson, Ruth Gilmore. *Golden Gulag: Prisons, Surplus, Crisis and Opposition in Globalizing California*. Berkeley: University of California Press, 2007.

Black Bodies, Art, and Community

Brian Bantum

ON JUNE 27, 2015, Bree Newsome climbed the flagpole in front of the South Carolina state legislature and took down the Confederate flag. Reciting Psalm 23 (as she was taken to jail) she said, "You come against me with hatred and oppression and violence. I come against you in the name of God. This flag comes down today." Photographs and artistic renderings of Newsome went viral. Newsome's act was only one instance of protest and art coalescing in the shadow of nine members of Emanuel African Methodist Episcopal Church being murdered by Dylan Roof, and in the wake of the murders of Trayvon Martin, Michael Brown, Tanisha Anderson, and Eric Garner (to name only a few). As protests filled the streets, there was also a proliferation of protest in the arts. Songs, murals, memes, digital art, installations all amplified the central tenant of a now global movement #BlackLivesMatter.

Newsome's act signified one moment in a long legacy of Black protest and the arts. A filmmaker and community organizer, Newsome displayed how the visualization of the Black body becomes the central point of counter-narrative against white supremacist discourses. The imagery of Newsome at the top of the flagpole removing the Confederate icon displayed the competing visualities of Black life in the United States, the mythic claims of white supremacy, and the refusals of Black flesh to be contained within those myths. The protests across the country, the protest art and songs, the memes, the gatherings in streets or in churches point to the thin membrane between art and Black life, that Black life is art.

In the face of a white gaze, Black people flicker from inconsequence to behemoth and back again, rarely being truly seen. And yet in the movement of light and shadow Black people have drawn depth and exuberance, the birth of cool, curated lives of rhythm and soul. If the Black body was the creation of white discourse about its visuality and its possibilities, that same Black body also spoke for itself. As bell hooks describes, "The practice of freedom in daily life, and that includes artistic freedom, is always a liberator act that begins with the will to imagine."[1] Stories and songs and dances and buildings and rituals, lives lived, countered the discourse of anti-blackness. Every day of living was a visualization that Black lives mattered.

The contestation between white supremacy and the meaning of Black bodies is the constant of the United States' genealogy, spilling into and out of sight throughout its history. And alongside these moments of protest, of accounting for Black personhood, Black citizenship, has also been art—as spirituality, as assertion, as protest, as icon, as counter-narrative. All of the arts—literature, song, dance, visual—have served to carve out space to articulate and celebrate Black personhood. And in all of these, there is a constant theme of subverting the racist discourses pressed against the flesh of the people of the African diaspora who live in the United States.

This invocation of art in order to tell a different story, to erect mirrors that reflect the beauty of, to make known what is not always on the surface, to tinge the whitewashing of state-sanctioned murder—this is the work of Black art in America, and while the discourse of white supremacy has been a constant, so too have been Black refusals and a determination to depict Black personhood in its fullness and beauty.[2] Black art participates in this economy of the icon that is Black flesh, navigating a world of being and being seen.

Called to see the world, the artist not only observes but must create, cut, bind, crush, layer, build, and fold until there is something where there was nothing. But in the wake of the colonial project, for the Black artist, or any artist of color, this task is an extension of being seen in the world, navigating the visceral nodes of contact that render one's body an aesthetic or an-aesthetic presence.

---

1. hooks, *Art on My Mind*, 97.

2. This is not to say that images of Black life are unsullied by narratives of whiteness or American mythologies, but see hooks, *Art on My Mind*, 95.

In a way, visual artists witness to the reality of a current of visuality that permeates all human life. That is, we see and are seen, we touch and are touched—taste, sight, sound are all fundamental aspects of being human. In the midst of these senses, visuality is a curious site of identity and identification that requires a theological accounting given the claim that we are made in the image of God.

Of course, most of us know the question of God's visuality was an aspect of the controversy and scandal surrounding the claims of Jesus' divinity—and would continue in the debates regarding the role of images throughout the church's history.

As Maria-José Mondzain points out, the question of the icon was never simply about images in churches, however. The iconoclastic controversies were also about empire and the power of the emperor's image in the world—and in this process, most interestingly, Jesus' face imaged frontally. In the turning from profile, Jesus' Jewish features become submerged, hidden . . . making possible new visual associations of power and lordship.[3]

Visuality permeates, surges, undulates in and under our everyday lives. We cannot escape it, but what do we do with it? And what do we do in the midst of a world where this visuality is never about images alone, but also the significance of our bodied lives, seeing and being seen each day? What do we do in the midst of a world where certain bodies—men, women of color, white women—where our bodies have been collected, probed, painted, and shaped so thoroughly that we enter into the world with "garments of skin" we did not ask for, and yet everyday feel and navigate—and yet transfigure?

Understood in dialogue with a theology of the icon, Black flesh, Black life, Black art moves in and out of one another, speaking and creating, being seen in a world that continually seeks to dismember its presence.

Icons, Christianity, and Black Bodies

While the curiosity and classification of the Black body is a more modern invention, beginning its violent questions in the fifteenth century, the question of image and body has been an enduring one in Christian life. In some respects, it could be considered the fundamental question of Christian life: how can a body reflect God's presence? How can a body

---

3. Mondzain, *Image, Icon, Economy*, 216.

be God's presence? And is it appropriate to image that presence? This has been an ongoing question of Christian life. Whether a consideration of images, or the Lord's Supper, or the ordination of women, and the inclusion of LGBTQ+ people. Who can reflect and mediate the presence of God in the world? To consider the theological significance of Black art and community, it would be helpful to consider two sketches of theological accounts of image and body in Christian history.

The Icon

The first response was the theology of the icon—a deep and generative attempt to consider the truth of Jesus' person as human and divine as a visual and anthropological phenomenon. As we gaze at the icon, as we kiss it, we are drawn into the image it reflects and into contemplating; we pray that we might, too, come to reflect this true image. The image is living, if you will. Pavel Florensky describes the icon as "a transfixing, an annunciation that proclaims in color the spiritual world; therefore, icon painting is the occupation of a person who sees that world as sacred."[4]

In this response of icon writing, the writer, the artist (we cannot forget those who create) is the one who prays, who mediates this presence into the world through a union of contemplation and skill and insight.

Martin Luther

A second response can be seen in the Reformation, perhaps encapsulated best by Martin Luther. Like most Reformers, Luther had a suspicion of images and what he saw as the idolatry that they represented and inculcated. Luther was a bit more liberal in allowing vestments and banners, but like Calvin and Zwingli, he would whitewash his sanctuary walls, images and paintings of saints would be taken down, leaving only an ornately carved pulpit and altar, and the preacher standing before the gathered people sharing the good news to be "heard" and received. As art historian Joseph Koerner suggests, "Luther . . . judged images not for what they in themselves were, but for the function they served. Declaring that the 'argument is not about substance, but about the use and abuse of things,' he tolerated and finally even encouraged church art if it served to instruct."[5]

4. Florensky, *Iconostasis*, 78.
5. Koerner, *Reformation of the Image*, 26.

What is so fascinating about the Reformers is their continued openness to images, but for the purposes of education and formation. Whereas the Reformers refused images as objects of veneration, nonetheless, they emphasized their use for teaching. Thus, the Reformers unwittingly created an icon even as they destroyed the images within their churches. In stripping the walls of their churches, they transformed their preachers into icons, into images of the image that ultimately reified and enclosed the possibilities of what the preacher could look like. Luther and the other Reformers reflect an attempt to dam up the currents of visuality—to redirect its energy, and in doing so, created new icons and new images imprinted upon our bodies, work that the Enlightenment would build upon with tragic and enduring consequences for so many of us.

Even in these brief accounts of Christians wrestling with the significance of images, there are two important aspects of images and the body working. First, images are part of a broader economy of personhood and culture. The earliest Eastern Orthodox notions of image presupposed an inherent relationship between the image, Jesus, and the person viewing the image. Images participated in an economy of visuality, body, and God's life that drew people deeper into the life and love of God and one another.

In Luther we see a second aspect of images that would echo throughout Christian life, the idea of teaching and "seeing" the truth of God. Images teach us because they allow us to see the truth of who God is, or who we are, or who we are not. Luther and the other Reformers saw an economy of visuality as well but oriented the image in service to the "truth" of faith as revealed in Scripture. I point to these two ideas in Christian histories not to validate or invalidate any idea about Black art. Instead, I want to point to broader currents of visuality that even Christian understandings of art navigate. What does the image reflect? How does it shape the viewer? How does it shape our understanding of what is portrayed? Or not portrayed?

For Luther, the good and evil of the world could be depicted. He used images not only as teaching tools, but perhaps even as propaganda. One famous etching of the trees of good and evil depicts angelic creatures on one side and demonic figures on the other.[6] But the demonic figures often shared physical characteristics with Jews, their features twisted and animalized. The images Luther's movement employed were not simply teaching but representing the bodies that

---

6. Cranach the Elder, *Law and Gospel*, Herzogliches Museum, Gotha, Germany.

reflected good and evil in their flesh. And a most significant icon within this economy would become a white Jesus, looking benevolently upon European colonists and enslavers as a New World was conquered and Black bodies brought to its shores in chains.

The Economies of Black Art

While formal avenues of visual artistic expression were prohibited for the earliest Black Americans, there was, nonetheless, intention to display the beauty, care, intellect, and mastery of craft in objects that were seen and used every day.[7] The beauty of Black art was always present in the everyday. But as more Black artists (trained and self-taught) were able to engage in visual arts they began to depict their lives in ways they saw them. In images that subtly pointed or explicitly declared, their work began to make space for the beauty and true lives of Black experience. With opportunities to practice fine arts also came depictions of Black life that countered the caricature and propaganda of white supremacist discourses. Sculptors such as Edmonia Lewis (1844–c. 1911) and portraitist Joshua Johnson (c. 1763–c. 1827) traded in the neoclassical motifs and styles that dominated early American art. And yet, their subjects oftentimes identified Black faces and bodies in depictions of American possibility and nobility. Whether inclusion in the "American" project was a goal could be debated and would be debated. But in these early artists we see the possibility of agency and representation in Black personhood.

In the 1920s the depiction of Black life became a central topic of Black artists, forming a singular expression in the New Negro Movement and the Harlem Renaissance. Art such as Meta Warrick Fuller's *Ethiopia Awakening* (1914) began to point explicitly to Black identity and African identity, a Black diaspora that Black flesh participated within and could find images of pride, power, and wisdom.

This emphasis on the possibilities of images and art in Black life was championed by Harlem Renaissance writer Alain Locke, who saw an unequivocal relationship between the images we see and who we believed ourselves to be. Visuality was tied to Black life. During the Harlem Renaissance, Alain Locke believed that the key to Black uplift lay in the nurture of Black artists and the cultivation of a Black aesthetic. Encouraging,

---

7. See Farrington, *African American Art*, 15–27.

promoting, and mentoring Black poets, novelists, and visual artists, Locke hoped to cultivate a unique cultural aesthetic.

> Here is a double duty and function to Negro art,—and by that we mean the proper development of the Negro subject as an artistic theme—the role of interpreting the Negro in the American scene to America at large is important, but more important still is the interpretation of the Negro to himself. Frankness compels the admission and constructive self-criticism dictates the wisdom of pointing out that the Negro's own conception of himself has been warped by prejudice and the common American stereotypes. To these there is no better or effective antidote than a more representative Negro art of wider range and deeper penetration.[8]

Locke's reading of Black art and its critical telos from Black subjects and towards uplift shares a critical overlap in Luther's response to the problematic and idolatrous visuality—each saw art as primarily shaping their communities.

Artists such as Romarie Bearden and Elizabeth Catlett reflected this sense of aesthetic self-realization. Re-presenting the history, dignity, power, and story of Black life in its varied hues and styles, the Harlem Renaissance and then later the Black Arts Movement of the sixties and seventies cultivated art for uplift.

Perhaps with less explicit theological frameworks, these artists were products of communal hope and organization. In the thirties and forties community art centers such as the South Side Community Art Center directed by Margaret Burroughs, or The Harlem Arts Center founded by Augusta Savage, became incubators, a priestly formation—those who would visualize the humanity we knew we had, but so often did not see on a daily basis.

Images seemingly reified and distorted the truth of who a people were. To this end, visuality, image, art was not to be discarded or completely avoided, but should be oriented towards uplift, towards gospel, towards enlivening and an enlivened life. Although it shares a certain orientation towards formation and inculcation, Locke's formative posture includes a vital distinction that should inform how we begin to understand the relationship between art and the body more broadly.

Black existence is never without its body. Any truth, any text, any claim is never an escape but an extension of one occupation of a space

---

8. Locke, "Negro Art, Past and Present," 159.

and a moment. The Reformers' understanding of visual life sought to maintain and stabilize the gospel, a gospel that lay beneath words which laid beneath the tones and within the body of the one who declared those words of truth.

In Locke's didactic formula the artist is the medium of the gospel, integral to the imagination, the creative capacities, and the truth that underlies any image—the beauty and humanity of the one who created the image and the beauty that the image invites all who look like it are invited into. While didactic in his aims, Locke points us to the ways that Black art was explicitly participating in deep currents or economies of visuality, seeking to reimagine and re-image the truths of Black existence in broader American life.

In a way, Locke's gospel, even while resisting the idolatries of white supremacy, nonetheless maintained a certain "gospel" of what Black life looked like. Far from trying to imitate European classic "masters," Locke called artists to develop a unique style of "Negro Art," and he sought to build a visual culture that reflected the fullness of Black life and personhood.

Like any movement that attempts to identify the parameters of faithfulness, Locke's hope to create a visual culture of African American life also risked creating lines of representation and "inauthenticity" that can only be understood as random. How do we make sense of the Black artists who did not follow the stylistic sentiments of a Romarie Bearden or Elizabeth Catlett, of those who were not in the streets of the civil rights movement or volunteering their time creating posters and protest art? Does the use of classic forms or motifs disqualify the artist's Black genius or as a representative of Black artistic and intellectual life?

Black artists, much like icon writers, were writing a truth that white supremacy had sought to obscure—rather than the image being that of word or Word made flesh, the truth is the fulsomeness of Black life and its possibilities—the truth of God's life and presence in their lives. Black artists become priests, mediators of the truth of their bodies fashioned into image.

To draw again from theological understandings of the icon: the Black artist creates mediums that participate in an economy of freedom. The artists, through their skill and insight, create moments, windows that illumine, imbue, or awaken the wholeness in the Black viewer—or speak to their pain or simply tell their story.

The Post-Soul Aesthetic

While Locke's hope for cultivating a Black cultural aesthetic was critical in that moment, and perhaps one of the few responses one might image in the segregation and violence of the early and mid-twentieth century, it created questions for some. What are the resources? What are the aims of art?

Namely, those born after the civil rights movement, who often shared fundamental commitments to Black life and thriving, but at the same time did not always see their art as necessarily oriented towards protest movements or civil rights causes—nor did they see themselves as distinct from those hopes or rhythms. While it has been captured by many names—The New Black Aesthetic or Post-Soul—writers, artists, scholars share a family resemblance, or as Bertram Ashe suggests a "school" of thought that identifies three markers of a post-soul aesthetic:

1. A cultural mulattoesque sense.

2. Blaxporation arguing that blackness is constantly in flux and in that way the post-soul aesthetic "responds" to the 1960's call for affixed and iron-clad Black aesthetic.

3. Using an allusion/disruption strategy that takes familiar tropes and flips them or turns them inside out to disorient and create new meanings.[9]

The post-soul artist uses history with disregard and recognition, identifying the veils and shredding them, braiding them, and hoisting them anew. Like icon writers, they are attentive to the dogmas etched into the wood, cuts that were meant to be repeated and honored—they attend but fill in with new color or ignore shape even while displaying mastery of technique and depth of insight.

Kehinde Wiley, working from the neoclassical archetypes, paints everyday Black people into portraits they resonate with. Some might sit on a horse in a Napoleonic triumph or be surrounded with the pomp of monarchy. Again, the question arises, "Are these European markers of wealth and status needed to give the Black people imaged dignity?" But perhaps we could also reverse the question and ask, "Who is giving dignity to whom?"

Or, what do we do with the images intended to dehumanize? Artist Kara Walker created silhouettes based on the caricatures of the pickaninny

9. See Ashe, "Theorizing the Post-Soul Aesthetic."

and mammy in elaborate Southern scenes that highlighted the violence and absurdity of slaveholding society. Her use of the silhouette mocked the practices of phrenology and silhouette as a form of epistemological revelation in order to critique the foundations of the social order.

In both of these artists, we see the inclinations of the very earliest of Black artists and Black life navigating a white supremacist society; there is no tool unavailable and there is nothing that can't be deconstructed and rebuilt to point towards life. As bell hooks describes photographer Lorna Simpson's work, "Simpson's photographs name that which is rarely articulated—a technology of the sacred that rejoins body, mind, and spirit . . . Despite all that is imposed on black female flesh, no coercive domination is powerful enough to alter that state of grace wherein the soul finds sanctuary, recovers itself."[10] While Black art has not disentangled itself completely from histories and formations of patriarchy, homophobia, sexism, colorism, it nonetheless points to the possibilities of remaking, retelling, making manifest the fullness of Black life and personhood.

The art of post-soul artists participates in the currents of Black art that draw from the cultural waters they exist within, even the elements meant to marginalize or exclude or kill, and reappropriate them to sing a different song. Nothing goes to waste. The Black church has been a complicated incubator of this type of imagination. Whether in the spirituals or the prophetic rereadings of Scripture or the depictions of a Black Jesus welcoming people into worship—the Black church is itself a radical act of prophetic artistic imagination.

But the Black church hasn't been free from the evil that is colonial, patriarchal, racist imaginaries. The church has also been a space where notions of freedom and life have looked very particular, where, much like Martin Luther's theology of image, the economy of the visual points towards the cisgender, heterosexual man. This has meant women, gay, lesbian, bi, trans, nonbinary, and disabled people have been asked to quietly work behind the curtains, under guise because the kingdom of God did not seemingly look like them.

But if Black life points to anything, it is just how vividly the presence of God, God's kin-dom is manifest in the everyday liberations Black people can create in the midst of white society's refusals. But why would it repeat those refusals within its very walls?

---

10. hooks, *Art on My Mind*, 100.

Black Icons

Black life has constantly negotiated the economy of visuality that is the United States' racialized beginnings. As an aesthetic existence there is a thin membrane between the daily creations of Black joy that fill small kitchens or choir lofts or backyard barbecues and the artistic practices of song or paint or clay. Their power and possibility are all drawn from the same river.

This brings us back to the image of Bree Newsome at the top of the flagpole with the Confederate flag in her hand, reciting Scripture. She knew she would be arrested when she set the first foot back down. She knew the flag would most likely be raised back up again as soon as she was taken away. And yet she also understood the power of the image, a Black woman climbing up to yank down a symbol of anti-blackness and all the myths it tried to sustain. In an interview following that morning, she said,

> And David says to Goliath, you know, "You come against me with sword and spear and javelin, and I come against you in the name of the Lord." And that, for me, as a black woman in America, I mean, that's what that moment—that's what that moment felt like, because I come from a historically completely disempowered place. And so, I think that's why it was so power-ful to a lot of people, especially to black women, to see me up there holding that flag in that way.[11]

But Newsome's icon-writing was not done to be hung behind an altar or a pulpit. While the church has been a space of prophetic imagination it also finds itself in a moment where those creating such prophetic images are also doing so in spite of the churches they were raised in.

Movements like the New Negro, the Black Arts Movement, and post-soul all sought to visualize the realities and beauty of Black life, to image a truer history and a richer future for Black Americans. The church exists as a body, something to be seen and touched and felt that speaks to the liberating and welcoming and embracing presence of a God who loves and abides with us and in us. This is art in the truest sense. May we live into the deepest creative rivers of black life and God's life to create spaces of love where God is seen and felt and heard for all people.

---

11. Newsome, "Exclusive."

Discussion Questions

1. What are some of the strongest images or experiences of God you have seen or felt recently? What made those holy?

2. How have you seen a "non-church" song or image become part of worship? What was difficult or inspiring about that? What are some reasons to be concerned or hopeful about art from outside the church being incorporated into church life/worship?

3. Sometimes artists challenge our sensibilities of what is appropriate in a church setting. How might artists push us to see God and ourselves in new ways?

Works Cited

Ashe, Bertram D. "Theorizing the Post-Soul Aesthetic: An Introduction." *African American Review* 41, no. 4 (2007) 602–23.

Cranach the Elder. *Law and Gospel*. Herzogliches Museum, Gotha, Germany. 82.2 cm × 118 cm (32.4 in × 46.5 in).

Farrington, Lisa. *African American Art: A Visual and Cultural History*. New York: Oxford University Press, 2017.

Florensky, Pavel. *Iconostasis*. Translated by Donald Sheehan and Olga Andrejev. Crestwood, NY: St. Vladimir's Seminary Press, 1996.

hooks, bell. *Art on My Mind: Visual Politics*. New York: New, 1995.

Koerner, Joseph Leo. *The Reformation of the Image*. Chicago: University of Chicago Press, 2004.

Locke, Alain. "Negro Art, Past and Present." In *The Works of Alain Locke*, The Collected Black Writings Series, edited by Charles Molesworth 155–60. Oxford: Oxford University Press, 2012.

Mondzain, Marie-José. *Image, Icon, Economy: The Byzantine Origins of the Contemporary Imaginary*. Stanford, CA: Stanford University Press, 2005.

Newsome, Bree. "Exclusive: Extended Interview with Bree Newsome, Who Climbed Flagpole & Took Down SC Confederate Flag." Interview by Amy Goodman. *Democracy Now!*, July 2, 2015. Transcript: https://www.democracynow.org/2015/7/2/exclusive_extended_interview_with_bree_newsome

White Supremacy Is a Script We're Given at Birth[1]

Reggie Williams

Maybe, after the last few months, a broader portion of the US population can now understand what James Baldwin meant when he said, "To be a Negro in this country and to be relatively conscious is to be in a rage almost all the time."[2] The rage is useful to the extent that it helps generate new knowledge about the world that can help our efforts toward change for the good of all. In a nation with a history of slavery and lynching, the fact that Black people bleed and die isn't new information. What may be new to many people, however, is just how prevalent and persistent white supremacy is in this country. According to Baldwin, white people remain trapped within a history that they do not understand, one from which they need release—but they must act, must be committed. To act in response to this history, however, is terrifying. It requires engaging a complete recalibration of identity. Short of that, there is no exit.

Reality has been hijacked, and the result is a history of carnage. The place where I am writing this—Cook County, Illinois—is populated by the two demographics hardest hit by COVID-19: Black and brown people. And in the midst of so much death and uncertainty caused by the pandemic, we have been forced, yet again, to behold the spectacle of the state killing unarmed Black people. When forty-six-year-old George Floyd pleaded with police officers, "I can't breathe!" while calling out for

1. Reprinted with permission from *The Christian Century*.
2. Baldwin, from a 1961 radio address, "Negro in American Culture."

his mother as he lay dying in handcuffs, face down on the street with a white officer choking him to death, the world was shaken from its precautionary shelter-in-place.

The officer who killed Floyd knelt on his neck for eight minutes and forty-six seconds, before a watching public, as indifferently as one might wait in a checkout line. His left hand was casually in his pocket. He was serene as he dismissed pleas from onlookers and from Floyd himself. This casual, callous disregard for Floyd's life is hard to fathom, as are the opposition to Black Lives Matter and the wider indifference toward the deaths of many other unarmed Black people in recent weeks, months, and years—unless we recognize what is happening. These are not isolated incidents. Western history has devised a premise that merges them all.

The premise is white supremacy. Recent events have opened more eyes to its reality, but most people still struggle with language to name it. In everyday conversation about racial oppression, terms like *xenophobia*, *prejudice*, and *white supremacy* are often used interchangeably. This doesn't help. We're not likely to prescribe the right treatment without an accurate diagnosis. Misdiagnosing the problem makes it difficult to understand how profoundly insidious white supremacy is—and how embedded it is within the story this nation believes itself to be living. It's so much more than a few bad apples. White supremacy sits deep inside of the way we've been made to understand the world after centuries of reality-bending cruelty. If there is any possible way to address the problem, we must recognize what it is and what it is not.

First, although white supremacy often includes affect, it is not about your feelings, which is to say, it is not a matter of liking or disliking people of different races. History is replete with white supremacists who love Black people, sexually or otherwise. Nor is white supremacy the same as xenophobia or prejudice, though it often includes these ideological gangsters and others. Xenophobia is essentially the opposite of hospitality: it is an attitude of unwelcome for strangers, foreigners, or anything unknown. It is not selective about which foreigners or strangers to dislike. By itself, it is not white supremacy—though it may play a part in white supremacy by working to maintain exclusively white space.

As for prejudice, we practice it when we produce or embrace knowledge about people that is not based on actual experience with them. It is bias or contempt that results from unsubstantiated information about others. Howard Thurman's description of hatred in *Jesus and the Disinherited* is a good primer on prejudice: hatred includes (1) contact without fellowship, which leads to (2) unsympathetic understanding, which generates (3) ill will, finally giving rise to (4) hatred walking.[3] One might say that prejudice is a matter of the heart. But prejudice alone is not white supremacy. It is vital to understand the difference: any individual may harbor unfounded bias or contempt toward a person or group of people. And while an individual's affect toward others can change, that is not the kind of transformation that will end white supremacy. No amount of hugging will eliminate it, because white supremacy is not about affect—it's about anthropology. How do we understand what it means to be human? The historical answer to that question has been a hegemonic one: white supremacy.

White supremacy is the manufacture and maintenance of systems and structures for whites only. Hatred and harm are always secondary effects of this primary thing: a longing for an idealized community populated by a fetishized, white ideal. The term can be used interchangeably with *racism*; they describe the same phenomenon. In what follows, I will explain what I mean by this definition of white supremacy. It is not my intent to offer a comprehensive history of race in this brief space. Instead, I aim to help clarify terms in order to provide us with better tools to diagnose the problem—because diagnosis determines treatment.

To live in the United States is to be the default recipient of an old and appalling political ecosystem. The political, economic, and social systems of this nation are historically synchronized to work like a theatrical production that is played out at every level of social discourse in scripted encounters. Even when it seems that we are making free-will decisions, we are inevitably engaging the script. We've seen it all before, just as we have seen it recently: police and white vigilantes killing unarmed Black people; white people making petty police calls on Black people, as if the police were their personal enforcement service or a lynch mob on speed dial; A biased legal system with disproportionate, race-based prison sentencing. The list is long.

These racial conditions for the US populace are not random or disconnected. They are part of a script that informs the common understanding of human difference in the United States and our corresponding mode of social interaction. We are handed this script at birth, and we all learn our obligatory lines and roles from multiple life teachers. We learn that we are protagonists or antagonists in the story, not by choice

---

3. Thurman, *Jesus and the Disinherited*.

but because we cannot avoid it. The script is written in our flesh, interpreted through foundational social platforms, and rehearsed throughout history. It is the story of race. This long-running performance is as old as the United States. It is not entertaining, and it has no grounding in reality—other than the alternate reality it has created.

It is vital to see its plotline in the symmetry of events that tirelessly result in Black death and what follows. This is the plight of the antagonist, which loosely follows a pattern. First, there is a blatant killing of an unarmed Black person by a state official or vigilante or a lethal, disproportionate response to a baseless fear. This is followed by the corresponding hashtag moment for the Black victim's name. The killer's defenders inevitably discover some form of disparaging information about the character or behavior of the deceased. This newfound info is used to justify the killer and implicate the dead. The Black victim is subsequently tried in the court of public opinion, using the evidence of the racial script as evidence against them in their own killing.

To be white, after all, is by default to be the protagonist. Somehow, the Black dead deserved to die; they were destined for this kind of death. That is the plight of the antagonist. And to be the protagonist also means to be given the benefit of sympathy, even when caught in the act of murder. This is an evil loop that happens so often that each instance quickly commingles with the next evil loop in the pattern; wash, rinse, and repeat.

That's all in the script. The plotline may not always end with the white killer being acquitted, but that is not the point. What matters is the reality-bending rationality of race that makes it logical to blame the dead for their own killing. Ahmaud Arbery visited a home under construction and failed to follow the simple commands of the armed white vigilantes who stalked him as he jogged. Trayvon Martin weaponized a sidewalk. Walter Scott owed child support when he was shot in the back several times, at a distance of nearly twenty feet from a uniformed officer, while running away.

The opposing characters in this script are not individuals, they're demographics. And unlike many narratives, in this one the main characters don't have comparable power. This story reached its maturity during the slave trade, in the eighteenth and nineteenth centuries. People made sense of their quickly changing world by assembling what are now common beliefs about human difference. Theories joined with economic interests to become toxic ideology, organizing societies around the notion of *human being* as a hegemonic identifier, for whites only.

The science of human taxonomies gave foundational relevance to the ideology of race, and two prominent theorists are important in that endeavor. In the early eighteenth century, Swedish naturalist Carl Linnaeus assembled the first taxonomy of five human types, based primarily on their geography and physical qualities. Linnaeus singularizes one type he names *Europeanus*, who has, among other traits, blue eyes and an "inventive mind." What's more, *Europeanus* is not like the others, who are governed by caprice, customs, or opinions. *Europeanus* is "governed by laws."[4]

In the late eighteenth century, German naturalist Johann Friedrich Blumenbach followed Linnaeus with a taxonomy of his own. Blumenbach largely accepts Linnaeus's findings and introduces a new advancement: aesthetics. The introduction of the philosophy of beauty into the science of taxonomy formalizes a hierarchy based on appearance. Blumenbach connects the origin of Europeanus to the Caucasus region, because of the supposed beauty of its white inhabitants. They are the most beautiful and, as such, the template by which to measure human beauty. As Nell Irvin Painter details in *The History of White People*, with Blumenbach the European becomes beautiful, white, Caucasian.[5] This addition of the language of beauty scientifically linked to white as a racial trait helped enable European racial science to give intellectual support to the burgeoning ideology of white supremacy. But for race to become fully actualized as an argument for the ascendancy of white people in an ideology of human difference, it would need the Negro.

On Africa's west coast there are various ports where Europeans once loaded, ambushed, and kidnapped Africans into cargo ships headed for the Americas. The Africans had names, they came from families, and the families belonged to peoples like the Yoruba, Ewe, Mende, and Mandinka. They had traditions connected to places with cultures and histories, all of which formed an identity that was decimated by the slave trade. When they encountered Europeans, they entered a different reality. Their identity was placed on their skin, and race became how they were recognized. The Ewe, Mende, and Mandinka became Negro. Some scholars describe the slaving ports as wombs out of which the slave was born. Poet Aimé Césaire described them as sources for the creation of walking compost, a product that would be essential to the production of sugar cane, tobacco,

4. Linneaus, *Systema Naturae*, 29.
5. Painter, *History of White People*.

and the very lucrative cotton. In her book, *Lose Your Mother: A Journey along the Atlantic Slave Route*, Saidiya Hartman tells us that the British called them factories. It was at the ports, with their infamous "door of no return," that something new was let loose into the world.[6]

Ideology accompanied Black bodies as they left the African continent, in order to legitimize seeing them as livestock. By 1790, European colonists in the United States were using *white* as a legal identifier for themselves, aided in that description by the logic of the sciences and the practice of trading in African flesh. Whites became fully human, synonymous with *free citizens* in a new land for whites only, as distinguished from the partly human, noncitizen, Black slave. The logic of race was important: it was a financially incentivized anthropology to formally authenticate the ascendant status of white people and the natural, moral, even Christian practice of white domination of everything related to heaven and earth.

Slavery endured for nearly 250 years in the US, during which time the logic of race contrived a being who has never existed. It was a type of conjuring, which is to say, invoking the presence of a being by magic or ritual. The Negro was a conjured caricature of Black people that served to stabilize the slave industry as a moral good.

Sterling Brown's 1933 essay "The Negro Character as Seen by White Authors" offers a taxonomy, but not the pseudoscientific European sort that classified human life hierarchically.[7] Instead, Brown's taxonomy takes account of several ways that white people stabilize a contrived racial hierarchy by reading people of African ancestry through the lenses of white supremacy.

The "contented slave" represents white ideals of the Negro under the complete authority of white people. Accordingly, Black people were satisfied, as it suited their inferior constitution. The "wretched freeman" is the Negro outside of his God-ordained state of slavery. This was the condition of the Negro upon escape to the North, longing for the South and for slavery. "Dixie," the theme song of the Confederacy, is the voice of the wretched freeman.

The "comic Negro" depicts the supposed distance between Black and white people when it comes to their capacities for civilized, intellectual, and moral living. The comic Negro is trying to be civilized, and

---

6. Hartman, *Lose Your Mother.* Césaire is referenced in Hartman.

7. Brown, "Negro Character."

it's funny; his use of white people's big words and fancy clothes is all just comical. The "brute Negro" is the regressed condition of Black people after slavery. Once Black people are no longer under the parentage of the benevolent white sovereign ones, they regress to savagery.

The "tragic mulatto" is regarded with pity due to her likeness to white people and is concurrently torn apart by warring biological dissimilarities. Race mixing crosses a tragic boundary, creating a pitiful creature, simultaneously beastly and ill at ease with subhumanity. Thus, the mulatto is vindictive and rebellious. This is a type without a race, worshiping the whites yet despised by them, despising and despised by Negroes who are perplexed by the mulatto's struggle to unite intellect with Black sensuousness. There are other tropes not mentioned by Brown, tropes that specifically target Black women: the mammy, the jezebel, the sapphire.

The racial script required inventing these movable character markups of the Negro in order to manufacture the absence of key humanizing features that white supremacy wants to be found in whites only. This is anti-Black fiction. By manufacturing Negro subhumanity, Black caricatures help to identify the humanity of whites—to defend, in an ongoing way, the protagonist in the story of race. The constantly evolving lapses highlighted within the Negro help to protect the imagined ascendancy of whites.

Yet hidden within all of this is another conjuring: the continued invocation of a human template that is simultaneously white and non-existent. In preserving this template, white supremacy disfigures all embodied human life. Conjuring the Negro is what maintained violent, overt, anti-Black laws as part of the normal political and legal machinery of the US for another century after the end of chattel slavery. Today this figure haunts us as the afterlife of slavery and Jim Crow in an overtly racist nation. To resist white supremacy is to encounter centuries of embedded ideology masquerading as reality. It is difficult, and frightening, to change someone's reality. To reveal this reality as the fiction it is requires the right tools—and courage.

Historian George Frederickson tells us that the logic of race finally developed into three overtly racist regimes in the twentieth century: the Jim Crow South, Nazi Germany, and apartheid South Africa.[8] Today, those regimes are in the past. But the twisted reality that gave them life is not. The longing for an ideal community populated with the ideal human

8. Frederickson, *Racism*.

is what maintains the systems and structures that historically have been manufactured for whites only. It is this longing that makes possible the indifference toward the lives of Black and brown people that is now being captured on cell phone cameras, sparking protests.

If we are to make any headway toward a reality more representative of actual human life, we need to put down the script and ask how this history of white supremacy has shaped our understanding of ourselves as raced beings. We need to encourage others to do the same. And we need to work to dismantle hegemonic systems and structures that are assembled for whites only. There is no making America great again. There is only moving forward, out of the alternate reality that race has made.

Discussion Questions

1. What is white supremacy and how does it relate to anthropology (being human)?

2. What is the script that we have been given and how does this script relate to the ongoing killings of unarmed Black people?

3. What does it mean to resist white supremacy and how does one go about it?

Works Cited

Baldwin, James. "The Negro in American Culture." A conversation with James Baldwin, Langston Hughes, Lorraine Hansberry, and Emile Capouya. https://www.youtube.com/watch?v=jNpitdJSXWY.

Brown, Sterling. "Negro Character as Seen by White Authors." *The Journal of Negro Education* 2, no. 2 (April 1933) 179–203.

Frederickson, George M. *Racism: A Short History*. First Princeton Classics ed. Princeton: Princeton University Press, 2015

Hartman, Saidiya. *Lose Your Mother: A Journey along the Atlantic Slave Route*. New York: Farrar, Straus & Giroux, 2007.

Linnaeus, Carl Von. *Systema Naturae per Regna Tria Nature, Secundum Classes, Ordine, Genera, Species. Cum Characteribus. Differentiis, Synonymis. Locis.* 1735.

Painter, Nell Irvin. *The History of White People*. New York: W. W. Norton, 2011.

Thurman, Howard. *Jesus and the Disinherited*. Boston: Beacon, 1996.

Williams, Reggie. "White Supremacy is a Script We're Given at Birth." *The Christian Century*, September 15, 2020. https://www.christiancentury.org/article/critical-essay/white-supremacy-script-we-re-given-birth.

Communicating Culture

The Beauty in Black Speech

Y. Joy Harris-Smith

"Death and life *are* in the power of the tongue:"

—PROV 18:21 KJV

Introduction

IT IS WITHOUT QUESTION that words, spoken aloud, have power. From a child, I can remember this Scripture being used in Sunday school, sermons, and other religious settings. It was a caution to be mindful of the words I speak. Additionally, it was an invitation to claim and create by speaking in the same way God spoke to create the world according to the Judeo-Christian tradition. Since I am created in the image of God, I, too, have the capacity to create by speaking a word. This sentiment can be found in music. Gospel singer/songwriter Donald Lawrence in 2004 penned the popular song "I Speak Life," featuring Donnie McClurkin. The refrain "I speak life" throughout the song speaks to calling forth that which is not into being. It is creating the life, the world, your situation as you would have it to be even in the face of adversity.

The creation story, according to the Christian tradition, found in Genesis shows God speaking the world into existence. God does something extra special with humanity. God engages in a conversation with

God's self and creates humankind (Gen 1:26–27). Humanity is unique in that while all of creation communicates in some form—speech is particularly human. Thus, humanity, created in the image of God, also possesses the power to create through the spoken word. This creative power through speech satisfies a desire to commune with God, other human beings, and all of creation.

All human beings have a need to understand and be understood. Communication, though, is not limited to words only. It includes unintelligible words, sounds, and the actions or positions we take with our bodies. Since Black people are human beings created in the image of God, we too have the capacity to utilize our words, our speech to create—to understand and be understood—and we do. The words that come out of our mouths have the capacity to create beautiful wonders similarly as God created the universe through speech. Many would agree that while this planet has its challenges, there are many wonders to behold—Black beauty spoken into existence.

History is replete with exemplars of beautiful Black speech if we would only attune our ears to its utterances. From the motherland, the continent of Africa, to various places around the globe, Black people speak, sing, recite poetry, and utter thoughts on the world from their point of view. Here I will offer some examples in the form of poetry, philosophy, and song to begin and ground this conversation. First is the poem *I Give You Thanks My God*, as it is rendered in English translated from French, by Bernard Dadie. This is a powerful example of beautiful Black speech.

Each stanza in this poem begins with the line, "*I give you thanks my God for having created me black.*" This line expresses praise and thankfulness for an identity that others in the world find challenging. Dadie affirms his identity as a Black man, as a Black person in creation, and is not interested in changing his position. He is content having been made Black and the Christlike role he must play in the universe. It is unequivocally Black pride. The significance of this poem is that Dadie writes this at a very different time in history then this present moment and there are many who would agree with his sentiments today. Dadie affirms himself and the Black diaspora by penning such a bold piece. Black speech, beautiful Black speech is not just for the art or to hear oneself speak. It has a purpose, an objective. I, too, give you thanks, my God, for having created me . . . *Black*.

Consider the African philosophical concept of Ubuntu or "I am because we are."[1] This is in direct contrast to the belief "I think, therefore I am," popularized by René Descartes. The Ubuntu philosophy recognizes that one's identity is based on the relationships one has with others—community is paramount. It does not negate the challenges of individual thoughts, ideas, or even the arguments that people may have with one another. Yet, the goal is to move past individual and interpersonal challenges to focus on the community. Thus, when the community prospers, we all prosper.

This is an example of beautiful Black speech because it reinforces the notion of community. It reminds us of our interdependence and need for one another. In many families throughout the Black diaspora aspects of this philosophy are practiced even if some are not aware of the term. The Ubuntu philosophy is something that operates in beautiful Black speech. When Black people speak it is not just for the individual but also for the benefit of the community—to uplift, encourage, provide direction, and/or to remember.

For over a century African Americans have been singing the poem set to music, *Lift Every Voice and Sing,* by James Weldon Johnson and his brother J. Rosamund Johnson.[2] I remember first hearing this song in elementary school. Mrs. Jackson was our technology/computer teacher. She was a short Black woman, four feet, eleven inches, who was *not* to be played with. We learned this entire song for our fifth-grade graduation. We sang this song at assemblies, but for our graduation, she wanted us to hear these words anew. If for some reason our words were not clear she made us sing the song again and again. I remember her getting upset with us because she wanted us to understand the importance of the words—the beautiful Black speech that we were singing—and what it meant for our lives both now and in the future.

Sons and daughters of the Black diaspora have always had to navigate the spaces between a "dark past" and a "hope that the present" offers us here in these United States of America. This song, like many others, are proverbs of life put to music. These proverbs are meant to remind, instruct, and encourage us to stand in the power we hold as divinely created beings.

1. "I Am Because We Are."

2. For the lyrics to this anthem see https://sos.sdes.ucf.edu/wp-content/uploads/sites/62/2019/01/Lift20Every20Voice20and20Sing1.pdf.

Mrs. Jackson was teaching us beautiful Black speech that would resonate through the course of our lives every time we heard the words or sang the song. This song is a melodic recapitulation of our history as Black people in America and how our people have been sustained in the United States for so long despite the nation's hostility toward us.

The Relationship between Language, Communication, and Culture

To deepen our discussion of the beauty of Black speech, let us consider the etymology of the word communication. It derives from the Latin '*communis*' (noun) and '*communicare*' (verb). The former having to do with that which is common and the latter meaning to make common or known. Perhaps then words like community, communion, and commune, to name a few, are connected to one another. Communication involves relationship—even relationship building. It is making known one's thoughts so that someone else may receive and understand them. It is also comprehending the thoughts and feelings, verbalized or nonverbalized, by another. To be more succinct, communication involves the sending and receiving of messages—verbal and nonverbal.

Therefore, our speech, our language has the capacity to be beautiful and Black speech *is beautiful*. Language allows us to connect with one another. "Every culture attempts to create a universe of discourse for its members, a way in which people can interpret their experiences and convey it to one another."[3] Whether religiously or culturally speaking, there is an agreement that words spoken out into the atmosphere have power to create a reality.

When we consider the ways in which people throughout the African diaspora were/are treated by other groups—it is no wonder then that their language was one of the first things attacked. The attempt to strip a people of their language—their ability to communicate with one another, to understand, and be understood is to attempt to render them as nonpersons—inhuman. Yet the creative life force within these dear ancestors would not and could not be silenced. Language and culture are dynamic human phenomena. They change and adapt as needed by those of the group. So new ways of communicating were created, and

---

3. Barlund, "Toward a meaning-centered philosophy of communication."

new words came into being in order to combat the physical realities of their existence.

Culture is transmitted through communication, and one does not communicate in a vacuum. The culture in which one resides teaches the acceptable ways to engage in communication with others. We communicate in conversation, through poems, the telling of stories and songs. We communicate when we bow our heads in prayer, in call and response, in preaching, in shouting, and in sacred readings. This is not an exhaustive list but rather a few examples of the beautiful speech we engage in which reverberates throughout time, culture, and the legacy of the African diaspora.

Gospel recording artist Richard Smallwood released a song in the late 1990s called "Total Praise." It reflected a time in his life where he was a caregiver to multiple persons in his family and life was challenging. Smallwood took to the piano to work through his emotions. He begins by citing/paraphrasing Psalm 121:1–2 (KJV): "I will lift up mine eyes unto the hills, from whence cometh my help. My help cometh from the LORD, which made heaven and earth." The song reflects Smallwood's understanding of a higher source or power. It conveys Smallwood's reliance on this power, "You are the source of my strength . . . of my life." It is both a declaration and a prayer that allows for those who sing it to simultaneously engage in agency and surrender.

This song was an answer to questions Smallwood had at a challenging moment in his life, but many people can identify with the words in this song—and not just those in the Black Christian community. This song has gone beyond the walls of the church having been sung by R & B artists and sung in languages such as Italian, Russian, Japanese, Hebrew, and French. Hence, this example points to an earlier observation, which is that beautiful Black speech is not just about the orator or the rhetor but also about community. In this case, Smallwood's words have touched people throughout the world. Beautiful Black speech is communal and relatable. It is not speech solely for the edification of one's self but to and for all who encounter it.

Maya Angelou's "Phenomenal Woman" is another example of beautiful Black speech. This poem has become a sacred text for Black women. Angelou highlights the physical body, beauty, and spirit of women—and Black women in particular—because she refers to herself in this poem. As Dadie's poem was unequivocally Black pride—this poem celebrates pride for those attributes that make Angelou uniquely a woman. It is no accident the word "phenomenal" is used as the descriptor. The word phenomenal means remarkable, extraordinary. When something or someone is phenomenal, she or it is mind-blowing, intoxicating. She/it fills the senses—and we, Black women, are very much phenomenal.

Angelou explicitly notes aspects of Black women that have been exploited and viewed negatively by American society. She offers a contrast by making those characteristics positives. The shape of Black women's bodies, how we walk, talk, and do our hair. Black women have a significant presence as evident by the reaction of others to our presence. Angelou's celebration of the personality and totality of being a Black woman is all the more significant, for her words encourage and remind Black women of the beauty and power they possess.

On popular television, there are glimpses of beautiful Black speech. For example, actress Amirah Vann plays the character Ernestine on the WGN show *Underground*, which depicts the lives of slaves on a plantation. Ernestine is the mistress of the slave master/plantation owner. They have three children together. In episode 7, season 1, Ernestine tries to give her youngest child James a crash course in working in the cotton field.

The scene shows an anxious Ernestine, the slave mother and mistress, doing what any good mother does when attempting to prepare her offspring for a new experience. She offers wisdom in the form of a song, a spiritual to sing called "Move Moses." Here it isn't just the words that are significant. The rhythm and tempo are also essential as well. "Move, move, move Daniel, move. Go the other way say, go the other way." As Ernestine sings the song for James, she taps her foot to keep the rhythm. She tells James that singing this song will help him keep time so that he can make the weight requirement. This refers to the amount of cotton that James needs to pick so that he would not receive the lash. However, all of Ernestine's attempts, and even a promise from the slave master, his father, failed to spare James from the consequences of being in the cotton fields.

The scene portrayed in this episode mirrors the many accounts that come from the lived experiences of Black men, women, and children who sang spirituals like "Move Moses" to work and pass time in the cotton fields. Black speech, while beautiful, layered, and instructive, is also practical.

Black Speech That Creates and Shapes Reality

Speech is powerful because it creates and shapes reality. Often when referring to speech and rhetoric, the Greeks are considered the starting point but there are others. Many ancient cultures had rules that governed the kinds of speech and communication they were to engage in. For example, *nommo*, an African rhetorical concept, is used to explain the uniqueness of African American speech and rhetoric. *Nommo* comes from Dogon people's creation narrative.[4] The creator, Amma, is said to use *nommo* to organize the spiritual and material world and assist humanity in achieving harmony and balance. According to Dr. Maulana Karenga, the principle of *Maat* is another term referring to "rightness in the world.[5] *Maat* is said to be the ". . . ruling force between good and evil."[6] *Maat* provides order and direction in chaos. These principles demonstrate the kinds of speech that African diasporic peoples were, and are, to engage in—beautiful speech. Speech that uplifts and connects its people to the past, present, and future.

I am a beneficiary of the power and beauty of Black speech. I can remember riding in the car with my mother on our way to school and she would begin morning conversations like this, "When you go to college . . ." I think I was in third grade when she first said this to me. As I got older many of our conversations began with this phrase, "When you go to college . . ." It was like a refrain from a song. I knew it well. I can hear the intonation in her voice, even now, although she has been gone for twenty years. That phrase "When you go to college . . ." created an expectation, a hope in me and in her I suppose. I would be the only child she would witness graduate from college before her death.

My mother raised us, for the most part, on her own during the late 1980s through the 1990s. Society did not have high hopes for girls and boys of single parents—especially in the Black community. The statistics of the time were not positive. So, my mother spoke to us. She shaped us with her words. She told us we were intelligent and loved. I was told I was beautiful, and my brothers were told they were handsome. My mother created a world for us that was different to combat the messages of society at the time. The beauty of speech, and Black speech in particular, is that it confirms and affirms our identity and to whom we belong.

4. Karenga, "Nommo, Kawaida, and Communicative Practice," 8.

5. Karenga, "Nommo, Kawaida, and Communicative Practice," 11.

6. Alkebulan, "Spiritual Essence of African American Rhetoric," 25.

During the 1960s, singer/songwriter James Brown, the Godfather of Soul, sang "I'm Black and I'm Proud." The song speaks to the cultural and political challenges of the 1960s and the fight for equality by disenfranchised Black people. In the face of all the challenges, the devaluation of the contributions of Black people and the systems put in place to keep Black Americans from experiencing "life, liberty and the pursuit of happiness," James Brown led Black people in this communal affirmation.

In this song James Brown speaks directly to Black people and the larger society. This is one of the songs of the civil rights movement. It speaks to Black reliance and empowerment. The song attests to the Black experience of struggle for equality—in education, regarding the right to vote, and fair treatment by the United States government for example. James Brown used his music, his beautiful Black speech, to speak to Black people and the circumstances they were experiencing. Beautiful Black speech is contextually relevant. It speaks to the current moment.

Jesse Jackson made famous the poem "I am somebody." Jackson used this poem with his nonprofit, the Rainbow/PUSH Coalition. This organization, based in Chicago, pursues equality, civil rights and participates in social activism on behalf of those disenfranchised—which often were Black people and other people of color.

The reason for using this poem was to motivate Black students. One of Jesse Jackson's most notable recitations of this is on *Sesame Street* with children of various ethnicities. He leads them in a recitation of the poem. The refrain, "I am somebody . . ." stands in contrast to the negative stereotypes of Black children and children of color at the time, particularly in the public education system. Here again the identity of one's humanity is affirmed—regardless of ethnicity. However, this was especially necessary for Black students—and this motivation, this affirmation is still needed. Regardless of what station in life a child finds himself or herself—they are somebody—they are valuable and have a right to life and equality.

The poem was written originally written by Reverend William Holmes Borders, Sr. (1905–1993) during the 1950s. He was the pastor at Wheat Street Baptist Church in Atlanta, Georgia, and an advocate for civil rights and those who were socioeconomically challenged.

So Black speech and language varieties are beautiful because they are "modes of attending to Black life and Black suffering . . ."[7] It helps us identify and connect to those within the Black diaspora. For example,

7. Sharpe, *In the Wake*, 22.

many African American churches across the United States, regardless of denomination can feel a little like home for some visitors. Among many things that are recognizable from Black culture in the Black church are the speech, the energy, the cadence, and the call-and-response format. For example, across denominations it is possible to hear the phrase "God is good" come from the pulpit and the congregation will respond "All the time." Then the worship leader will say "And all the time . . ." and the people will respond with "God is good." The beauty of Black speech is that it reveals our hermeneutic of kinship, our connectedness to all living things—regardless of our religious affiliation.

The hermeneutic of kinship, as expressed by Dr. Melva Costen, is reflective of the cultural and religious beliefs about relationships throughout God's creation.[8] It is a belief that all of life is connected—the living and the dead. All of life is interrelated. We are both sacred and secular—holy, created by a higher power and members of this physical realm. There is no divide, no sacred/secular dichotomy. What is done in one area of life has bearing in another area. Memory and legacy are part of this hermeneutic of kinship. Perhaps a modern form that readers may be familiar with is how hashtags have been used via Twitter and on other social media platforms. For example, the hashtags #SayHerName or #SayHisName are used in order to keep in the minds and hearts of society those who have been murdered by police. This is also a chant during protests. A designated person will say, "Say his name" and the group will respond by saying, "George Floyd" or "Ahmaud Arbery." Or "Say her name" and the group will respond "Breonna Taylor" or "Sandra Bland." Saying the names of these people who were taken from this physical realm too soon invokes the righteous indignation that is needed to resist injustice and press for change. The call to "Say his name" or "Say her name" reminds us and those who hear that these people existed and that they still matter even if they are not physically with us now.

This is the beauty of Black speech that even in sorrow it attests to the humanity of Black people when the rest of society would easily forget. It calls for justice and action. American society has often tried to ignore this kind of speech. However, Black speech is compelling and demands a reckoning.

A few years ago, I had students in one of my speech classes say the Lord's prayer (Matt 6:9–13) at the same time. There were about seven to

8. Costen, *African American Christian Worship*.

nine students. While it was not exactly the United Nations in the classroom, there were enough similarities and differences for students to get the point. In just saying the first few lines, they could hear where they paused, placed emphasis, and took a breath. In some places it was the same and in other places it was different. While this might seem uneventful to most, the point I made to them was this: We are united as Christians because we all know the Lord's prayer and can recite it. We can even hear how we sound together when we say it in unison. However, we can also hear the differences—the differences are often a reflection of language, culture, and theology. The exercise reinforced our differences and some of our similarities as members of the body of Christ.

Language, culture, and communication are forever in a relationship. Relationships are dynamic—just like the relationship between language, culture, and communication. The impacts or effects experienced can be positive, challenging, and all of the above. Sometimes the effects are subtle and unnoticeable, while other times they can be seen and felt deeply.

Embedded in language are rules of the culture from which it emerges. It governs the communicative acts that we engage in. To whom do you speak? How do you speak to them? What titles, if any, do you use? What tone of voice should you use? What words can one use? We don't think often about these things, yet the rules and regulations of speech are still transmitted generation to generation. However, shifts can happen, and often do. We recognize this most notably in words and phrases that are used in different generations. Think about it. What words do/did your parents use? What words do (did) you use (as a teenager)? What words are phrases do you hear from members of Generation Z? Those words and phrases are examples of the ways in which language, culture, and communication are forever in a relationship. They impact one another, reinforcing certain behavioral practices and creates new ways for us to engage one another.

There is a need then to proclaim the beauty in Black speech because even the words that come out of our mouths are "imperiled and devalued by a racial calculus and a political arithmetic that were entrenched centuries ago."[9] Everything about Black people and Black life is attacked—even the words that come out of our mouths.

Stolen Africans were stripped of their languages when brought to the shores of the Americas. They were tasked by threat of the lash to take

---

9. Hartman, *Lose Your Mother*, 6.

a new name, learn a new language and with it a different worldview, and yet the hypocrisy was also that laws were established so that they *could not* learn to read and write this new language. These barriers did not stop these precious ancestors from learning anyway. And while time may have eroded the memory, the remnants of words and phrases from the motherland that remained were passed and integrated into the vocabulary. Yet, this ". . . racial calculus and political arithmetic . . ." can be seen in the fight for equality for education—from *Brown v. Board of Education* into this current day with failing schools that serve mostly Black and brown children.

Therefore, celebration of the beauty of Black speech is necessary. It is necessary because it contains our history and our story. We must remember so that we do not lose our history and our story. This is rightfully ours.

Black Death and Black Speech

The assault on Black life seems unending. As the world entered the 2020 coronavirus pandemic and places began to shut down, the headlines in the media read in an all too familiar fashion of Black lives taken way too soon by those who felt they wielded such power to do so.

In response to the deaths of Ahmaud Arbery, George Floyd, Breonna Taylor, and countless others, the refrain "Black Lives Matter" reverberated again, but this time the world—on pause—was watching and listening. The treatment of people of African descent throughout the world has come up for discussion as institutions, houses of worship, government, and other facets of society consider the part they play in the continued subjugation of Black and brown people.

Consider why the phrase, "Black Lives Matter" provokes such a reaction. Why are people angered? Why is there such a strong visceral response? Those who hear "Black Lives Matter" and get angry are often those who are white or those who have consciously, or subconsciously, subscribed to the notion that Black people are ontologically inferior to whites and other human beings. This is beyond a mild case of ethnocentrism or perhaps bias or unconscious bias. The often visceral reaction to the phrase "Black Lives Matter" should be enough for folks to stop and check themselves. When people respond with "X Lives Matter" or some other group's lives matter it attempts to deny, erase, and discount the history of mistreatment of Black people in America—and the ways Black people *continue to be mistreated*. It is an implicit statement that Black people cannot be the center—even when they are mistreated—Black people and Black life cannot be the lens through which humanity looks at herself.

To say "BLACK LIVES MATTER" is to speak a cosmological and ontological truth to power—the power we can see and the power we cannot see. It disrupts the foundation that was laid centuries ago. The phrase, Black Lives Matter, pulls back the curtain on the dissonance that many experience despite their best efforts to proclaim that they are not racist or "not like that" or they have "a Black friend" or are "married to a Black person" or "date Black people." The unnerving feeling that rises for certain people, and those who align themselves with white supremacist thinking, is because for a moment they feel decentered—the same de-centered feeling that Black and other peoples of color feel on a regular basis. This is why saying "Black Lives Matter" is powerful and important.

The phrase "Black Lives Matter" pays homage to the fact that Black people are intentionally part of the created universe. It is by design that we, Black people, exist. We are not leftovers, a forgotten and disregarded group. Nor is our function on this earth to be slaves or to struggle for our entire existence. Saying Black life does matter is a push back; it is resistance to the oppressive belief of the opposite. For those co-conspirators, and or allies, who also stand and utter "Black Lives Matter" they realize the lies that exist about Black people and the unjust treatment we have received as a group. To say Black Lives Matter while everything shouts back death is exercising one's given right to vote—vocally—in the opposite direction.

The phrase Black Lives Matter is a beautiful phrase, speech par excellence. Black Lives Matter is a proclamation, a cry, a demand for recognition—once again from a people who have consistently been denigrated both in the United States and abroad. The phrase empowers us and our allies (or co-conspirators). It echoes the Rev. Dr. Martin Luther King, Jr.'s statement that "Injustice anywhere is a threat to justice everywhere. We are caught in an inescapable network of mutuality, tied in a single garment of destiny. Whatever affects one directly, affects all indirectly."[10]

Black Lives Matter is moral speech and calls on humanity, in all expressions, to give an account. It is a quest for what is good, divine, and right in the world. Like scripture, Black speech, is a sharp two-edged

---

10. King, "Letter from a Birmingham Jail."

sword "piercing even to the dividing asunder of soul and spirit, and of the joints and marrow, and is a discerner of the thoughts and intents of the heart" (Heb 4:12 KJV).

Black speech is beautiful because it is one of the forces that has kept Black people alive despite the efforts of some to rid us from the face of the earth. When we are hard pressed on every side, the beauty of Black speech is that it reminds us of who we are. It reminds us of where we come from and to whom we belong. It reminds us of our humanity, our creative potential, and our resilience. The beauty of Black speech is that it can repurpose the master's tools.[11] The tools that were meant to destroy now have the power to heal. The tools that were meant to divide can now be used to unite.

When they thought they had taken our language, we devised new words and phrases to communicate our thoughts. When they thought they had taken our cultural memory, we managed to preserve some and pass it on. When they thought they had taken our dignity and self-respect, we created words of affirmation, engaged the readings of sacred texts, and sang songs to restore it.

We need to reclaim again and again the beauty of Black speech and Black language because *Black lives do matter*. They always have and they always will. This reclamation is not just for us today but for future generations. Generations unborn need us to preserve what has kept our people for centuries—long before we ever touched American soil. We need to use the tools we have at our disposal—like social media, and other platforms and share our similarities in the Black diaspora (and our differences) because we need both. This is what contributes to the beautiful cacophony of sounds and the tapestry of African diasporic culture. Language, the words we speak, are like seeds. We sow them, and consciously or unconsciously, we grow them.

> "Beautiful, also, are the souls [and words spoken] by my people."[12]

---

11. Lorde, "Master's Tools Will Never Dismantle the Master's House."
12. Hughes, *Collected Poems of Langston Hughes 1902–1967*.

Discussion Questions

1. Where do you hear (or see) echoes of black language/black speech in society?

2. What do you think black people are famous for in relation to black language/black speech?

3. How have you changed in your own speech over the course of this past year?

4. What words or phrases do you use that are reflective of Black language/culture?

5. What is your starting point (theological or otherwise) for understanding the purpose and power of the spoken word?

Bibliography

Alkebulan, Adisa. *"The Spiritual Essence of African American Rhetoric."* In Understanding African American Rhetoric: Classical Origins to Contemporary Innovations, 23–39. New York: Routledge, 2003.

Angelou, Maya. "Phenomenal Woman by Maya Angelou." Poetry Foundation. Accessed July 10, 2021. https://www.poetryfoundation.org/poems/48985/phenomenal-woman.

Barlund, D. "Toward a meaning-centered philosophy of communication." *Journal of Communication*, 12, no. 4 (1962) 197–211.

Conflict Of Interest. Accessed July 10, 2021. https://www.issues4life.org/blast/2012009.html.

Costen, Melva Wilson. *African American Christian Worship*. Rev. ed. Nashville: Abingdon, 2007.

Gorman, Amanda. "The Hill We Climb" (Presidential Inauguration of Joseph Biden/Washington, DC, January 20, 2021). https://www.cnbc.com/2021/01/20/amanda-gormans-inaugural-poem-the-hill-we-climb-full-text.html.

Hartman, Saidiya. *Lose Your Mother: A Journey Along the Atlantic Slave Route*. New York: Farrar, Straus, and Giroux, 2007.

Hughes, Langston. *The Collected Poems of Langston Hughes 1902–1967*. New York: Knopf, 1994.

"'I Am Because We Are': The African Philosophy of Ubuntu." To The Best Of Our Knowledge. September 30, 2020. Accessed July 10, 2021. https://www.ttbook.org/interview/i-am-because-we-are-african-philosophy-ubuntu.

"I Give You Thanks My God—Bernard Dadie." African Soulja. July 30, 2013. Accessed July 10, 2021. https://afrilingual.wordpress.com/2011/01/25/65/.

Jaffe, Clella. *Public Speaking: Concepts and Skills for a Diverse Society*. Boston: Cengage Learning, 2016.

"James Brown—Say It Loud: I'm Black and I'm Proud." Genius. Accessed July 10, 2021. https://genius.com/James-brown-say-it-loud-im-black-and-im-proud-lyrics.

Karenga, Maulana. "Nommo, Kawaida, and Communicative Practice: Bringing Good into the World." In *Understanding African American Rhetoric: Classical Origins to Contemporary Innovations*, 3–22. New York: Routledge, 2003.

King, Martin Luther. 1968. *"Letter from a Birmingham Jail."* https://www.africa.upenn. edu/Articles_Gen/Letter_Birmingham.html.

"Lift Every Voice and Sing." *PBS*. Accessed July 10, 2021. https://www.pbs.org/black-culture/explore/black-authors-spoken-word-poetry/lift-every-voice-and-sing/.

Lorde, Audre. "The Master's Tools Will Never Dismantle the Master's House." *History Is a Weapon*. https://www.historyisaweapon.com/defcon1/lordedismantle.html.

Marovich, Bob. "Genesis of a Gospel Song: 'Total Praise' by Richard Smallwood." *The Journal of Gospel Music*. October 14, 2015. Accessed July 10, 2021. http:// journalofgospelmusic.com/gospel/genesis-of-a-gospel-song-total-praise-by-richard-smallwood/.

Sharpe, Christina. *In the Wake: On Blackness and Being*. Durham, NC: Duke University Press, 2016.

Samovar, L., R. Porter, and D. Barlund. "Communication in a Global Village." In *Intercultural Communication: A Reader*, 5–14. Belmont, CA: Wadsworth, 1988.

"I Am Black and Beautiful"

A Biblical Haymanot (Theology) of Blackness

Vince Bantu

Introduction

WHAT DO THE CHRISTIAN tradition and Black identity have in common? Many non-Christians in Black communities around the world understandably question the role of Black people in the Christian faith, given the implications of the religion's Western constituency in acts of oppression. Recently, a pastor of a prominent white evangelical denomination decried his denomination's "foolish" repentance of the "'sin' of whiteness." While the US government has placed "Negros in residences that they could not otherwise afford" and granted "them unmerited entry into classrooms and boardrooms," the response has been, "Giveusmo!" Despite the alleged privileges of African Americans, the letter proclaimed, "Yet, they remain savages," and that improving denominational life is "beyond the Negroes' intellectual capacities."[1] The racist response from this white pastor was in reaction to a Black pastor who, among many, has challenged the Southern Baptist Convention's claim that the belief in systemic racism is incompatible with the Christian faith. Such statements and beliefs from prominent white Christian institutions continue to engender questions about the role and value of Black people in the Christian church. Unlike much of Western Christendom, the Word

1. Blair, "Dwight McKissic receives letter urging SBC to bid black members 'goodbye and good riddance.'"

of God intentionally affirms the role of Black people in God's household and the value of unique Black expressions of faith.

The Black People of the Bible

The eighth chapter of Acts presents us with the NT's only account of a sub-Saharan, Black Christian. Luke's account tells us that the apostle Philip was led by an angel to the Gaza Road, where "he met a Black eunuch, an important official in charge of all the treasury of the *Kandake* (which means 'Queen of the Black People')" (Acts 8:27).[2] The word *aithiopios* literally means "burnt-faced one," in other words, "Black person." This word was used to refer to a variety of ethnic communities that were from regions south of Egypt, including Kush/Nubia, Axum (modern Ethiopia), Southern Arabia, and the Indian subcontinent. Therefore, when Luke said that this eunuch was "Ethiopian," Luke was not indicating that this man was from ancient Axum (modern Ethiopia) but, rather, that this man was Black. Translating *aithiopios* as "Black" more accurately reflects the broad racial category that this term reflects, rather than the confusing English word "Ethiopian," which refers to a modern nation-state that Luke did not have in mind. In addition, the mention of the *Kandake*—the Meroitic Kushite title for the queen—further specifies that this Black man was from ancient Kush, later known as Nubia (modern Sudan). In the Masoretic Hebrew Scriptures, the Hebrew word *kush* is used to refer to the kingdom of this eunuch as it existed in pre-Christian times. However, in the Septuagint version of the OT, *kush* is translated as *aithiopios* (Gen 2:13; Esth 1:1; Ps 68:31). This use of *aithiopios* for *kush* demonstrates the regularity with which Nubians were called "Ethiopians" by Greek-speakers within the Roman Empire.

Indeed, the fact that Kushites, and no other ethnic group in the OT, came to be called "Black people" (*aithiopios*) in the Septuagint demonstrates the degree to which *Kushites* was synonymous with *Blackness* in the OT and NT. And this is not only the case in the OT. Black skin and sub-Saharan features are consistently associated with Kushites in ancient Near Eastern and Hellenistic material culture.[3] Kushites, therefore, rep-

---

2. Unless otherwise noted, all biblical citations are from the New International Version (NIV). In this case, I have chosen to translate *aithiopios* as "Black" rather than "Ethiopian" for reasons that are explained below.

3. Redford, *From Slave to Pharaoh*, 6.

resented how the ancient world saw Blackness. To study how the ancient world saw Blackness is to study Kush. In ancient Near Eastern and Hellenistic material evidence, Blacks/Kushites were overwhelmingly depicted as slaves in chains who were brought as spoils of war. Hellenistic writers saw the Greek, and later Roman, people as biologically superior and destined to rule all other people. This kind of biological determinism also took the form of constructing "whiteness" as a marker of superiority and "Blackness" as a sign of depravity. When the name "Kush" was mentioned in ancient texts, images of Black skin, African phenotype, and the social meaning added to Blackness immediately came to mind. An ancient writer did not need to take the extra step of mentioning Black skin every time the name Kush appeared; the two were already intertwined in the ancient collective consciousness. Modern names like "Chinese," "Samoan," or "Jamaican" similarly connote racial characteristics accompanied by modern racialized tropes beyond the ethnic identities these names refer to. This would have been the case even more so in the ancient world when Kushites were one of the only sub-Saharan African people groups that Hellenistic and Near Eastern societies interacted with. The surrounding ancient world predominately depicted Black people as voiceless pieces of property, intellectually inferior, and spiritually depraved.

The depiction of Black people in the Bible is precisely the opposite. In fact, Black skin is the only skin color specifically mentioned in the Bible (Song 1:5). I do not think that it is coincidence that the only skin color specifically referred to in Scripture is also the skin color most exoticized and denigrated in the ancient world. Rather, God in providence makes a habit of taking that which the world sees as inferior to shame that which is touted as superior (1 Cor 1:27). In full awareness of how the ancient world denigrated Black skin, God chooses to specifically call out Black skin as a beautiful reflection of God's image. God's Word uplifts Black skin in the same way that the poor, ill, sojourners, orphans, and widows are especially given attention. This does not mean that God loves Black skin more than any other, any more than it means that he loves the poor more than the rich. There is a way in which God's kingdom economy enacts a reversal of worldly social capital. The bride of Solomon boldly declares:

> I am black and beautiful, daughters of Jerusalem, black like the tents of Kedar, like the tent curtains of Solomon. Do not stare at me because I am black, because I am blackened by the sun. My mother's sons were angry with me and made me take care

> of the vineyards; my own vineyards I had to neglect. Tell me,
> you whom I love, where you graze your flock and where you
> rest your sheep at midday. Why should I be like a veiled woman
> beside the flocks of your friends? (Song 1:5–7)[4]

In addition to disparaging sub-Saharan Africans, it was common in the ancient Near East to engage in practices of colorism. This too, the Bible expressly condemns. When she disparages Moses's Kushite (i.e., Black) wife, God punishes Miriam with an affliction of leprosy that turned her skin white—an intentional irony that should not be overlooked (Num 12:10).[5] Just as God stands with Moses' Black wife and punishes the anti-Black sentiment undergirding Miriam's rebellion, Blackness is boldly affirmed in the face of lighter-skinned Hebrew women disparaging the dark-skinned bride of Solomon: "I am black and beautiful." Black people (Kushites) in the Hebrew Scriptures were prophesied to be an integral component of the people of God. Kushites are chief among those who are said to have a share in Zion (Ps 87:4; Isa 11:11). Indeed, the Psalms declare that "Kush will submit herself to God" (Ps 68:31). The salvation of the Black eunuch in Acts was the fulfillment of OT prophecy that Black Africans will be among the first to share in the heavenly Zion through faith in Jesus Christ (Heb 12:22; 1 Pet 2:6; Rev 14:1). The OT prophets understood that not only Kushites, but further regions of Africa, would become part of the covenant people of God: "From beyond the rivers of Kush my worshippers, my scattered people, will bring me offerings" (Zeph 3:10). As the oldest Black, sub-Saharan African civilization in the world, Kush can rightly be considered the motherland of all Black people, on the continent and in the diaspora.

Among Black people across the world, there are followers of Jesus Christ that have become his co-heirs. God said through the prophet Zephaniah that "my worshippers, my scattered people" would bring offerings of worship to him. Blacks from around the world have been scattered. Yet, from beyond the rivers of Kush, we have been gathered unto him

---

4. This passage is taken from the NIV except for the above use of the word "Black" to translate the Hebrew *shachor* and the use of the word "and" instead of "yet" to translate the Hebrew preposition *waw*.

5. While the challenge was to Moses' leadership, verse one says that it was "because of his Cushite wife." Such challenges were not issued to Moses' Midianite wife, Zipporah, who was also not a Hebrew. Therefore, Miriam's problem with the wife of Numbers 12 was likely not simply because the wife was foreign, but that she was dark-skinned.

through faith in Jesus. And our unique forms of worship are the offerings we bring to him. The Black eunuch in Acts went to Jerusalem to worship. After being saved, he went on his way, continuing in worship. The story of the first Black (sub-Saharan African) Christian begins and ends with him worshipping. A central theme of African religion is the belief in a supreme God who is worshipped through vibrant, emotive praise.[6] It is not surprising, then, that the first Black Christian is presented as one with a heart for worship. Black worship is centered on verbal expression and embodied response. The Bible speaks of Black people in a reverent way. Isaiah 18 is perhaps the most direct biblical reflection on the values and characteristics of Kushite (Black) people. Kush is described as a "land of whirring wings," a reference to the bustling commercial trade along the Nile river.

Biblical Theology of Blackness

The land of Kush is "divided by rivers," indicating the fertile nature of African soil. The people of Kush are described by three principal characteristics:

1. Tall and smooth-skinned,

2. Feared far and wide,

3. Powerful.

These attributes are listed at the beginning of Isaiah's woe to Kush and again repeated at the end while reflecting on the Kushites who will worship the Lord at Zion: "At that time gifts will be brought to the Lord Almighty from a people tall and smooth-skinned, from a people feared far and wide, a conquering and powerful people, whose land is divided by rivers—the gifts will be brought to Mount Zion, the place of the Name of the Lord Almighty" (Isa 18:7).[7] Of the three attributes that are used in this passage—twice each—the Hebrew term *qaw-qaw* is the most unique. This rare phrase has often been translated as "strange speech" in Bible translations referring to the language of the Kushites. However, this phrase is more aptly translated as "powerful," in the sense of a reinforced

---

6. Mbiti, *African Religions and Philosophy*, 58.

7. I have rendered *'am* as "people" instead of "nation" and *mebusah* as "conquering" instead of "aggressive"; *qaw-qaw* will be discussed below. Otherwise, this citation is from the NIV.

measuring line.[8] (Cf. the use of *kaw* in 2 Kgs 21:13; 2 Chr 4:2; Job 38:5; Ps 19:4; Isa 28:10). Rather than seeing the speech of Black people as "strange," the prophet Isaiah defines Kushites as a powerful people. Indeed, during Isaiah's lifetime, the Kushites were experiencing unprecedented growth as they had conquered Egypt. During the Kushite rule of Egypt, King Taharqa also rescued the Hebrew King Hezekiah from the Assyrians (2 Kgs 19:9; Isa 37:9). Therefore, the Hebrew perspective of Kushites/Black people during the pre-exilic period would have been one of great reverence and admiration as this was the period in which Kush reached its apex.

Similarly, Isaiah makes note of the unique skin quality of Black people. The prophet's estimation of Black skin is rather different than his ancient Near Eastern counterparts, which often depict Black skin in an exoticizing manner. Rather than characterizing Black skin and features in dehumanizing ways common to antiquity, Isaiah describes sub-Saharan Africans as people who are "tall and smooth-skinned." The prophet is likely noting the relative lack of facial and body hair common to sub-Saharan Africans in contrast to Hebrews of the Near East. Isaiah also describes Kushites as a people "revered far and wide." The biblical view of Blackness is overwhelmingly and consistently positive and humanizing.[9] As in modern times, the ancient world associated Blackness with stereotypes of sexual and physical prowess, especially in athletic competitions.[10] Therefore, when a Kushite is mentioned as a running messenger to deliver news to King David of his son Absalom's death, an ancient reader would expect the Kushite runner to be very fast. Yet, this Kushite—who had a running head start—was outran by Ahimaaz (2 Sam 18:19–33)! This surprising result of the race to deliver news to David actually comes as a very humanizing representation of the Kushite: Black people are not biologically different from the rest of the human race and our value is not tied to physical and athletic abilities. The fact that Ahimaaz outran this Kushite humanizes him and all Kushites in the mind of ancient Near Eastern cultures that would otherwise cast sub-Saharan Africans as a physically, superhuman "Other."

The humanization of Blackness in Scripture is also evident in how Kushites are equally subject to divine judgment for sin (2 Chr 14:12–13;

---

8. See also Smith, *Isaiah 1–39*, 48.

9. Goldenberg, *Curse of Ham*, 40. Goldenberg even claims that Isaiah was essentially calling Kushites "good-looking."

10. Crowther, *Sport in Ancient Times*, 22.

Isa 20:4; Ezek 30:4–5; Zeph 2:12). Like all other gentiles that are obedient to the covenant stipulations of YHWH, Kushites are also equally afforded the opportunity for inclusion in the people of God (Isa 11:11; Ezek 38:5). This is because, as the Lord said to Israel: "Are not you Israelites the same to me as the Kushites?" (Amos 9:7). The Lord commands that Israel see Black people as he does—a people equally made in God's image and called to become part of God's household. Not only does the Bible depict Black people as an integral part of the covenant people of God, but Blackness is not diminished and is magnified alongside all other racial and ethnic identities as a part of God's image on humanity. Even after becoming a part of the Hebrew people through her marriage to Moses, the Kushite identity of this Black woman is still highlighted (Num 12:1). The Kushite messenger of the general Joab was likely a Hebrew citizen, as he was present in battle in the employ of the Hebrew army (2 Sam 18:21). Yet his ethnic identity is constantly referred to in the biblical account.

When the prophet Jeremiah prophesied the fall of Jerusalem to the Babylonians, the imperial house of the King of Judah was presented in the text as full of leaders rebellious to the law of YHWH. Of notable contrast was Ebed-Melek, the Kushite (Black person), who petitioned King Zedekiah to release Jeremiah from the cistern (Jer 38:7). The Lord spoke directly to Ebed-Melek through Jeremiah and declared that this Kushite Hebrew was a faithful servant of the Lord and under divine protection: "I will save you; you will not fall by the sword but will escape with your life, because you trust in me, declares the Lord" (Jer 39:18). While Judah was under rebellious leadership, this Black Hebrew was singled out at the hour of Jerusalem's fall as being a faithful servant of the Lord. And his Kushite identity—his Blackness—was highlighted several times in the account.

Moreover, in Jeremiah 13:23, the prophet Jeremiah asks the rhetorical question, "Can a Black person change his skin or a leopard its spots?"[11] In this verse and in countless others—including those surveyed above—individuals and whole communities are identified by their ethnic and racial association. Again, in the case of Jeremiah 13, Blackness is identified and highly valued, though a cursory reading would seem to indicate otherwise. In a cursory reading, Jeremiah likens the permanent Blackness of a Kushite to the inevitable sinfulness of the Hebrews. While it may appear that the Scriptures are making a racialized association of

---

11. The NIV here quotes from the Septuagint, which uses the term *aithiopios*, which, as we have seen, literally means "burned-faced one," i.e., "Black person." The Hebrew of the Masoretic Text behind the Septuagint says, "Kushite."

Blackness with depravity—common to ancient Near Eastern cultures—the opposite is actually true. This rhetorical question of Jeremiah is mirrored in the fifth-century BCE *Instructions of Onchscheshonqy*, in which it is declared: "There is no Negro who lays off his skin."[12] The rhetorical question in this ancient Egyptian text expects the answer: "No one." That is, Black skin is so valuable that no Kushite would desire to get rid of it. Therefore, like Jeremiah, this quotation demonstrates the degree to which certain contexts actually valued sub-Saharan African skin and saw it as a treasure. This interpretation of Jeremiah 13:23 is congruent with the other biblical examples in which Blackness is highlighted, such as the exclamation of the bride of Solomon: "I am black and beautiful."

The seventh-century prophet Zephaniah is introduced in a manner that indicates his identity as another Hebrew citizen of Kushite ancestry: "The word of the Lord that came to Zephaniah son of Kushi, the son of Gedaliah, the son of Amariah, the son of Hezekiah, during the reign of Josiah son of Amon king of Judah" (Zeph 1:1). Given the rarity of the name "Kushi," several OT scholars have argued that this name, in fact, refers to Zephaniah being of Kushite descent.[13] The genealogy is added to the prophet's introduction to indicate that he is indeed a Hebrew citizen. If it is true though that Zephaniah was a Hebrew of Kushite ancestry, then this would be yet another example of how Kushite members of God's household yet retain Blackness as a feature that is highlighted. Put another way: when Black people become part of the people of God, our Blackness does not fade or diminish; rather, it finds its truest expression. God created Blackness. Black people, along with the entire human race, became separated from God because of sin. Therefore, the only way to be fully Black is to be made right with God by grace through faith in Jesus. God's plan of salvation entailed restoring humanity by bringing every tribe into the covenant people of God. Like Ebed-Melech or Zephaniah, when this adoption occurs it does not necessitate the diminishment of one's racial or ethnic ancestry. Rather, since God intentionally created racial and ethnic difference, Black people, like all other racial groups, are not assimilated but are celebrated. The inclusion of Black children of God like Zephaniah is one of many biblical examples which fulfill God's prophecy that Kushites will "stretch their hands out to God" (Ps 68:31) and "will bring offerings to the Lord" (Zeph 3:10).

---

12. Sadler, *Can a Cushite Change His Skin?*, 90.

13. Sadler, *Can a Cushite Change His Skin?*, 67; see also Sweeney, *Zephaniah*, 49.

At the beginning of the world, the Scriptures describe a river whose tributaries flowed from the garden of Eden and touched much of the known world during the time of Moses. One of the principal regions described in the creation account was Kush, the land of Black people: "The name of the second river is the Gihon; it winds through the entire land of Kush" (Gen 2:13). The creation account describes Black people as an integral branch of the human family that was connected to the rest of the human race through the rivers of Eden.

In the same way, the book of Revelation depicts Black people as an integral part of the heavenly multitude that will be nourished by the River of Life flowing through the streets of heavenly Jerusalem (Rev 22:1). The people of God that will be healed by the river and tree of life in glory are defined in John's celestial vision as retaining their racial and ethnic characteristics: "After this I looked, and there before me was a great multitude that no one could count, from every ethnicity, tribe, people and language, standing before the throne and before the Lamb" (Rev 7:9).[14] Racial and ethnic differentiation is not a temporary, this-worldly reality; rather, it is an integral part of how God made us and will be with us for eternity. The eschatological vision not only indicates physical diversity, but cultural diversity as well. Languages and cultures are human inventions that are always changing and adapting. The human capacity to create languages and cultural forms of expression are perhaps the defining aspect of what it means to be the only creature made in the image of God. Just as God is the Creator, so too are we creators. When God created humanity, his mandate was to "fill the earth and govern (*kabash*) it" and to "cultivate (*radah*)" the elements of creation (Gen 1:28). God intended for diversity. God chooses to be glorified through diversity. God eternally exists in diversity, as exemplified in the Trinity.

The Father, Son, and Holy Spirit are distinct and yet unified persons of the triune God. There can be no unity without diversity; there is a need for differing entities to be distinct in order to be unified. Uniformity is not the same as unity. Indeed, uniformity works against God's mandate of diverse unity. For example, as the various peoples of the world began to spread and fill the earth, there was a movement towards the construction of a homogenous empire at Babel (Gen 11:1–9). It is noteworthy that the cultural and linguistic homogeneity of Babel was a condition of the

14. I have translated *ethnous* as "ethnicity," a concept more closely mirroring ancient concepts of social identity, rather than the uniquely modern concept of "nation." Otherwise, this quotation is taken from the NIV.

community in the midst of rebellion against God's command and their arrogant attempt to glory in their own empire. However, after being dispersed by the Lord, the people went out with different cultures in order to continue forming diverse cultural communities. Therefore, rebellion in Genesis 11 took the form of cultural homogeneity, while God's intervention resulted in the global migration and cultural diversity intended from the beginning. Therefore, cultural homogeneity confutes God's intentions for humanity, while cultural diversity fulfills God's creation intent. Cultural diversity was already well underway before Babel, as the account of the various people groups in Genesis 10 makes clear. The story of Babel further demonstrates God's desire for humanity to spread out and cultivate the earth, as Abraham—by contrast to Babel one chapter later—did by faith when he left his land for the home God would show him (Gen 12:1–9).

Furthermore, God demonstrated his heart for human cultural distinction when the reverse-Babel occurred in Acts 2. Rather than humanity attempting to "reach heaven" in cultural homogeneity, God descends to humanity, and the Holy Spirit fills the people of God as the gospel is proclaimed in the languages of "every ethnic group (*ethnous*) under heaven" (Acts 2:5). Similarly, the multiethnic, multilingual heavenly multitude described in Revelation as quoted above symbolically reflects the multiethnic community of Pentecost.

Conclusion

As mentioned above, the writer of Acts describes the first Christian mentioned in the Bible from sub-Saharan Africa as *aithiopios*, or Black. Being a Christian does not entail some sort of competition between racial and religious identity. Christianity is not a challenge to Black identity, nor a threat. Christian identity is not antithetical to Black identity. God is the one who created Blackness as a reflection of his image. Because of sin, humanity became separated from God, which entailed various distortions and perversions of what it means to be Black. By grace through faith in Jesus, humanity has the opportunity to be made fully human again by the Son of Humanity. This includes Black people who, through the regeneration of the Holy Spirit, are brought into the fullness of Black identity. There is no tension or conflict in being Christian and Black; rather, the only way to be truly Black is to be a Christian. The only way to come into the fullness of Black identity is to be brought back into fellowship with the God who created Blackness.

Some statements common to modern Western Christianity that are not resonant with the anthropology of Scripture include: "I don't see color." "When will we get past race?" "Racial justice is not a biblical concept." Such statements typically come from a naïve, underdeveloped theology of culture that denies the role of cultural values in Christian faith while simultaneously imposing culturally specific expressions of Christianity throughout the world. Rather than ignoring racial and ethnic distinctions, the Bible highlights them.

Discussion Questions:

1. In the world of the Bible, who was considered "Black"?

2. How does the Bible describe Kushites/"Ethiopians"?

3. What is the Bible's view of Blackness?

4. How do you think the Bible's view of Blackness compared/contrasted with other ancient Near Eastern or Greco-Roman perspectives of Blackness?

Works Cited

Blair, Leonardo. "Dwight McKissic Receives Letter Urging SBC to Bid Black Members 'Goodbye and Good Riddance.'" *The Christian Post*, February 3, 2021. https://www.christianpost.com/news/dwight-mckissic-receives-letter-disparaging-blacks-in-sbc.html.

Crowther, Nigel B. *Sport in Ancient Times.* Westport, CT: Greenwood, 2007.

Goldenberg, David M. *Curse of Ham: Race and Slavery in Early Judaism, Christianity, and Islam.* Princeton: Princeton University Press, 2003.

Mbiti, John S. *African Religions and Philosophy.* 2nd ed. Oxford: Heinemann, 1982.

Redford, Donald B. *From Slave to Pharaoh: The Black Experience of Ancient Egypt.* Baltimore: The Johns Hopkins University Press, 2004.

Sadler, Rodney S. *Can a Cushite Change His Skin? An Examination of Race, Ethnicity, and Othering in the Hebrew Bible.* New York: T & T Clark, 2005.

Smith, Gary V. *Isaiah 1–39.* The New American Commentary: An Exegetical and Theological Exposition of Holy Scripture 15A. Nashville: B&H, 2007.

Sweeney, Marvin A. *Zephaniah: A Commentary.* Hermeneia: A Critical and Historical Commentary on the Bible. Minneapolis: Fortress, 2003.

Migration, Adaptability, and the Utilization of Media

Black Pentecostalism Goes Global

MARCIA CLARKE

"CHRISTIANITY IS AND HAS always been a global religion . . . It is important never to think of Christianity *becoming* global."[1] Western Christian history has a tendency to depict what began as a multicultural first-century movement in Palestine as taking a Western trajectory, ultimately with the West as its epicenter. Christian proselytization then is perceived as the result of Western missionary efforts flowing into Asia and Africa. The contemporary shift in demographics has led to what is understood as the "emergence of the global south." This, however, is deemed a misconception, as stated in the opening sentence. Vince Bantu demonstrates that the earliest biblical manuscripts and ecclesial hierarchy were Egyptian, i.e., African, emerging no later than the second century. Additionally, what is now present-day Ethiopia was, in the fourth century, a predominantly Christian nation, which, along with Nubia, functioned under the ecclesial hierarchy of Egypt. While certain Black people and groups have presented Christianity as being the religion of "white oppression," Bantu seeks to "[deconstruct the] Western, white cultural captivity of the Christian tradition" and "[elevate] . . . non-Western expressions of Christianity.[2] Such a task requires a rejection of an incomplete history

1. Bantu, *Multitude of All Peoples*, 1.
2. Bantu, *Multitude of All Peoples*, 6.

of Christianity, thereby shifting focus to embrace the "image of Christ among every tongue, tribe, and nation."[3]

Similarly, then, this chapter discusses Pentecostalism as a global force as demonstrated in the rise and expansion of the Church of Pentecost (CoP). This Ghanaian (i.e., African) denomination, with its membership of over three million people traversing over one hundred and twenty countries, is an example of a global Black church whose origin is not Western. While remaining conservative, the denomination takes seriously the need to attend to migration and its concomitant challenges. Additionally, its response to the growing number of members who are educated and/or are primarily English speakers has been the implementation of Pentecost International Worship Centers (PIWCs), which I outline further below. The worldwide expansion of the CoP offers a contemporary challenge to the perception of the West as the epicenter of missionary undertakings and offers the Black church as a principal actor. It is an example of an African Pentecostal denomination that, in its local and national context, has grown and thrived.[4] What follows is a focused discussion of Pentecostalism through an exploration of the CoP. The CoP presents an example of a Black denomination, the proliferation of which has been achieved through migrant grassroot missionary efforts alongside the utilization of technology and media. Additionally, 40 percent of this classical Pentecostal denomination is under the age of thirty-five. How was this achieved? After a short introduction, the section continues with a historical overview, concluding with a description of CoP governance.

The history of global Pentecostalism has for the most part been written from a Western, predominantly North American, perspective. The impact and influence of William Seymour (1870–1922) and the Azusa Street Revival (1906) is central to the historical Pentecostal narrative; it cannot and should not be undermined. However, the movement does not have a singular origin but is rather polycentric, each center being "equally important to the formation and expansion of Pentecostalism."[5] Pentecostalism was not "primarily a [Christian] movement from the Western world to 'foreign lands' but more significantly movements within these

---

3. Bantu, *Multitude of All Peoples,* 6.

4. Anderson, *Spreading Fires,* 10.

5. Deininger, *Global Pentecostalism,* 49.

continents themselves."[6] This movement includes the continent of Africa and its Pentecostal influencers, such as William Wade Harris of Liberia and Simon Kimbangu of present-day Congo. The idea of Pentecostalism being a movement within continents is especially applicable to the present case study of the CoP.

Brief History of the Church of Pentecost

The CoP ascribes its founding to Peter Newman Anim (1890–1984). Anim, after reading a periodical published in Philadelphia called *The Sword of the Spirit*, contacted the magazine's editor, Pastor A. Clark. Clark was also founder of Faith Tabernacle ministry. Although not Pentecostal, Clark did emphasize holiness and healing, a teaching unfamiliar to Anim, who was Presbyterian.[7] Up until that time Anim's spiritual formation had been principally cerebral; however, Clark emphasized the discipline of "prevailing prayer." Anim, who had a history of stomach issues, was healed from chronic stomach pain and guinea worm disease after prayer.[8] In 1921, following his healing experience, Anim resigned from the Presbyterian church and relocated to another town, where he joined others who had also experienced healing. In time, others in need of healing also joined Anim's group. In 1922, convinced of Clark's teaching, Anim adopted Faith Tabernacle as the name for his organization.[9] Anim and Clark never met in person, communicating only by letter. In October 1923, Clark issued Anim a certificate of ordination, conveying rights to baptize and appoint workers. In time, Faith Tabernacle expanded to Nigeria, and Clark continued to ordain leaders by correspondence.[10]

Anim's movement, Faith Tabernacle, continued to spread throughout Ghana. In 1926 Anim began receiving copies of *The Apostolic Faith*, a magazine published in Portland, Oregon. It was through this publication that Anim was introduced to the Pentecostal practice of speaking in unknown tongues. Anim believed this was necessary for "deeper faith and greater spiritual power."[11] Although Clark emphasized the Spirit's work

6. Anderson, Tang, and Robeck, *Asian and Pentecostal,* 157.

7. Larbi, *Pentecostalism,* 1; Daswani, *Looking Back, Moving Forward,* 37.

8. Larbi, *Pentecostalism,* 100.

9. Larbi, *Pentecostalism,* 100.

10. Larbi, *Pentecostalism,* 100.

11. Larbi, *Pentecostalism,* 103.

in the inspiration of Scripture, he did not espouse the gifts of the Holy Spirit. In 1930, Anim separated from Faith Tabernacle and adopted the name The Apostolic Faith. In 1932 a member of Anim's group, Stephen Owiredu, experienced Spirit baptism after going to the bush to pray for one of his sick children. Anim and a few others went to visit Owiredu in order to experience Spirit baptism. During that visit, two of Owiredu's sons were baptized in the Spirit, along with two women that accompanied Anim. However, Anim did not receive the baptism at that time.[12] Anim returned to his base at Asamankese, where he organized a revival which ran from August 31 to September 12. While many of his followers experienced Spirit baptism, Anim did not and would not for some years.[13]

Anim subsequently met with representatives from the Apostolic Church UK, which in 1937, upon Anim's request sent James McKeown (1900–1989) to Ghana as a resident missionary. McKeown fully participated in the life of the Anim's Apostolic Faith movement, even in building the mission house where he lived.[14] Anim's movement had four foci, which consisted of a strong emphasis on prayer, the experience of glossolalia, and a robust evangelistic ethos. Additionally, there was a firm belief in divine healing, to the extent that there was to be no recourse to any form of preventative or curative medicine.[15] At one point, McKeown became extremely ill after contracting malaria, and Anim escorted him to the hospital despite it being a theological problem for Anim's followers. After eleven days, McKeown was discharged, but it was clear his theological perspective differed from that of Anim and his church.[16]

Anim and McKeown could not resolve their theological differences, and after two years a church split occurred. Those who followed Anim became the Christ Apostolic Church, and those who followed McKeown became the Apostolic Church, Gold Coast. McKeown continued as a missionary supported by the UK Apostolic Church for fifteen years.

In 1953 the UK church made two changes in its constitution that would affect the Apostolic Church, Gold Coast. First, the actions of prophets were restricted to their jurisdiction, hence they could not prophesy beyond it. Second, Africans could only be Apostles to other

12. Larbi, *Pentecostalism*, 105.
13. Larbi, *Pentecostalism*, 105.
14. Larbi, *Pentecostalism*, 109.
15. Larbi, *Pentecostalism*, 109.
16. Larbi, *Pentecostalism*, 109.

Africans and not to the wider church. McKeown was unable to accept the changes, and this led to him seceding and the church being renamed the Gold Coast Apostolic Church.[17] Upon its independence from Britain, the Gold Coast was renamed Ghana, and the Gold Coast Apostolic Church became the Ghana Apostolic Church. In 1962, the church adopted the name the Church of Pentecost.[18] It is said that while McKeown led the church, his role was mainly facilitatory, while others suggest his relationship was paternalistic in nature.[19]

It is clear that Anim's thought and action was influenced by literature from the West and the presence of McKeown. Additionally, the British colonized Ghana until 1957, when it became the first African nation to regain its independence. It is also probable that the *Apostolic Faith* magazine was that of Florence Crawford (1872–1936), an original member of William Seymour's Azusa Street Mission until she left and founded the Apostolic Faith Church in Portland, Oregon. While the impact of colonization on Anim cannot easily be quantified, it is evident that the reading, interpretation, and application of the literature was conducted in and developed from Anim's cultural context. The fact that the church continues to be a "grassroots" church supports this assertion.

Governance Change and Expansion

From its humble beginning, the CoP has become the largest Pentecostal church in Ghana. As of 2017, in addition to its local base of nearly 21,000 local assemblies, it has organized over 150 congregations across the US and Canada.[20] It is centrally governed with a strong clerical and bureaucratic structure to ensure "accountability, administrative and pastoral discipline."[21] Theologically, the CoP emphasizes the Four-Square Gospel: holiness, salvation in heaven, the gifts of the Spirit, and belief in Jesus

---

17. Church of Pentecost, "Brief History."

18. McKeown was the first leader and arguably founder of the CoP as a registered denomination. It should be remembered that without Peter Anim, the movement would not have been.

19. Onyinah, "Pentecostalism and the African Diaspora," 227.

20. Asamoah-Gyadu, "'On Missions Abroad,'" 89, 91; CoP Headquarters, "Statistics": Church of Pentecost, 2018, http://www.theCoPhq.org/index.php/statistics/.

21. Asamoah-Gyadu, "'On Missions Abroad,'" 91; Daswani, *Looking Back, Moving Forward*, 16.

as soon-coming King.[22] It takes a strong theological stance against neo-charismatic churches, i.e., those that emphasize the promise of health, wealth, and prosperity. Such churches, state Girish Daswani, are understood as "responding to new soteriological needs created by the advance of capitalism in Ghana."[23] There is concern that people in general and Ghanaians, in particular, are turning to Pentecostalism on the basis of a promise of financial success and the expectations of miracles. An additional concern stems from the new-charismatics emphasis on malevolent spirits and witchcraft in the lives of believers. While the CoP—which is considered as classical Pentecostal—believes in the existence of the latter and the former, it holds that a commitment to Jesus Christ, along with baptism in the Spirit frees believers from such control.[24]

The CoP is primarily a grassroots church, conducting its services in the local language, Twi. While this continues to be its main demographic, in a bid to engage younger, educated, and urban members, the CoP introduced the Pentecost International Worship Center (PIWC) service model.[25] PIWC worship services are conducted in English and, as such, attract not only younger congregants but non-Ghanaians. Further, while the traditional model is conservative as it relates to dress, head covering for women, separation of the sexes during worship, and the wearing of make-up and jewelry, the PIWC, designed to appeal to a different demographic, has done away with the aforementioned traditions.[26]

The implementation of PIWC's stand alongside migration, adaptability, and utilization of media as modes of the CoP's contribution to the contemporary globalization of Pentecostal Christianity. It is to this contribution that I now turn.

Discussion

Global Pentecostalism is adaptable to modern world systems and, concomitantly has an increasing visibility in the public sphere. Underlying the assertion of cultural adaptability is the assumption that the world's economic, political, and other societal structures have shifted (and

22. Daswani, *Looking Back, Moving Forward*, 16.
23. Daswani, *Looking Back, Moving Forward*, 17.
24. Daswani, *Looking Back, Moving Forward*, 17.
25. Asamoah-Gyadu, "'On Missions Abroad,'" 91.
26. Asamoah-Gyadu, "'On Missions Abroad,'" 94.

continue to shift), and Pentecostalism as a religious orientation can accommodate, or maybe even leverage, those shifts.[27] By discussing the ideas of adaptability and accommodation, visibility in the public sphere, and shifting societal structures as it relates to migration, Deininger's assertion provides the framework for the remainder of this essay.

Migration

Using a functional definition of migrant as "people who have lived outside their homeland for one year or more," scholars of globalization are in general agreement that "migration patterns of those seeking an 'economy of life' flow into areas where democratic capitalist systems are dominant, not out of them."[28] Before the 1950s, the migratory flow was from highly developed contexts to pre-capitalist locales. While Jehu Hanciles is clear that the factors reversing the flow are complex, "colonialism and the expansion of global Western powers are pivotal" factors.[29] Conversely, the reasons for migrating from South to North are also complex and diverse, so much so that it is "impossible to disentangle elements of 'compulsion' and 'expulsion.'"[30] Migration to rich countries represents such a strong pull that people from poorer countries are willing to risk their lives. An average person from one of the hundred poorest countries can increase their income five or six times by moving to one of the twenty-two wealthiest countries.[31]

Migration is said to be deeply embedded in the African experience. "[C]alamitous economic conditions in the subregion, epitomized by widespread unemployment, severe income inequalities, impoverishment of the middle class, declining standards of living and low human development" have contributed substantially to the human flow.[32]

Migration has contributed to the change in the demographic make-up of countries in the North and transformed the religious landscape of urban areas and capitalist democracies throughout the world. Hanciles argues that the impact of contemporary non-white immigration on the

27. Deininger, *Global Pentecostalism*, 2–3.
28. Hanciles, *Beyond Christendom*, 182; Stackhouse, "Sovereignty of Grace," 9.
29. Hanciles, *Beyond Christendom*, 172–73.
30. Hanciles, *Beyond Christendom*, 181.
31. Hanciles, *Beyond Christendom*, 178.
32. Hanciles, *Beyond Christendom*, 221.

American religious landscape is surpassed only by that of the original European migrants.[33] This is because as Christians from Africa, Asia, and Latin America migrate, their worship style and Christian expression migrate also.[34]

The CoP has contributed to this impact and change. Many Christians migrate for economic reasons. An important point to make regarding the CoP is its mainly poor but effective rural base. For many CoP members, it is the CoP that serves as the first point of contact when migrating to urban areas of Accra and Kumasi and further.[35] Unlike twentieth-century Pentecostal missionaries whose sole intent was spreading the gospel message in advance of the Parousia and subsequently building churches, the CoP's expansion was not intentional. Its global expansion was a result of migrating members sharing their faith.[36] Opoku Onyinah comments that while the CoP did not have a systematic theology, matters of faith were transferred and shared by means of practices of worship, prayer, and community.[37] What happened in London is a case in point. Migrant CoP members in London requested the Mother Church in Ghana establish a branch for them in London. Part of the motivation was accommodation. A CoP branch accommodated the worship of God in a way that was relevant to CoP members and helped maintain links with fellow Ghanaians at home and abroad.[38] Through such requests across the world, a missionary network was established under the leadership of an International Missions Director (IMD).[39] Aside from assisting in the establishment of churches, the IMD is responsible for the CoP's "international mission activities among the Ghanaian diaspora."[40] National worship styles practiced outside their locale inculcate a sense of belonging as well as a communal platform from which to respond to migrant social needs, including marital conflicts, bereavement support, and immigration issues. Onyinah, the first IMD, further states that diasporic churches create conditions that prevent members from falling victim to drug abuse, drug trafficking, and

33. Hanciles, *Beyond Christendom*, 277.

34. Hanciles, *Beyond Christendom*, 277; Asamoah-Gyadu, "'On Missions Abroad,'" 89.

35. Daswani, *Looking Back, Moving Forward*, 15.

36. Onyinah, "Pentecostalism and the African Diaspora," 228.

37. Onyinah, "Pentecostalism and the African Diaspora," 229.

38. Onyinah, "Pentecostalism and the African Diaspora," 217–18.

39. Onyinah, "Pentecostalism and the African Diaspora," 217.

40. Onyinah, "Pentecostalism and the African Diaspora," 218.

excessive use of alcohol. Further, they are successful in reaching diasporic communities; hence they become springboards to evangelize their local contexts.[41] The migrants represent a means of impacting the broader society by their model religious commitment, the application of the gospel to their immediate exigencies, and as a marginalized community that has an opportunity to interact with other marginalized groups.[42] In the US, this is perhaps extenuated because of its proclivity for voluntary associations along with a capacity for religious pluralism.

However, whether in London, New York, or Bangladesh, the CoP is connected to a transnational Pentecostal network. Birgit Meyer suggests that while earlier mission churches advocated for local appropriations of Christianity, Pentecostal and charismatic churches strive for global connections with English as the lingua franca. The CoP accommodated this move in the establishment of PIWCs, which provided space for educated Ghanaians and English-speaking foreigners.

CoP's Adaptability

At the end of 2019, the church had a global membership of over three million, located in over one hundred different countries.[43] How did the African denomination achieve this? Partly through the implementation of PIWCs.

During a conversation with one of CoP's national leaders, I was told that initially, PIWC was the brainchild of Opoku Onyinah when he served in the role of International Missions Director in the 1980s. When he first presented the idea, the leadership dismissed it as divisive. Yet PIWC played a major role in the CoP UK. In the year 2000, two CoP assemblies merged to form a PIWC. The move was necessitated by the fact that the church was not growing and was inaccessible to non-Twi speakers. As a PIWC, the church began to grow with non-Ghanaians attending. The eventual establishment of PIWCs was a recognition of the CoP's expansion, but also attends to cultural globalization and its attendant necessity for adaptability. A central thread running through the study of global Pentecostalism is its adaptability to the modern world system

---

41. Asamoah-Gyadu, "'On Missions Abroad,'" 90; Daswani, *Looking Back, Moving Forward*, 7.

42. Asamoah-Gyadu, "'On Missions Abroad,'" 278.

43. Church of Pentecost, "Statistics."

and, concomitantly, its increasing visibility in the public sphere, which I discuss in the next section through the CoP's media presence.

Increased Public Visibility through Media

The use of mass media has given the Pentecostal movement a higher public visibility, profile, and influence. Media intersects with both the public sphere and that of adaptability. Further, it provides a platform for the CoP's primary function of evangelism. The utilization of media reflects a Pentecostal response to emergent culture, both local and globalized.[44] Through this medium, popular culture is represented in "Christian terms." This practice is not dissimilar to the way multinational companies re-present sporting events, pop stars, and children to capture their target audiences. African Pentecostals are not dissimilar to Pepsi marketers in their quest to reach the world with their message. Ogbu Kalu traces the connection between Jim and Tammy Bakker's *Praise the Lord (PTL)*, which aired from 1974 to 1987, and Nigerian Pentecostalism. Bakker extended programming into Nigeria through the ministry of Benson Idahosa.[45] An added benefit of liberty from colonial authority was that freedom of religious expression was tolerated.[46] Control of their own productions carried with it at least three benefits. First, African Christians had greater cultural agency with the audio, DVDs, and music produced and broadcasted. Second, audio material such as sermons or music could be easily replicated and produced. And third, the absence of state regulation and access to inexpensive media technologies gave rise to a new economy.

The medium of television became a new instrument for forging transnational relationships, greater mass reach, direct encounter, potential promotional attraction, and world evangelism. This medium reinforces both the message of the gospel and the vision of the church.[47] Television represented a break or rupture with traditional methods of evangelism. In Ghana, it is the newer charismatic churches that dominate religious broadcasting.[48] African Christians are contesting for public space. This

---

44. Kalu, *African Pentecostalism*.

45. Kalu, *African Pentecostalism*, 106.

46. Kalu, *African Pentecostalism*, 107.

47. Kalu, *African Pentecostalism*, 105.

48. Asamoah-Gyadu, "Anointing through the Screen," 11.

"coming out" displayed a rejection of the classical Pentecostal withdrawal into enclaves of faith. The CoP began broadcasting intermittently on Ghana Broadcasting Company's *Radio 2* in the 1970s. The denomination has now developed so that it has a media arm, Pentecost Media or Pent-Media. Through PentMedia it produces its television programs, records documentaries, personality profiles, and interviews, and duplicates audio CDs alongside recording CoP's programs and activities.[49]

A church's approach to media and technology reveals much about its spirituality, mission, and worldview. Social media, as a response to the emergent culture, has been utilized by the CoP for Christian outreach, as well as a means of maintaining relationship with members in the diaspora.[50] Religious relationships form the most important way Africans interact with the rest of the world. Far from being peripheral, churches that have a positive approach to media claim that it is at the heart of new developments. Media in general and the internet in particular offer opportunities to maintain homeland pastoral and religious connections through church websites. Through web pages, members globally follow the activities of the mother church, solicit prayers for survival in their international contexts, and offer their appreciations through online tithes and offerings.[51]

The globalism/modernity discourse links the Pentecostal utilization of media to transnational and homogenizing cultural flows and global networking.[52] The late Ogbu Kalu highlights a couple of concerns. First, that through media African Pentecostalism would become an extension of the American electronic church and a vanguard of the political agenda of the American moral majority.[53] Though there may be some truth in this as it pertains to those churches who are dependent upon American support, this is not the case for the CoP, which is self-supporting. Scott Thomas explains that there has been a global shift towards local concerns and national politics, and as such, it is unclear if countries will align with American foreign policies solely on the basis of a shared faith.[54] Second, market theory profiles the religious space as a marketplace. This

49. White and Assimeng, "Televangelism."

50. Deininger, *Global Pentecostalism*, 31.

51. Asamoah-Gyadu, "'Get on the Internet!' Says the Lord," 227.

52. Kalu, *African Pentecostalism*, 108.

53. Kalu et al., *African Pentecostalism: Global Discourses, Migrations, Exchanges, and Connections*, 108.

54. Thomas, "Globalized God," 100.

theory promulgates religion as a commodity packaged as messages and religious products in a competitive marketplace, which leads to a contest for public space.[55] In the religious "market" space, religious leaders and denominations, like their secular counterparts, use secular marketing techniques to convince customers to buy books, DVDs, and religious paraphernalia. In so doing, glitz is added to religion, which transforms the religious space to secular space as a means of entertainment. The persona of the preacher and that of the television star become more and more indistinguishable. Hence, evangelism and the sharing of the gospel can be threatened or become secondary in the light of materialism and financial gain.[56]

In response to this charge, Martyn Percy, in applying advertising theology revises the religious use of media. The goal of media is not to bring about conversion but rather invites the viewer to take a second look. In a pluralistic modern world characterized by freedom of choice and competition, the invitation to take a second look renders the use of media in religious space legitimate. Percy argues that posters, handbills, television, goods, and clothes as advertisement can inspire, evoke affection, and impart useful public information, and as such, is beneficial to religious groups in a pluralistic age.[57]

Kalu is critical of African Pentecostals that have not adequately dealt with funding media intensive evangelization. Unlike in the West, there is no secular sponsorship, no fan base, or elaborate structures for mailing and contacting consumers. In the Western religious domain, the media ministry and the church can be separate entities, whereas in Africa, the funding comes from the tithes and offerings of the members and earnings received from business ventures.[58]

Economics

In 2018, Ghana had one of the fastest growing economies in the world. Although the trickle-down is yet to impact her more impoverished citizens, there is reason for hope. The CoP has contributed to that economy and has engendered a sense of optimism that comes from such growth.

---

55. Kalu, *African Pentecostalism*, 108.
56. Kalu, *African Pentecostalism*, 108.
57. Kalu, *African Pentecostalism*, 111.
58. Kalu, *African Pentecostalism*, 116.

The denomination has established the following: Pentecost University College, Pentecost Convention Centre, Pentecost Press Limited, Pentecost Hospital in Accra, and other smaller clinics across Ghana. Along with one hundred educational facilities, the CoP established the Pentecost Television Station (Pent TV) and the Pentecost Theological Seminary (PTS) in Birmingham, England, among many other projects. All of their endeavors are part of an effort to give back to society and holistically disseminate the gospel of Christ to the unreached. Moreover, it has chaplains appointed to two company holdings: Tobinco Group of companies and Jospong Group of companies.

Conclusion

Through this case study of the CoP, we see an example of how Black migration has transformed the outreach potential of African churches and Christian ministries.[59] From its humble beginnings, the CoP has become the largest Pentecostal church in Ghana. In addition to its local base of nearly 21,000 local assemblies, this African church has organized close to 150 congregations across twenty US states and Canada, and has a presence in 104 nations across the world.[60] It has a thriving chaplaincy and a social services arm, through which it offers multiple services, including development and relief and a credit union. The development of PIWCs is an example of Pentecostalism's adaptive qualities and the creativity of the Black church while maintaining and preserving its distinct religious feature of commitment to Christ and Holy Spirit-empowered evangelism, through which the CoP has become a global force.

For Further Discussion

1. Discuss the group's images of the African church *prior* to reading this chapter.

2. How has this chapter changed your view of the African church?

3. Identify any cultural and or social changes to which your church/denomination has had to adapt.

59. Hanciles, *Beyond Christendom*, 351.

60. Church of Pentecost, "Statistics"; Asamoah-Gyadu, "'On Missions Abroad,'" 89, 91.

Works Cited

Anderson, Allan. *Spreading Fires: The Missionary Nature of Early Pentecostalism.* Maryknoll, NY: Orbis, 2007. http://catdir.loc.gov/catdir/toc/ecip0711/2007006860. html.

Anderson, Allan, Edmond Tang, and Cecil M. Robeck. *Asian and Pentecostal: The Charismatic Face of Christianity in Asia.* Regnum Studies in Mission. Oxford: Regnum, 2005.

Asamoah-Gyadu, J. Kwabena. "Anointing through the Screen: Neo-Pentecostalism and Televised Christianity in Ghana." *Studies in World Christianity* 11, no. 1 (2005) 9–28.

———. "'Get on the Internet!' Says the Lord': Religion, Cyberspace and Christianity in Contemporary Africa." *Studies in World Christianity* 13, no. 3 (December 2007) 225–42. https://doi.org/10.3366/swc.2007.13.3.225.

———. "'On Missions Abroad': Ghana's Church of Pentecost and Its USA Missions." In *African Christian Presence in the West: New Immigrant Congregations and Transnational Networks in North America and Europe*, edited by J. Kwabena Asamoah-Gydu and Frieder Ludwig, 89–100. Religion in Contemporary Africa Series 8. Trenton, NJ: Africa World, 2011.

Bantu, Vince L. *A Multitude of All Peoples: Engaging Ancient Christianity's Global Identity.* Missiological Engagements Series. Downers Grove, IL: IVP Academic, 2020.

The Church of Pentecost. "Brief History." https://thecophq.org/brief-history/.

———. "Statistics." https://thecophq.org/statistics/.

COP Headquarters. "Statistics | The Church of Pentecost." http://www.thecophq.org/index.php/statistics/.

Daswani, Girish. *Looking Back, Moving Forward: Transformation and Ethical Practice in the Ghanaian Church of Pentecost.* Toronto: University of Toronto Press, 2015.

Deininger, Matthias. *Global Pentecostalism.* Online resource (108 pages). Hamburg: Diplomica Verlag, 2014. http://public.eblib.com/choice/publicfullrecord. aspx?p=1640417.

Hanciles, Jehu. *Beyond Christendom: Globalization, African Migration, and the Transformation of the West.* Maryknoll, NY: Orbis, 2008. http://catdir.loc.gov/catdir/toc/fy0904/2008013931.html.

Kalu, Ogbu. *African Pentecostalism: An Introduction.* Online resource (xvi, 359 pages). Oxford: Oxford University Press, 2008. http://public.eblib.com/choice/publicfullrecord.aspx?p=4664076.

Kalu, Ogbu, Wilhelmina Kalu, Nimi Wariboko, and Toyin Falola. *African Pentecostalism: Global Discourses, Migrations, Exchanges, and Connections.* The Collected Essays of Ogbu Uke Kalu 1. Asmara, Eritrea: Africa World, 2010.

Larbi, Emmanuel Kingsley. *Pentecostalism: The Eddies of Ghanaian Christianity.* Studies in African Pentecostal Christianity. Dansoman, Accra, Ghana: CPCS, 2001. http://hdl.library.upenn.edu/1017.12/366318.

Onyinah, Opoku. "Pentecostalism and the African Diaspora: An Examination of the Missions Activities of the Church of Pentecost." *Pneuma* 26, no. 2 (2004) 216–41.

Stackhouse, Max. "The Sovereignty of Grace: A Protestant View of Globalization." Lecture, Reformed Institute of Metropolitan Washington, January 27, 2007. http://www.reformedinstitute.org/images/Documents/Stackhouse07.pdf.

Thomas, Scott M. "A Globalized God: Religion's Growing Influence in International Politics." *Foreign Affairs* 89, no. 6 (2010) 93–101.

White, Peter, and Abraham Anim Assimeng. "Televangelism: A Study of the 'Pentecost Hour' of the Church of Pentecost." *HTS Teologiese/ Theological Studies* 73, no. 3 (2016) 1–6.

Black Protest Theology

Considering Bourdieu's Habitus *Theory with a Comparative Analysis of Protest Approaches in the Civil Rights Movement and the Hip-Hop Generation*

Antipas L. Harris

Introduction

Effecting change through protest is intricately and permanently woven into the fabric of American life. The very freedom that America celebrates today emerged from protest against British rule. From the Boston Tea Party of 1773 to the Tea Party of 2016, from the March on Washington for Jobs and Freedom in 1963 to the March on Washington for Lesbian, Gay, and Bi Equal Rights in 1993, the power of protest has undeniably shaped the course of history. Protesting women won the right to vote; protesting students helped end the Vietnam War; protesting African Americans helped curb prison brutality through the First Step Act.

Indeed, the sanctity of "the people's voice" is embedded in this paraphrase of the First Amendment: "Congress shall make no law . . . abridging the freedom of speech . . . or the right of the people peaceably to assemble, and to petition the Government for a redress of grievances." The denotation of protest assures the freedom to speak, to assemble, and to petition for redress (change). The Montgomery Bus Boycott (1955–1956) is just one illustration in which protest led to change: the desegregation of public transportation in Birmingham, Alabama. Protest became the "weapon of choice" in the modern civil rights movement.

In general, methods of protest have changed with the times. This chapter applies French philosopher Pierre Bourdieu's theory of *habitus* to principles of black protests throughout the civil rights and hip-hop eras. It then contrasts protest schemes that changed as experiences and perceptions evolved with the times. This analysis identifies an epistemological ecosystem that bridges the civil rights and hip-hop eras, employing a narrative comparison method with particular attention given to *habitus*, which is governed by the interplay of structures and experience.[1] Probing fundamental factors in the broad historical landscapes that surround black protest helps to bolster intergenerational collaboration toward a common vision of true "freedom and justice for all."

Similarities

For several years, scholars have discussed similarities between the civil rights and hip-hop eras. The epistemological thread between the eras is *habitus*, as Bourdieu explains it: "a system of lasting, transposable dispositions which, integrating past experiences, functions at every moment as a matrix of perceptions, appreciations and actions."[2] The *habitus* "system" is an epistemological ecosystem that is reflexive of the black experience, secular and sacred perceptions of life, and freedom actions. Black freedom protests may be explained as ritualistic[3] acts of *habitus* that reflect and produce black self-understanding and the way blacks understand the world around them. Black protests reveal 1) the conviction that God favors the oppressed, 2) the search for refuge, elevation, and freedom in community, and 3) the need for physical engagement in freedom demonstrations.

1. Bourdieu, *Outline of a Theory of Practice*, 95.

2. Bourdieu, *Outline of a Theory of Practice*, 82–83.

3. I am using Ronald Grimes's definition of rituals to label black freedom protests as rituals. See Grimes, *Craft of Ritual Studies*, 195–96. Ritual is *embodied, condensed, and prescribed enactment*. Protests are rituals in that they involve human activity; they shift from ordinary human action; they are shaped by black culture and communal agendas; and they evoke communal cause-oriented action (cf. Grimes).

God Favors the Oppressed

The conviction that God favors the oppressed acknowledges the basis of God's activity in everyday life. This foundational conviction in a holistic vision of black epistemology has Scripture as its foundation. Negro Spirituals are the primary locus for the study of black theology. James H. Cone has long argued that the meaning of God in black spirituals emerges from black biblical hermeneutics. Cone explains that slaves embodied a Job and Habakkuk-type reverence for a God who fights against suffering and will ultimately win that fight.[4] Deeper still, the essence of God as liberating, as expressed particularly in the exodus narrative, and in the resurrecting power of Jesus, is the overarching divine nature in Scripture. Cone explains,

> In the Bible, the black slaves found the God . . . whose will was the liberation of the oppressed. This same God also came to humanity in Jesus Christ the Oppressed One. . . . This biblical disclosure the slaves appropriated as speaking directly to their own condition . . . That this theme of God's involvement in history and the liberation of the oppressed from bondage should be central in black slave religion and the spirituals is not surprising, for it corresponded with the black people's need to know that their slavery was not the divine Creator's intention for them. In fastening on this knowledge, they experienced the awareness of divine liberation.[5]

This liberation involves personal and communal, private and public participation and benefits.

Consistent with Cone's observation, Melva Wilson Costen points out that people of African descent, including black slaves, have tended to view life "holistically, rather than in separate compartments, as created by a secular-sacred dichotomy."[6] Insightfully, civil rights scholar Aldon Morris locates civil rights protests within the context of black institutional life and posits that the protests were not meant merely to draw

---

4. Cone, *Spirituals and the Blues*, 56.

5. Cone, *Spirituals and the Blues*, 66.

6. Costen, *African American Christian Worship*, 1. Also, Cone posits that the black holistic worldview is reflected in the blues, which are "secular in the sense that they confine their attention solely to the immediate and affirm the bodily expression of black soul. . . . They are spiritual because they are impelled in the same search for the truth of black experience." See Cone, "The Blues: A Secular Spirituality," in *The Spirituals and the Blues*, 112.

white leaders' attention to a "worthy cause" expressed by nebulous and disgruntled black people.[7] They emerged out of deep thoughtfulness within black institutions, particularly churches, and with the resourceful genius of black religious leaders who sought to advance society toward a more just way of life.[8]

Similarly, hip-hop employs the black epistemological integration of secular and sacred.[9] Hip-hop scholar Todd Boyd tends to distance civil rights from hip-hop on the basis that "Hip Hop has rejected and now replaced the pious, sanctimonious nature of civil rights as the defining moment of Blackness."[10] In an essay review of Boyd's work, Derrick P. Alridge's "Hip Hop Versus Civil Rights?" challenges Boyd's assumption that civil rights died and hip-hop replaced it.[11] In a later essay, Alridge keenly argues for a linking "nexus of ideas" between civil rights and hip-hop.[12] Alridge, Daniel White Hodge, and others have long pointed to evidence in hip-hop music for similar goals of freedom and human dignity that existed in civil rights.[13] Alridge explains, "Hip Hop pioneers such as Kool Herc, Afrika Bambaataa, and Grandmaster Flash and the Furious Five, among others articulated the post-civil rights generation's ideas and response to poverty, drugs, police brutality, and other racial and class inequalities of postindustrial U.S. society."[14]

However, there remains a deeper connection than Aldon's insights on the intellectual and institutional forces behind the civil rights protests and Alridge's attentiveness to the "nexus" of similar social concerns between the eras. Within a nation built on the separation of church and state, the black community is formed with a fundamental understanding that all of life is a journey with God.[15]

7. Morris, *Origins of the Civil Rights Movement*, 5.

8. Morris, *Origins of the Civil Rights Movement*, 4. Also, see chapter 4.

9. Hodge, *Soul of Hip Hop*, 22–23.

10. Boyd, *New H.N.I.C.*, xxi.

11. Alridge, "Hip Hop Versus Civil Rights?"

12. Alridge, "From Civil Rights to Hip Hop," particularly 228.

13. Later, I will explain how hip-hop music integrates the secular and sacred dynamics of black epistemology.

14. Alridge, "From Civil Rights to Hip Hop," 226.

15. See Sorett, *Spirit in the Dark*, particularly chapters 1 and 6. Sorett attends to the long-standing integration of the secular and the sacred in black life, with particular attention given to black poetry and black preaching. He observes that in black history social spaces and cultural performances echo the interconnection of all of life.

People from the African diaspora are indigenously religious people with spirituality that involves the moral pursuit of freedom. Black practical theologian Dale P. Andrews points to a breakdown between evangelical Protestants and early black Christians on the basis of divergent meanings of liberation from sin and spiritual bondage.[16] He explains that African Americans were attracted to American revivalism, expecting its promise of liberation to be a holistic one.[17] Their holistic worldview was impervious to the American revivalist notion that God cares about human salvation and liberation but limits such divine activity to otherworldly, intellectual, or spiritual classifications. Andrews further explains that "preaching freedom from personal sin not only recognized human value, but also inspired transformation of the social order. Deliverance from spiritual bondage was understood within the drive for human freedom, in soul and body."[18] The black epistemological ecosystem integrates spirituality with everyday life. God is always present and on the side of the oppressed. In such a world, the political, moral, and religious are intermingled as a single composition.

Black life has gradually evolved into a complicated gap between generations, yet the underlying *habitus* that forms the black holistic view of life persists. In Evelyn L. Parker's essay on "Bridging Civil Rights and Hip-Hop Generations," she echoes hip-hop scholar Bakari Kitwana, who posits that the difference between the civil rights generation and the hip-hop generation involves a shift in black worldview.[19] Parker's article cites the hymn "Walk with Me, Lord" and hip-hop artist Kanye West's "Jesus Walks" as different genres and different religious messages. The hymn invites Jesus to be with God's people and the other affirms that Jesus is with struggling people in their pain. On the one hand, "Walk with Me, Lord" attends to a traditional approach to Christian prayer:

> Walk with me, Lord, walk with me
> Walk with me, Lord, walk with me
> I'm on this tedious journey, Lord
> Walk with me, Lord, walk with me, Lord.

16. Andrews, *Practical Theology*, 45.

17. Andrews, *Practical Theology*, 45.

18. Andrews, *Practical Theology*, 45–46.

19. Parker, "Bridging Civil Rights and Hip Hop Generations," 20–21. The reference to Kitwana is Kitwana, *Hip Hop Generation*, 28.

The traditional approach suppresses most of the details or codifies the need, in this song, with the word *tedious*. On the other hand, "Jesus Walks" is much more matter of fact with unrestrained explicit language while also making claims about Jesus' presence in the everyday life of suffering people.[20] For example, West sings of police harassment, including verbal assaults, as he hustles to manage his life. He views the offenses he faces as attacks from Satan.

Although the religious approaches are different, both share common concerns about the vicissitudes of life. Also, they share a common understanding that Jesus cares enough to live life with ordinary, suffering people.

African American understanding of God "walking" with them cannot be overstated. In black epistemology, spirituality has no boundaries. A higher power than white supremacy comes down to experience life among the oppressed. God is not with "them"; God is with "us" because God is always present and always, as Cone puts it, "partial toward the weak."[21] Blacks approach "redress of grievances with the conviction that God has already prepared the way to victory, particularly in a society where "black life" has never had equal significance to "white life." For centuries, dating back to slavery, the black community has developed with the long-standing perceived insignificance in the broader society. So, protest emerged as a cultural ritual in the fight to live as fully human and with equal dignity to white people.

The struggle for human dignity has taken on different forms but shaped by similar experiences. Bourdieu posits that "the *habitus*, a product of history, produces . . . practices—more history—in accordance with the schemes generated by history. It ensures the active presence of past experiences."[22] An example of Bourdieu's point is the seventy- and eighty-year-olds who often speak of racial problems in the mid-to-late 1900s, and the black millennials who are today convinced that black life does not matter the same as white life in America. Stated differently, during the civil rights era, segregation demanded that black people drink from fountains labeled "Colored," and could not eat in certain restaurants nor attend certain schools.

The social situation is clearly not the same today with desegregation, fair labor laws, and other laws meant to protect the liberty and interests

20. West, "Jesus Walks." See the lyrics at https://genius.com/Kanye-west-jesus -walks-lyrics.

21. Cone, *God of the Oppressed*, xi.

22. Bourdieu, *Logic of Practice*, 54.

of black Americans. Yet, young blacks often struggle with the constant threat of "driving while black" and "doesn't fit the profile." Consider Philando Castile, who was "living while black," and murdered at the hands of a Mexican-American Minnesota police officer, or Botham Jean, who was murdered in his apartment by a white Dallas police officer, or Trayvon Martin, who crossed invisible racial lines and was murdered because of it. In Bourdieu's words, "The *habitus*—embodied history . . . [that] is the active presence of the whole past of which it is the product."[23] This suggests that while the timing and particularities of generational experiences separate them, freedom protests from the past and present share a common *habitus*.

Kelly Brown Douglas points out that at the inception of the Black Lives Matter protest—after Trayvon Martin's accused killer was acquitted—Trayvon's father, Tracy Martin, uttered through his deep pain, "My heart is broken, but my faith is unshattered."[24] Martin's faith is deeply interwoven in the black epistemological ecosystem in which the secular and sacred intermingles *habitus*. Douglas evokes the theology of preacher and abolitionist Henry Highland Garnet, who delivered a captivating "Address to the Slaves of the United States of America" in Buffalo, New York. Garnet reasoned:

> If a band of heathen [people] should attempt to enslave a race of Christians, and to place their children under the influence of some false religion, surely, Heaven would frown upon the [people] who would not resist such aggression, even to death. If, on the other hand, a band of Christians should attempt to enslave a race of heathen [people], and to entail slavery upon them, and to keep them in heathenism in the midst of Christianity, the God of heaven would smile upon every effort which the injured might make to disenthrall themselves.[25]

Garnet, furthermore, asserts, "It is your solemn and imperative duty to use every means—moral, intellectual, and physical—that promises success."[26] The preacher's words radiate with a militancy reminiscent of Rev. Nat Turner's 1831 rebellion. Turner preached that God was in favor of violent protest. Frustrated with the horrors of

23. Bourdieu, *Logic of Practice*, 56.

24. Douglas, *Stand Your Ground*, 137.

25. Garnet, "Address to the Slaves," 5.

26. Garnet, "Address to the Slaves," 9; also cited in Douglas, *Stand Your Ground*, 152.

slavery, both Garnet and Turner were convinced that God supports an action-oriented faith that fights for freedom. Turner's violent methods were short-lived, but the fundamental conviction that faith requires transformational action was enduring.

For the most part, the Christian sentiment of nonviolence continues in black protest; however, the Black Panthers of the 1960s influenced hip-hop's sense of black pride. Over the course of the hip-hop era, there have been both nonviolent and violent protests. The marches and demonstrations led by Dr. Martin Luther King, Jr. reflected a commitment to nonviolence. However, the 1992 riots following the televised beating of Rodney King in Los Angeles exemplified hip-hop's objection to police brutality when the accused officers were acquitted. While all blacks do not support violence, black *habitus* exists at the intersection of structural opposition and lived experience in which they draw from a deep spiritual reservoir to cope with what many consider state-sanctioned violence.

Building on Cone's black liberation theology, Douglas conjectures that the spirit of black radical resistance has been sustained throughout black history on the basis that oppression "hurls defiance in the face of God."[27] God, therefore, favors the oppressed and not only nods at their resistance but empowers their fight against domination and abuse. Relating the fight to the hope of a better day, Douglas explains that "black faith is . . . a testimonial of the divine/human interaction between God and black people. As such, it is a witness to black reality and black hope."[28] Moreover, Trayvon Martin's parents' resolute faith in the face of unimaginable horror of losing a son bears witness to faith recycled throughout black history—a different day but a continuity of faith. Black hope, of which Douglas speaks, helps sustain black Americans through senseless violence and unrelenting oppression.

Douglas argues that black faith in the wake of the deaths of Trayvon, Jordan, Renisha, Johnathan, and others is to "weep for divine justice. God's justice means an end to the very culture that has declared war on innocent, young black bodies. This means an end to the systemic, structural, and discursive sin of Anglo-Saxon exceptionalism, which makes black bodies the target of war."[29] It is acting like God is in control, "thus to be where God is, standing up . . . so that our sons and daughters might

27. Garnet, "Address to the Slaves," 5; also cited in Douglas, *Stand Your Ground*, 152.

28. Douglas, *Stand Your Ground*, 139.

29. Douglas, *Stand Your Ground*, 232.

live."[30] This resilient faith is engrained in the epistemological materials that stirred the mothers and fathers of the civil rights movement and hip-hoppers of the Black Lives Matter Movement to take to the streets in sociopolitical protest.

Refuge, Elevation, and Freedom

Black people of both the civil rights and hip-hop eras place a high value on community. Solidarity serves as a coping mechanism in the presence of unending racism. During the civil rights era, blacks found such refuge, elevation, and freedom in their faith communities, mostly black churches, but some found it in mosques, as well.

Hip-hoppers, however, find religious fulfillment in a number of other places. Hip-hop art, music, and literature influence and are influenced by a number of lived experiences that lead to alternative religious satisfaction. Sociologist of religion Grace Davie points to the need to understand the ways in which religion, or more accurately, religions, not only influence but are influenced by behaviors and situations.[31] Black religious scholar Onaje X. Offley Woodbine explains that the hip-hop movement ushered in new avenues for young people to find a similar satisfaction. Woodbine argues that the new sense of refuge, elevation, and liberation forces new meaning for black religion. Consistent with guidance from sociologists, Woodbine postulates that "religions in the African Diaspora . . . [are] primarily practical traditions of 'healing, ritual, and community' for those seeking 'refuge, elevation . . . [and] liberation' in an anti-black world."[32] Andrews adds that the black church evolved as a place of refuge for blacks in social pain. This explains *why* and *in what ways* the black church has been a healing balm, a place of refuge, escape, and connection.

Comparably, the central thesis of Woodbine's chapter, entitled "An Invisible Institution," is that sports have become a place of refuge, elevation, and liberation for black youth, becoming their "religion."[33] Stated differently, while basketball and football may be classified as mere

---

30. Douglas, *Stand Your Ground*, 232.

31. Davie, *Sociology of Religion*, 1.

32. Woodbine, "Invisible Institution," 183. Woodbine draws upon Peter R. Gathje, "Teaching African American Religions."

33. Woodbine, "Invisible Institution," 173.

American pastimes, they also qualify as religion for many Americans,[34] especially young black men. Woodbine explains,

> To promote Black survival, rituals have played a critical role across the African Diaspora, providing a set of non-discursive bodily techniques . . . to displace ego wounds related to slavery, loss, and systemic racial abuse to rediscover connections to something greater in themselves and the world.[35]

Sports function as part of the epistemological ecosystem in that they are mechanisms of embodied knowledge of the social world. Such embodied knowledge is not merely a reaction to social situations but rather formative amid them. Embodied knowledge is centered on unearthing practical knowledge in "a set of non-discursive bodily techniques." This is accomplished in protests, as well as sports. Bourdieu emphasizes how bodily knowledge is a product of *habitus*, advancing social realities. Bodily knowledge as expressed in sports becomes religion, fulfilling the need for refuge, elevation, and liberation for many hip-hoppers. Sports are a coping mechanism at the intersection of the secular and sacred, providing urban youth with spiritual insight into the meaning of life. As active players or devoted spectators, young people often "find themselves" through sports. They are also connected to something greater than the sum of their problems: God.

Although published before the National Football League's (NFL's) kneeling protest, Woodbine's argument sheds light on the racial division regarding that protest. White America, in general, views the kneeling protest as unpatriotic. However, black urban youth understand the black-led kneeling protest as solidarity in this ongoing struggle. The tension lies in opposing "religious views" of sports. So, while Woodbine is correct to highlight sports as a religion within the hip-hop community, one must acknowledge that sports are a religion in all of America.[36] Woodbine's argument for sports as religion leads to the conclusion that from the perspective of urban black youth, mingling sports with black protest is appropriate. The religious dynamism inherent in sports empowers protest just as the church, spirituals, and civil rights songs did in the civil rights era.

---

34. For more on sports as religion in America, see Higgs, *God in the Stadium*, particularly chapter 1.

35. Woodbine, "Invisible Institution," 182.

36. Prebish, *Religion and Sport*, 25–26. Also, see Higgs, *God in the Stadium*, 19.

Physical Engagement in Freedom Demonstrations

Physical demonstrations—active, vocal, determined voices—characterize the black struggle for freedom. Both civil rights and hip-hop protests
involve physical defiance.[37] For example, Rosa Parks refused to surrender
her seat to a white man in 1955; King and Ralph Abernathy were arrested
for marching against segregation in 1963. King defended black resistance
based on Christian convictions in his "Letter from a Birmingham Jail."
King believed that Christians are called to be social agitators for the common good. Andrews concludes,

> Survival need not limit itself to a passive and impotent accep-
> tance of historical conditions. Survival may in fact be part of
> humanity's proactive participation in the redemptive activity of
> God. Redemptive suffering is not acquiescence to the atrocity of
> suffering . . . . Survival and refuge need not be in dialectical op-
> position to sociopolitical liberation ethics. In faith identity, the
> former nurtures, expects, and even pursues the latter.[38]

Leaders of different faith traditions do not always concur on defensive tactics toward liberation. Some are nonviolent; some violent; others
draw upon both.

Black epistemology involves the inseparability of reflection and action. Thus, the work of *habitus* over the course of black history has also
been reflective and action-oriented praxis. It has been expressed in slave
gatherings in the house of meetings, call-and-response code singing in
the fields of the plantations, the Montgomery Bus Boycott and Freedom
Fighters, the marches on Washington, the Selma to Montgomery march,
Bloody Sunday, Black Lives Matter protests, the kneeling protest, and
others. Blacks believed that the sum of the weak equals strength. Their
collective strength in protest would break the back of legalized white he-
gemony. Unlike whites who deify law and order, blacks possess an intui-
tive critique of laws. For them, laws have potential for civility and justice
but have rested in the hands of uncivilized, immoral agents in power.

Moreover, black individuals tend to see protest as a disruption of
corrupt normalcy. In *God's Long Summer: Stories of Faith and Civil Rights,*
theologian Charles Marsh explains that blacks used massive protests as a
unified front to disrupt and destroy the yoke that Jim Crow segregation

---

37. Andrews, *Practical Theology,* 46.
38. Andrews, *Practical Theology,* 46.

had on blacks.[39] In this way, even nonviolent protests had a violent intent in that the goal was to destroy inhumane systems with nonviolent tactics. Similarly, in *Ferguson and Faith: Sparking Leadership and Awakening Community*, practical theologian Leah Gunning Francis explains that in the protests that resulted in St. Louis from the police killing of Michael Brown, citizens were compelled by a common judgment among millennials that something is not right. The moral fortitude of the community was a call to action. Francis reflects on her empirical research among the protesters:

> I do not suggest that young leaders emerged within the movement because of the clergy. Actually, I think the argument could be made that the young leaders ignited the leadership among the clergy; they created space and impetus for the clergy I talked with to live into the roles as leaders.[40]

Francis emphasizes that the call to faithful witness amid realized tragedy in the black community demanded action that young people could not resist when church leaders moved slowly. The irony is that, at least if reading Francis correctly, the moral impulse to fight against injustice was beating more fervently among those who were not clergy.

Francis points out that a crescendo of concerned citizens grew restless with the nation's bankrupt justice at a time when a young black teen lay voiceless in the streets, killed by an officer sworn to protect him. Story after story, the percolating consensus was that the moral conscience of the community demanded action. T. D. Jakes interviewed Andrew Young, one of the few surviving civil rights leaders from the 1960s, at Jakes Divinity School. Jakes asked Young for an assessment of the Black Lives Matter movement. Young commented, "They have the same spirit we had during the civil rights movement."[41] He further expressed the need for "deep spiritual reflection"[42] to crystallize the Black Lives Matter agenda.

Conclusion

Throughout American history, public protests—whether violent or nonviolent, massive or confined, indoors or out, have altered the course of the nation. Cone and Costen agree that a history of black protest for

---

39. Marsh, *God's Long Summer*, 129.
40. Francis, *Ferguson and Faith*, 5.
41. Jakes, "Chancellor's Master Class."
42. Jakes, "Chancellor's Master Class."

human rights is biblically rooted in the community's embodied herme-neutic. Alridge and others add that the intent of protests have remained constant: to right an obvious wrong, to challenge injustice, or to be a voice for the voiceless. This analysis reveals an epistemological continu-ity not merely limited to the goals of protest but also to the theory of knowledge that is foundational to the black community's understanding of God, self-perception, and vision of the world.

While black protest methods have changed over time, the integrated secular and sacred epistemological ecosystem has persisted in black thought and practice. This epistemological orientation informs protests that raise awareness and unite people in battles deemed worth the fight. During the fifties and sixties—the civil rights era—protests proved to be an effective weapon for African Americans to create social change. Then, in the late seventies and eighties, the phenomenon known as hip-hop arrived, dominating the "free speech, assembly, and redress" scene with its own approaches to leadership, religion, and justice.

The black church remains central to galvanizing disparate segments of the community, although the church is no longer the epistemic sym-bol it once was. Christian narratives and symbolism occupy a different position in the justice discourse. Yet, those protests that strategically and effectively harness the sacred and secular ecosystem, which runs through multiple generations, will continue moving toward historic black biblical views about lived freedom and justice.

This chapter explored the power of protest to effect change across the broad social-historical landscapes. Regardless of the chronology, the two generations are connected with an epistemological ecosystem that involves the *habitus*. In the final analysis, the black experience draws from the rich heritage of lived wisdom and embodied biblical hermeneutics. Both are sometimes explicit and other times implicit in black American culture and manifest in everyday life and protests. Bourdieu's insights about *habitus* involve its dependence on the strength and wisdom from "historically and socially situated conditions of its production."[43] When African Americans from both the civil rights and hip-hop eras, with a wide range of socioeconomic statuses and talents, discover their common epistemological foundation and historically linked *habitus,* it will be easier to sit together (rather than separate) at the "table of [sister/]brotherhood,"

---

43. Bourdieu, *Outline of a Theory of Practice*, 95.

and benefit from the life-giving wisdom and embodied biblical hermeneutics to finally achieve the goals of the variety of freedom protests.

Works Cited

Alridge, Derrick P. "From Civil Rights to Hip Hop: Toward A Nexus of Ideas." *Journal of African American History* 90, no. 3 (Summer, 2005) 226–52.

———. "Hip Hop Versus Civil Rights?" Essay Review of Boyd's *The New H.N.I.C. Journal of African American History* 88 (Summer 2003) 313–16.

Allen, Donna E. "Rituals of Resistance to Strengthen Intergenerational Relations." In *Black Practical Theology,* edited by Dale P. Andrews and Robert London Smith, Jr., 47–55. Waco, TX: Baylor University Press, 2015.

Andrews, Dale P. *Practical Theology for Black Churches: Bridging Black Theology and African American Folk Religion.* Louisville: Westminster John Knox, 2002.

Boyd, Todd. *The New H.N.I.C.: The Death of Civil Rights and the Reign of Hip Hop.* New York: New York University Press, 2002.

Bourdieu, Pierre. *Distinction: A Social Critique of the Judgement of Taste.* London: Routledge, 1984.

———. *The Logic of Practice.* Translated by Richard Nice. Stanford, CA: Stanford University Press, 1980.

———. *Outline of a Theory of Practice.* Translated by Richard Nice. New York: Cambridge University Press, 1977.

Breitman, George, ed. *Malcolm X Speaks: Selected Speeches and Statements.* Broadway, NY: Grove, 1965.

Cone, James H. *A Black Theology of Liberation.* Maryknoll, NY: Orbis, 2010.

———. *God of the Oppressed.* Maryknoll, NY: Orbis, 1997.

———. *Said I Wasn't Gonna Tell Nobody.* Maryknoll, NY: Orbis, 2018.

———. *Spirituals and the Blues.* Maryknoll, NY: Orbis, 1992.

Costen, Melva Wilson. *African American Christian Worship.* Rev. ed. Nashville: Abingdon, 2007.

Craven, Julia. "More Than 250 Black People Were Killed by Police in 2016." *HuffPost,* January 1, 2017. https://www.huffingtonpost.com/entry/black-people-killed-by-police-america_us_577da633e4b0c590f7e7fb17.

Davie, Grace. *The Sociology of Religion.* Los Angeles: Sage, 2007.

Diamant, Jeff, and Besheer Mohamed. "Black Millennials Are More Religious than Other Millennials." *Pew Research Center: Numbers, Facts and Trends Shaping Your World,* July 20, 2018. https://www.pewresearch.org/fact-tank/2018/07/20/black-millennials-are-more-religious-than-other-millennials/.

Douglas, Kelly Brown. *Stand Your Ground: Black Bodies and the Justice of God.* Maryknoll, NY: Orbis, 2015.

Francis, Leah Gunning. *Ferguson and Faith: Sparking Leadership and Awakening Community.* St. Louis: Chalice, 2015.

Garnet, Henry Highland. "An Address to the Slaves of the United States of America." https://digitalcommons.unl.edu/cgi/viewcontent.cgi?article=1007&context=etas.

Garza, Alicia. "A Herstory of the #BlackLivesMatter Movement." *The Feminist Wire,* October 7, 2014. http://www.thefeministwire.com/2014/10/blacklivesmatter-2/.

Green, Derryck. "Evangelicals, Black Lives Matter and *The New York Times.*" In *Juicy Ecumenism: The Institute on Religion and Democracy's Blog.* https://juicyecumenism.com/2016/01/26/evangelicals-black-lives-matter-and-the-new-york-times/.

Grimes, Ronald L. *The Craft of Ritual Studies.* New York: Oxford University Press, 2014.

———. *Rite Out of Place: Ritual, Media, and the Arts.* New York: Oxford University Press, 2006.

Higgs, Robert J. *God in the Stadium: Sports and Religion in America.* Lexington: The University Press of Kentucky, 1995.

Hodge, Daniel White. *The Soul of Hip Hop: Rims, Tims, and a Cultural Theology.* Downers Grove, IL: InterVarsity, 2010.

Jakes, T. D. "Chancellor's Master Class: An Interview with Ambassador Andrew Young." Jakes Divinity School, November 5, 2020.

King, Martin Luther, Jr. *A Gift of Love: Sermons from Strength to Love and Other Preachings.* Boston: Beacon, 2012.

Kitwana, Bakari. *The Hip Hop Generation: Young Blacks and the Crisis in African American Culture.* New York: Basic, 2002.

Lange, Matthew. *Comparative-Historical Methods.* Thousand Oaks, CA: Sage, 2013.

Marsh, Charles. *God's Long Summer: Stories of Faith and Civil Rights.* Princeton: Princeton University Press, 1997.

Morris, Aldon D. *The Origins of the Civil Rights Movement: Black Communities Organizing for Change.* New York: Free Press, 1984.

Parker, Evelyn L. "Bridging Civil Rights and Hip Hop Generations." In *Black Practical Theology,* edited by Dale P. Andrews and Robert London Smith, Jr., 19–34. Waco, TX: Baylor University Press, 2015.

Prebish, Charles S. *Religion and Sport: The Meeting of Sacred and Profane.* Westport, CT: Greenwood, 1992.

Price, Emmett G. III, ed. *The Black Church and Hip Hop Culture: Toward Bridging the Generational Divide.* Lanham, MD: Scarecrow, 2012.

Sorett, Josef. *Spirit in the Dark: A Religious History of Racial Aesthetics.* New York: Oxford University Press, 2016.

Taylor, Keeanga-Yamahtta. *From #BlackLivesMatter to Black Liberation.* Chicago: Haymarket, 2016.

Woodbine, Onaje X. Offley. "An Invisible Institution: A Functional Approach to Religion in Sports in Religion in Wounded African American Communities." In *The Black Church and Hip Hop Culture: Toward Bridging the Generational Divide,* edited by Emmett G. Price III, 173–84. Lanham, MD: Scarecrow, 2012.

Section Three

Sermons on Blackness

Jesus and the Borders

(Luke 14:7–14)

LUKE A. POWERY

WHEN ONE ENTERS A neo-Gothic cathedral like Duke University Chapel, designed by Black architect Julian Abele, it is easy to notice at first sight the beautiful stained-glass windows or the high vaulted ceilings or the worn wooden pews or even the elevated pulpit covered by a wooden canopy. But there may also be things one may not notice initially, like a green devil in one of the stained-glass windows, or the two wooden mice that are in residence in the building, or even the video cameras, or the water stains on the walls from leaks throughout history. These latter mentioned parts of the iconic building at Duke are marginal. They are not front and center; they are not obvious at first; they are on the borders, and we might not even notice that they are there because we think they do not matter.

Yet, margins, borders, matter. In a 2016 Olympic tennis match, Jack Sock was playing Lleyton Hewitt. Hewitt served the ball, and the umpire called it out. It was so close that to Sock it looked in, so in an unusual fashion, Sock told Hewitt to challenge the call. You can see the chair umpire looking at Sock as if he was crazy, and you can hear the audience chuckling in surprise. They can't believe what's happening. The umpire reviewed the call, and the ball was shown to hit the line; thus, it was actually in, giving Hewitt a point. Sock risked losing a point in order to be just. He chose to go against the grain and investigate what happened on the borderline, on the margins, and not ignore what happened there, because just as in tennis, what happens on the margins, on the borderlines of society, the borderlands of human existence, matters. It can change the game and it can change your life. If we neglect the margins, we won't see the full picture. Margins matter in tennis and even around dinner tables.

We often find Jesus around a table because he was an ancient foodie (Luke 7:34). He'd love all of the eating options in the South, especially the barbeque. At a last supper with his disciples, he even told them that he wanted to be remembered by a meal—"Do this in remembrance of me"(Luke 22:19). In this story, he's going to eat a meal, then tells a parable about a meal, and then another story about a meal. But what's telling about Jesus is not the actual meal but who is at the meal. He eats with religious leaders, but when he moves beyond his respected and expected acquaintances, he raises eyebrows: "Why do you eat and drink with tax collectors and sinners?" (Luke 5:30). In some settings, that might be like asking, "Why are you hanging out with those Black people?" He gets critiqued for how he minds the margins because as the saying might go, "Show us who you eat with, [and] I'll tell you who you are."

At the table, Jesus shows us who he is through his two instructions. The first is: "When you are invited, go and sit down at the lowest place . . . For all who exalt themselves will be humbled, and those who humble themselves will be exalted" (Luke 14:10–11). I know that humility gets a bad rap in our day. "Are you kidding me? This was not my approach to getting into college or being hired at a consulting firm or winning this research grant—I wasn't chosen because I was humble." None of us get a job offer because we're humble! On the contrary, you get accepted or are chosen for boasting about your achievements, demonstrating how gifted you are, how much you did in the community, how you excelled in the classroom or on the field, what you created and for which you have a patent. If I think about the Duke-Carolina basketball rivalry, Duke fans will sometimes say to their Tar Heel opponents, even if we lose: "That's alright, that's okay, you will work for us some day!" Not much humility there.

What Jesus teaches goes against the grain, and this is what Christians are often called to do. "Go and sit down at the lowest place"? Who would boast, "I'm a marginal reader, choose me!" No one wants to be marginal or marginalized. We all want to be the best, extraordinary movers and shakers in the world.

The London Underground, also known as "the Tube," is the oldest rapid transit system in the world. In 1968, a recorded voice was installed to warn travelers to watch out for the space between the platform and train every time the train stops. That voice says, "Mind the gap." Mind the gap because if you don't, you may fall and hurt yourself. In life, if you don't mind the social gaps and those on the margins, you may fall because the margins or the fringes shouldn't be ignored. It's not just those who are honored who deserve a better seat around the table of humanity but those who are dishonored on a daily basis, even because of the color of their skin. If we don't mind the margins, mind the social gaps, we miss the collective picture of humanity that affirms Black lives matter.

"Go and sit down at the lowest place"? Go and empathize with Black lives? Yes. Go and see what it's like to feel what others feel on the borderlands of human existence and increase your empathy with those who always have to sit or be told to sit at the lowest place or who have a knee jammed into their neck just because they are Black. Put yourself in someone else's shoes to see the world from another perspective. Empathize with those who carry burdens on the borders of society, "with their backs against the wall"[1] just because their backs and bodies are Black. Mind the margins.

Inhabit the lowly places because they are actually central to society. Talk of borders has been in the national discourse of the United States and elsewhere. Borders in life or on a page are significant. Former Duke President Richard Brodhead appeared on *The Colbert Report* with Stephen Colbert. They discussed the American Academy of Arts and Sciences report on the importance of the humanities and social sciences in education.[2] At one point, Colbert picked up the report and pointed to the size of the margins on each page and challenged Brodhead by claiming he was stretching the report, making it longer with bigger margins. Colbert claimed that if the margins weren't so large, the report, which is about eighty-eight pages long, would only be eight pages long. But swiftly and wittingly, Brodhead responded by saying, "All serious readers know that margins are to keep your notes in." The margins on a page are a part of the reader's experience, a part of the full page, the full picture, the full story that must be told.

When we read a book, we may use the margins to emphasize what's important to us as readers. "We have all," in the words of former US Poet Laureate Billy Collins,

> seized the white perimeter as our own

---

1. Thurman, *Jesus and the Disinherited*, 11.
2. https://www.cc.com/video/8ax5jq/the-colbert-report-richard-brodhead.

and reached for a pen if only to show
we did not just laze in an armchair turning pages;
we pressed a thought into the wayside,
planted an impression along the verge . . .[3]

The margins can have lasting impressions on the borders of a book and a society.

But some may never pay attention to the borders, especially the footnotes or endnotes, those notes on the margins of a page, because they are in smaller font, revealing somehow that they may not be as important as the "main text" or "majority." When publishing books, editors may even encourage writers to limit the number of footnotes because what's in the margins seemingly doesn't matter and is viewed as getting in the way of the reader, breaking the flow of the "real content." Yet the irony is that the marginal footnotes tell you the source for the information in the main text; they feed into what is central and tell you where to go for the source of knowledge. They are the backbone to what is considered most significant. Without the footnotes, without the margins, without the borders, you wouldn't have all of the necessary information at hand. You wouldn't have the whole story because without the fringe of a page or a community, you can't see the whole and know the fullness of God.

The marginal information is sometimes commentary on the main body of the text. The margins matter, and maybe it's the margins, the borders, that tell us what kind of society this really is. The margins tell us who Jesus was and is because the marginalized were Jesus' tribe. As Howard Thurman reminds us in *Jesus and the Disinherited*, Jesus was a poor Jew, a member of a minoritized, marginalized group, living under Roman oppression, and whose spirit gave the oppressed courage.[4] Jesus hung out with the least, the last, and the left out, which is why his second instruction is, "When you give a luncheon or a dinner, do not invite your friends or your brothers or your relatives or rich neighbors, in case they may invite you in return, and you would be repaid. But when you give a banquet, invite the poor, the crippled, the lame, and the blind. And you will be blessed, because they cannot repay you . . ." (Luke 14:12–14).

Invite those who aren't connected to power. Invite those who can never repay you. Be careful of befriending others just because you can get something from them but aren't really interested in them. Invite those

---

3. Collins, "Marginalia."
4. Thurman, *Jesus and the Disinherited*, 11–35.

who can't give you anything but themselves—they have no money, their health is bad, they are reliant on you, they are not in the right network, or don't have the right net worth. Invite those who aren't your usual associates. Engage those who are different. And by inviting the poor, the crippled, the lame, the blind, those without college degrees and with great material and physical needs, you are telling them, "You are accepted."[5]

Whether it be where you sit or whom you invite, the message is clear—embrace places and people out of the normative cultural, racialized, hierarchical bounds. Embrace Blackness and every single Black life. And tell them, "You are accepted!" Choose the margins, the socially unacceptable, the periphery, and the unpopular, and tell them, "You are accepted!" If you want to be first, be last. Go against the grain and choose the lowly seat and invite the outcasts because God wants to broaden your relational social borders.

Choose the way that won't win you any awards or honorable mentions. Choose the way that may reward you with a burden or just make you a footnote. Choose what you really don't want in order to receive what you really need. Don't worry about seeking greatness; seek humility. If you want to be great, be great in service. If you want to be great, be great in loving your neighbor. If you want to be great, be great in respecting the one who cleans bathrooms, sweeps floors, serves food in the cafeteria, and has to clean up after you at your workplace. If you want to be great, be great in complimenting someone else, be great in loving, be great in listening, be great in giving, and perhaps you'll work your way toward a PhD in love. Do you want to be great? Mind the margins. Mind the social gaps. Mind Blackness and bless the borders like Jesus. Pay attention to what and who is on the border, for we need them if we want to see the whole picture of life and experience the beautiful beloved community of God. If Black lives do not matter, then we can never say all lives matter. We need the inclusion of Black lives, Black human beings on the borders, to gain a fuller sense of the beauty of God.

Our destinies are intertwined, and without those on the margins—refugees, strangers, immigrants, widows, orphans, the hungry, the thirsty, the naked, the sick, the prisoner, the most vulnerable among us, Black lives—our future will be anorexic, and the dream of a beloved community will die.

---

5. Tillich, "You Are Accepted."

But I still hold fast to that border-crossing dream captured in the words of the sonnet "The New Colossus," inscribed on a plaque on the inner wall of the pedestal of the Statue of Liberty, the "Mother of Exiles":

> From her beacon-hand
> Glows world-wide welcome . . .
> Give me your tired, your poor,
> Your huddled masses yearning to breathe free,
> The wretched refuse of your teeming shore.
> Send these, the homeless, tempest-tost to me,
> I lift my lamp beside the golden door![6]

In other words, to channel Kanye West: "I'm just tryna say the way school need teachers / The way Kathie Lee needed Regis, that's the way [we] need Jesus" and the margins.[7] We need each other as the promise of our future is the expansion of our heart's borders. And maybe, just maybe, we'll recognize that borders and Black lives aren't actually dangerous but sites of hope where the dream of God can come true. I hope to see you at the border.

Works Cited

Collins, Billy. "3 Poems and Analysis: 1. Marginalia." *Billy Collins—The People's Poet.* https://billycollinsbalderdash.weebly.com/3-poems-and-analysis.html.

Lazarus, Emma. "The New Colossus." *Poetry Foundation.* https://www.poetryfoundation.org/poems/46550/the-new-colossus.

"Richard Brodhead." Episode. *The Colbert Report.* New York: Comedy Central, August 15, 2013.

Thurman, Howard. *Jesus and the Disinherited.* Nashville: Abingdon, 1996.

Tillich, Paul. "You Are Accepted." In *A Chorus of Witnesses: Model Sermons for Today's Preacher*, edited by Thomas G. Long and Cornelius Plantinga, 92–101. Grand Rapids: Eerdmans, 1994.

West, Kanye. "Jesus Walks." *AZLyrics.com.* https://www.azlyrics.com/lyrics/kanyewest/jesuswalks.html.

6. Lazarus, "New Colossus."

7. West, "Jesus Walks."

Rise of the Liberating Church

Efrem Smith

The LORD said, "I have indeed seen the misery of my people in Egypt.
I have heard them crying out because of their slave drivers, and I am
concerned about their suffering. So I have come down to rescue them
from the hand of the Egyptians and to bring them up out of that land
into a good and spacious land, a land flowing with milk and honey—the
home of the Canaanites, Hittites, Amorites, Perizzites, Hivites and
Jebusites. And now the cry of the Israelites has reached me, and I have
seen the way the Egyptians are oppressing them. So now, go. I am
sending you to Pharaoh to bring my people the Israelites out of Egypt."

(EXOD 3:7–10 NIV)

THE HASHTAG AND MOVEMENT Black Lives Matter has come under attack by a segment of the body of Christ. A segment of evangelicalism,
to be specific, has spent enormous energy writing blogs, developing
podcast episodes, crafting statements, and preaching sermons on why
Christians should not support Black Lives Matter. These critics have
pointed to the website of Black Lives Matter, the organization, to make
the case that there are principles presented that are antithetical to the
Scriptures. They have accused the founders of the organization of being
anti-American. Some of these critics have even stated that the Black Lives
Matter movement is racist. But the criticisms have not just been limited

to Black Lives Matter the organization. Pastors who have posted on social media the hashtag Black Lives Matter under a picture of George Floyd, Breonna Taylor, or Ahmaud Arbery have been the objects of attack as well. Sermons that acknowledge systemic racism and call for justice and reforms have been deemed political and not biblical by some. Pastors of predominately white, evangelical congregations, who in this moment are for the first time preaching more concretely on issues of racial reconciliation and biblical justice, are being accused of replacing the gospel with politically liberal ideology, cultural Marxism, and critical race theory.

The purpose of this sermon is not to answer all of the accusations of these critics. Neither is it to defend all the principles and points of Black Lives Matter the organization. The purpose of this sermon is to explore a biblical foundation for God as One who cares deeply about Black bodies. To present a liberating God who hears the cries of the enslaved, the oppressed, and the marginalized. To make it clear, that Black Lives Matter is a cry that God hears and responds to, because God hears and responds to the cries of the oppressed, the dehumanized, and the demonized by those in power, who abuse power. With this being the case, there is a biblical calling upon the church to align its mission with the liberating God. The gospel is liberating news. God is a liberating God. So, in order for the church to better align itself with the mission of God, she must become a liberating church. The church must rise and join the liberating God in hearing and responding to the shout, Black Lives Matter!

Some in the body of Christ respond to the proclamation Black Lives Matter with the colorblind-based and deflecting statement of All Lives Matter. Of course, all lives matter because all human beings are made in the image of God. All human beings are image-bearers of the creator of the universe. All human beings are loved by God, gifted by God, and have the potential to live out a transformative life mission.

Genesis chapter one, beginning with verse 26, makes this clear:

> The God said, "Let us make mankind in our image, in our likeness, so that they may rule over the fish in the sea and the birds in the sky, over the livestock and all the wild animals, and over all the creatures that move along the ground." So God created mankind in his own image, in the image of God he created them. God blessed them and said to them, "Be fruitful and increase in number; fill the earth and subdue it. Rule over the fish in the sea and the birds in the sky and over every living creature that moves on the ground." (Gen 1:26–28 NIV)

The issue is not whether all lives matter to God. The issue is that in a sinful, fallen, and upside-down world, all lives don't matter equally. Sin disrupts God's desire for how human beings are to live—in relationship with God and with one another. It even disrupts how God desires that individual humans would see themselves. A holistic understanding of sin, as presented in Scripture allows us to gain clarity on why it's biblical to proclaim Black Lives Matter and expect a liberating response from God and God's people.

The Need for Liberation: Supernatural, Soulish, and Systemic Sin

Sin is not just housed in the souls of human beings. Sin is housed in systems, structures, institutions, and ideologies within this fallen world. Evangelicalism, as well as the United States of America, in a general sense, has functioned within an ethos of rugged individualism. This is important because evangelicalism has had an impact both on the development of the Black church, going all the way back to the antebellum church of slavery, and on the multiethnic church, especially in its more visible form beginning in the 1980s and 1990s. An individualistic understanding of sin is not only prevalent within evangelicalism but also on some level in both Black church and multiethnic church ecclesiology. Sin is primarily seen as situated in the souls of human beings. So, the focus is on saving individual souls. The belief is that people only need to repent of sins they individually committed. With this limited view of sin, it makes sense why issues such as systemic racism, sexism, and classism are offensive and rejected by far too many in the body of Christ. It makes sense why a segment of the body of Christ would be unable to engage Black Lives Matter as both a missional and biblical justice opportunity. A holistic and biblically rooted understanding of sin is a proper starting point.

Sin is supernatural to the degree that it is introduced to human beings through the temptation of an otherworldly being in the form of a serpent (Gen 3).To understand the origins of sin is to acknowledge Satan, demonic forces, and spiritual warfare. Both fallen and regenerated human beings are in a battle, whether they realize it or not, for their identities, beloved-ness, and true purpose. The apostle Paul paints a picture of this spiritual warfare dynamic of sin in Ephesians, chapter 6:

> For our struggle is not against flesh and blood, but against the rulers, against the authorities, against the powers of this dark world and against the spiritual forces of evil in the heavenly realms. Therefore put on the full armor of God, so that when the day of evil comes, you may be able to stand your ground, and after you have done everything, to stand. (Eph 6:12–13 NIV)

Yes, sin is a demonic, supernatural force. Sin, in this way, is an invisible force of temptation towards human beings in order to influence our behaviors and decisions. But sin is also housed in the soul of human beings. The temptation of the serpent in Genesis 3 leads to sin entering into the collective souls of humanity. Sin is not just the tempting tool of Satan; it is also what separates humanity from God. Sin is a sign of the disobedience of human beings; of rejecting the desires and commandments of God. All human beings are sinners. We cannot simply blame Satan for sin. Human beings are co-conspirators in this sinful world. Sin disrupts our relationship with God and with one another. One of the ways this shows itself is in how we sin against each other.

Sin impacts the relationships between the first human beings we read about in Scripture. It brings dysfunction into the relationship between Adam and Eve and it leads to murder among their children, when their oldest son, Cain, kills his own brother Abel (Gen 4). Sin infects the family system. Sinful human beings also build sin-filled structures, communities, institutions, and ideologies. The murderer, Cain, eventually builds a city. Years later, sinful human beings set out to build a tower and another city in Genesis chapter 11:

> Now the whole world had one language and a common speech. As people moved eastward, they found a plain in Shinar and settled there. They said to each other, "Come let us make bricks and bake them thoroughly." They used brick instead of stone, and tar for mortar. The they said, "Come let us build ourselves a city, with a tower that reaches to the heavens, so that we may make a name for ourselves; otherwise we will be scattered over the face of the whole earth." (Gen 11:1–4 NIV)

Sinful people collectively build and develop sinful systems, structures, institutions, and ideologies. Systemic sin is visible in society through idolatry and injustice. Idolatry is expressed through the worship of false gods in the form of objects and deities formed by human beings or in replacing the one true God with the leaders of nations and empires as gods in the forms of Pharaoh and Caesar. So, with a holistic understanding of sin, we must acknowledge how sin exists in our own nation. If we live in a sinful world, this includes the United States of America. There are many wonderful things about this nation, but we are also infected by sin—sin in our souls, systems, and structures. The journey of Black bodies in this nation from slavery, through Jim Crow, and in this present moment, gives us one picture of the impact of systemic sin. Sin has infected every area of our society. Idolatry and injustice are real demonic and human-driven realities. We are in need of salvation and deliverance from our being held captive to the fallen and sinful systems and structures of this world. But God, as a Liberator, has a solution to systemic idolatry and injustice. God's solution is liberation, righteousness, and justice.

This is what we come to understand in the book of Exodus. In the book of Exodus, see the Liberating God raising up a human liberator in Moses. In Moses, we have an opportunity to see what our response should be to the shout, Black Lives Matter. This is a burning bush moment for the church. God is once again speaking in this moment and calling for liberators who will rise up as reconciling and justice-oriented disciple-makers in response to the continued dehumanizing and demonizing of Black bodies.

A Liberating God Raises Up Liberators

Moses is tending sheep for his father-in-law Jethro when God calls out to Moses from within a burning bush. God explains to Moses that he has seen the misery and heard the cries of the Israelites suffering in Egypt. God states that he is coming down to rescue them from the oppressive hand of Egypt. God also lets Moses know that Moses is the vessel that God is going to use for this liberating mission. Moses has a decision to make. Will he continue with the comfortable occupation he is currently in, or will he say yes to the liberating opportunity burning in front of him? The current painful expressions of injustice through the deaths of unarmed African Americans at the hands of law enforcement is a burning bush opportunity. George Floyd crying out for his life on the corner of 38th and Chicago Avenue in Minneapolis, Minnesota, is a cry heard by God. God hears and responds to the cries of George Floyd and many others. The blood of Ahmaud Arbery and Breonna Taylor cry out to God from the ground like Abel's after being murdered by his brother Cain. This is a burning bush moment. This is why the church must rise up as a liberating church and join in the shout that Black Lives Matter! But we aren't simply called to shout, but also to serve. We are called by God to participate in liberating ministries of reconciliation and justice. We must ask ourselves, "What is keeping us from saying yes to the call and rising up as God's liberating people?"

A Liberating Story

Moses was reluctant in saying yes to God's call to a liberating mission. In Exodus chapter 4, Moses begins to debate with God over why he doesn't believe he is qualified to go to Pharaoh and demand the liberation of the Israelites. The liberating call upon the church includes stepping into a courageous life of speaking truth to unjust systems of power. Moses questioned if he indeed had the God power to confront earthly power structures:

> Moses answered, "What if they don't believe me or listen to me and say, 'The LORD did not appear to you'?" Then the LORD said to him, "What is in your hand?" "A staff," he replied. The LORD said, "Throw it on the ground." Moses threw it on the ground and it became a snake, and he ran from it. Then the LORD said to him, "Reach out your hand and take it by the tail." So Moses reached out and took hold of the snake and it turned back into a staff in his hand. (Exod 4:1–4 NIV)

When Moses threw the staff on the ground and it became a snake, he ran from it. Could it be that the snake was an image of the tempting serpent back in Genesis, which introduced sin to humanity in the first place? This snake at the feet of Moses could very well have been the one reminding Moses of his fears and insecurities. Reminding him that he grew up not knowing his biological parents. Reminding him that he was a murderer and a fugitive. But yet, when God tells Moses to pick up the snake, it becomes a staff again. It becomes the tool in Moses' hand that God will use in the liberating mission to deliver the Israelites. Our life stories can hold us captive or we can allow God to liberate them so that we are able to humbly, lovingly, and courageously stand against injustice. God can take our sinful past, our broken life stories, and instead of them being an accusing serpent at our feet, God can redeem them and use them as transformative tools in our liberating mission.

A Liberating Soul

Then God directs Moses to put his hand inside his cloak. When he does and pulls his hand out, his skin is leprous. Then God told him to put his hand back inside his cloak again and when he pulled it out the second time, his hand was restored (Exod 4:6–7). Could it be that this moment is pointing us to the state of the soul of Moses? When Moses pulled out his hand the first time and it was diseased, this was Moses seeing what his life would look like if his outside looked like his inside. Moses may have very well been dealing with identity crisis. He grew up in Pharaoh's palace but was not an Egyptian. He watched his people, whom he wasn't raised with, suffering under the oppression of slavery. He killed an Egyptian and ran away to find a new life. His soul is damaged. It's possible to experience the call to the liberating life of God and be held back by a wounded soul. There are far too many people who are seeking to be reconciling and justice-oriented servants with damaged souls. I know that I can say that I have struggled in my own soul in this challenging season. Watching the video of George Floyd crying out for his life is deeply traumatic to the African American soul. I have needed to lean into spiritual direction, prayer, and the community of godly friends like never before. Allow God to heal and liberate your soul consistently, so that you are able to stay emotionally healthy in the liberating work.

A Liberating Voice

Moses presents one last excuse to God for not being qualified to serve as God's vessel of liberation. He brings up the fact that he is not a very good communicator. Not only is he not an eloquent speaker, he has a stuttering problem. But God reminds Moses that it is God who gives human beings their abilities and uses them in spite of weaknesses and struggles. God lets Moses know that he will empower him to speak (Exod 4:10–12). Before Moses finally accepts God's liberating calling, though, he draws the anger of God. This part of the story raises two questions.

One, "Will you allow God to liberate your voice?" You don't have to be a powerful preacher or the most excellent public communicator to live as God's liberating mouthpiece. Maybe your liberating call is going to be lived out in one-to-one relationships or smaller groups in your neighborhood, on your job, or at your school. Maybe your liberating call is focused on one politician, one police officer, one CEO of a company, one family member, or one neighbor next door. The point is, surrender your voice to God. Allow God to liberate and empower your voice. Whether a shout or a still calm voice, speak for truth, reconciliation, and justice in the place of influence God has already given you.

The second question is, "Will you stop arguing with God?" When will you stop denying that God hears the cries and sees the injustices in this sinful world? When will you join God in hearing the cries and seeing the injustices? When we deny the cries and refuse to see the injustices, we are arguing with God. When we keep bringing up excuses for not living as cross-cultural, reconciling, and justice-oriented disciple-makers, we are arguing with God. We must move from lives of arguing with God to living in the liberating and justice-oriented anointing of God. Because when we live as liberators, we are aligned with Christ. The story in the book of Exodus is a story of liberation and deliverance, and it also points to the coming of the most excellent Liberator, Jesus the Christ.

Conclusion: The Liberating Mission of Christ

God is revealed as a liberating God throughout Scripture. Ultimately this is shown in the Liberating Savior. In Christ, human beings are liberated from a life of sin, but also liberated from sinful and oppressive institutions and structures. Christ receives proclamations of "Messiah" and "King" at the moment of his birth, making it both a spiritual and political event. He disrupts the oppressive religious structures of the day through His use of the words of the prophet Isaiah to launch His public ministry. This moment is captured in Luke 4 in the following manner:

> Jesus returned to Galilee in the power of the Spirit, and news about him spread through the whole countryside. He was teaching in their synagogues, and everyone praised him. He went to Nazareth, where he had been brought up, and on the Sabbath day he went into the synagogue, as was his custom. He stood up to read, and the scroll of the prophet Isaiah was handed to him. Unrolling it, he found the place where it is written: "The Spirit of the Lord is on me, because he has anointed me to proclaim good news to the poor. He has sent me to proclaim freedom for the prisoners and recovery of sight for the blind, to set the oppressed free, to proclaim the year of the Lord's favor." (Luke 4:14–19 NIV)

The public ministry of Christ that follows his pronouncement in Luke 4 is the liberating words of the prophet Isaiah becoming active. Christ demonstrates his pronouncement through casting out evil spirits, healing the sick, raising the dead, and challenging the abuse of the poor by religious leaders in the temple. The liberating mission of Christ is both salvific and one of social justice. This liberating mission informs the evangelism, discipleship, and outreach ministry of the liberating church. It calls for the church to go beyond individualistic salvation initiatives to ministries focused on meeting the physical and social needs of the marginalized and poor. The liberating church is one that addresses the class and racial disparities within its community in some transformative way. Transitional housing programs for the homeless, tutoring young people below grade level in math and reading in order to address racial disparities in education, providing free healthcare services, or working for police reform are ways in which the liberating church can participate in the liberating ministry of Christ. In order to launch and sustain these kinds of ministry initiatives, members of the church must be equipped and mobilized. Therefore, the equipping and releasing of cross-cultural and justice-oriented disciple-makers is the continuation of the liberating ministry of Christ. Church, there is a burning bush in front of us, and it's calling us to rise up as liberators.

Feast Day for Saint Harriet

Donyelle McCray

BASED ON HEBREWS 11:1–16, this sermon's central theme is living by faith.[1] Yet one of the sermon's aims is to demonstrate the minimal attention liturgical calendars tend to assign to African American witnesses, other than Dr. Martin Luther King, Jr. and figures like Bishop Richard Allen and Rev. Absalom Jones. What might it mean to bring the life stories of other African Americans who embody Christian virtues into our liturgies—people like Pauli Murray, Bayard Rustin, Howard Thurman, or in this case, Harriet Tubman? Should we adhere to the traditional process of selecting dates for these observances or chart a different path? Ultimately, such feast days ought to honor the ancestors, inspire the contemporary church, and strengthen the spiritual bonds between the living and the dead.

> In the Name of the Living God
> Who was, and is, and is to come . . .

In late September—we don't know exactly what day—but late September 1849, the woman we now know as Harriet Tubman set off into the dark on her first trek towards freedom. She left at night towards an unseen land and an unknowable future. And, like so many other fugitives whose names are unknown to us but cherished by God, Harriet offers a testimony as firm as our spiritual ancestors in Hebrews 11 about what it means to live by faith.

---

1. This biographical sermon was first preached on September 25, 2019, at Bethany Theological Seminary as part of a preaching series on race.

In the Episcopal Church, Harriet shares a feast day in July with Sojourner Truth, Elizabeth Cady Stanton, and Amelia Bloomer, but I wish today were her feast day. I wish pilgrims commemorated the hundred-plus-mile journey with two weeks of night walking from Maryland's Eastern Shore, up through the Delmarva Peninsula and over into Philadelphia—maybe crossing the same rivers or brushing up against some of the same trees that felt Harriet brush by on her first escape. But American vanity being what it is, I worry that such a pilgrimage would quickly devolve into T-shirts and car decals, and selfies at the Pennsylvania border.

When the *Harriet* film was released, I had hoped that it wouldn't squeeze her into an American success narrative because that would mean squeezing her into someone who was fearless, invincible, and self-assured in the triumphalist sense. She was brave, but not fearless. Too much had happened to her and to the people she loved. And she was not invincible because she had the "deep scars on her spirit" that came from being hated, as well as a physical disability—headaches and fainting spells stemming from being hit in the head with a two-pound counterweight.[2] It's true Harriet was confident, but more in God than herself. She spoke of "asking of Him" or "consulting Him" in an intimate way—the way we talk of speaking to one another.[3] One time she bid on a piece of land at auction, and won, despite not having the money, and when asked how she'd pay up said, "I'm gonna talk about it with Jesus tonight . . ." One of her Quaker friends, Thomas Garrett, said, "I never met anyone of any color who had more confidence in the voice of God."[4]

Harriet Tubman was one of those people who packed the achievements of twenty lives into one. Risking her own life, she made more than a dozen trips on the Underground Railroad and liberated more than seventy people—actually closer to a thousand if we count the additional 750-plus people she liberated at the Combahee River (near Charleston) during the Civil War. Eventually she became known as "Moses" for bringing so many out of "Egypt," but on this night in September, she was more like her spiritual ancestor Abraham who set out into the unseen and found God there.

When "Minty," as she was known in 1849, set out that late September evening, she was not seeking to become anyone's hero. She couldn't

2. Thurman, *Luminous Darkness*, x.
3. Clinton, *Harriet Tubman*, 91.
4. Clinton, *Harriet Tubman*, 91.

have known what the next hour would hold—much less any further into the future. But lack of control did not mean lack of clarity: "I had reasoned this out in my mind," she said, "there was one of two things I had a right to, liberty or death; if I could not have one, I would have the other."[5]

She left at night. Without a map. Without the ability to read road signs. Without expertise in mid-Atlantic geography. On the clear nights she had the moon and the North Star, and when it was cloudy, she could trust the mossy side of trees to guide her or squat down next to a stream and feel the current. She thought they all flowed South, and she was mostly right—right in her belief that nature could be trusted.

Her best ally was the darkness. Under that blanket, she could walk ten miles a night—maybe more. Not racing, because she needed her stamina. And not standing still, because she had to "keep going," but moving carefully, because there was a whole life world around her that she could not see . . . giant spiderwebs, raccoons and hooting owls. Crickets, bats, delicate insects wisping by on nightly errands of their own . . .

And slavecatchers stalking the night for Black flesh. She'd had dreams about these. Before she learned to listen to God in nature, she listened for God in dreams. First, there were the dreams of a woman screaming. Maybe this was her own screaming, or her mother's or her two older sisters who were sold South. Her mother never stopped mourning for them. God could've been screaming in her dreams at what was happening to them. We don't know if the screaming dreams intensified during those times when Edward Brodess (the family's owner) considered selling members of her family. All we know is that the dream was recurrent and that it announced an unspeakable, irreparable loss—Rachel screaming for her children who are no more (Jer 31:15; Matt 2:18).

Then, there were the galloping dreams of horse hooves coming closer and closer behind her. These she says little about beyond the sense of threat. It makes sense that she'd feel hunted by a force she could not see. Horror was and remains central to Black experience in the Americas.

Most mysterious were the flying dreams. Years before she tried to escape, she'd dream of flying "over fields and towns, and rivers and mountains, looking down upon them 'like a bird,' and reaching at last a great fence, or sometimes a river, over which she would try to fly," but she said it appeared "like I wouldn't have the strength, and just as I was sinking down, there would be ladies all dressed in white over there, and they

---

5. Bradford, *Harriet Tubman*, 29. Spelling and dialectal variations in the original account have been emended for clarity.

would put out their arms and pull me across."[6] She'd make it, but not in her own power; she'd have to be carried.

Now I don't know, but I like to believe the ladies dressed in white who put out their arms to pull Harriet across are the ancestors who lived by faith in a hostile land, those whom our Scripture says, "died in faith without having received the promises, but from a distance they saw and greeted them . . . God is not ashamed to be called their God; indeed, He has prepared a city for them" (Heb 11:13, 16). Though dead, the saints are very much alive and still bearing ardent witness. Through these flying dreams, they give Harriet the confidence to step out by faith.

Harriet was one of those Christians who believed in direct revelation. She was not embarrassed to talk about dreams or visions or signs from another shore. Her God was God of the temporal and the eternal; able to hold the things we understand and able to hold the things we will *never* understand. God was the only one who was utterly trustworthy in the dark.

To walk for hours in the dark, sometimes through thick forest, is to be drawn not only out of place but out of time, and to be swallowed in the enormity that is God. A Buddhist teacher I know says we find the strength to face the thing we cannot face when we can imagine something large enough to hold it. Harriet finds that "Something Larger" in God. Moving out into the dark was moving into the hidden will of God where there is no grid, no coordinate, no calendar—just the ocean of divine unknowing. And Hebrews suggests every saint sails into it. In the dark it becomes clear that only God is God.

What if God's gift to us, in a saint like Harriet, is to lead us away from preoccupation with assured outcomes into a way of being that is freer, nimbler, and more joyous? Shouldn't our practice of Christianity give us that? What if God's gift to us in a saint like Harriet is a pathway out of the life-stealing clutches of control?

I don't know if you've ever found yourself outside walking alone in the dark and heard the wind rustle the leaves or looked up into a black sky and suddenly felt tiny. There's a quiet beauty and a touch of fear that arises when we tap into the fact that we are all finite. And finitude, as my friend Susan Dunlap says, involves more than bodily mortality and fragility.[7] We have emotional limits, cognitive limits, limited power to

---

6. Clinton, *Harriet Tubman*, 38. Spelling and dialectal variations in the original account have been emended for clarity.

7. Dunlap, *Caring Cultures*, 189–90.

predict the future, limited powers to cure or hold what's precious. Painfully limited power to protect those we love.

In the daylight these ever-present limits recede into the background, but in the dark they are thrown into full view. The illusions of control are pierced.

White supremacy feeds fantasies of control and pressures all of us to spend enormous amounts of energy trying to look like we are in control and pretend we have the answers. We don't. And the performance of that fiction does violence to the soul.

I also see this pattern of clinging to control in contemporary conversations about race when there's a rush to resolution and a refusal to go deep. This is a problem because race operates in the realm of memory. Some of the most important work happens when submerged memories thaw and flood into consciousness, and there's enough trust in the room to share that memory. When this happens, what we need is to wobble and sway in the new depth of what's been shared. But sometimes the desire to be in control clamps down the energy, and there's a rush to move on, talk about something else . . . What we need is to develop sea legs so that we can tolerate more depth and more uncertainty without shutting down.

Or what we need is to move like Saint Harriet into the night and find God there. And maybe we won't find God as Father or King or a Shepherd keeping the sheep in control, but as the Dark Mystery who envelops us, as the Endless Depth, as the Inner Music, as the Night Companion, the Unfolding Way . . . I think that's who God was for Harriet. What if God is using Harriet to expand our understandings of divine presence? Because that's what it'll take to live *by faith*.

One of the church's failures when it comes to race—particularly the white mainline church—is its unwillingness to go into the dark. The church is content with learning good racial etiquette rather than pressing forward and dismantling systems in ways that will require fundamental change. Beautiful Christian words like "reconciliation" and "hope" have been infected by white supremacy. I mean, the idol of control has corrupted the church's use of these terms. I don't want to bristle when I hear the word "reconciliation," but I often do because "reconciliation" so often means "Get over it." And this leaves people of color with the burden of pretending the past doesn't inform our present-day interactions as much as it does. Reconciliation has been reduced to just one more layer of American racism. And the continued emphasis on reconciliation keeps the church from moving out into the dark where something newer and freer can happen, where a divine vision can emerge.

The church's language around hope suffers, too. I see this when white Christians look at the wreckage of American racism and prevail on people of color to give them hope. Yet often, what's desired is not hope but anesthesia. The sun has to set on hope-as-optimism before living *by faith* becomes possible.

What if today, around this 170th anniversary of Harriet's first venture into the dark, what we are to be reminded of is that faith is not an abstract concept? It is a lived reality that is most clearly perceived in messy lives—people making the most of impossible situations. Faith is Abraham setting off to an unseen land. Noah building an ark for a flood he couldn't imagine; Enoch being taken who knows where. Sarah conceiving past her time. Faith is clearing a path through thick brush. Faith is a Black woman walking in the darkness and finding she is not alone. Such feats give us a window into who Jesus is and more. They summon the best from those of us who seek to live by faith.

And what more can I say? For time will not let me tell you about how God soothed Harriet's heartbreak when her first husband remarried. Or how God helped her rig a box, a board, and a mule together into a horse and buggy to help her elderly parents escape. Or how God helped her at almost eighty years old to create a Black nursing home in New York. Or how God gave her an apple orchard to provide jobs for family and friends. And time will not let me tell you about how God sustained her in a decade-long struggle to get her veteran's benefits and how she couldn't pay her bills but survived.

Her life story is a lesson in how to move in cold, dark spaces; how to hold on to your tenderness while navigating tough terrain; how to climb softly and deliberately despite your fear; how to clear new territory and enter it—claiming the fullness of the freedom God bestows on us.

For the gift of Harriet Tubman and for her witness of living by faith and moving into the darkness, let us thank the Lord. Amen.

Works Cited

Bradford, Sarah H. *Harriet Tubman: The Moses of Her People*. Secaucus, NJ: Citadel, 1974.

Clinton, Catherine. *Harriet Tubman: The Road to Freedom*. New York: Back Bay/Little Brown, 2004.

Dunlap, Susan J. *Caring Cultures: How Congregations Respond to the Sick.* Waco, TX: Baylor University Press, 2009.

Thurman, Howard. *The Luminous Darkness: A Personal Interpretation of the Anatomy of Segregation and the Ground of Hope.* New York: Harper and Row, 1965.

A Decriminalizing Gospel and Empowering Maneuvers[1]

David D. Daniels III

Is it not the rich that oppress you? Is it not they who *drag you into court*?
You do well when you really fulfill the royal law according to
the scripture, "*You shall love your neighbor as yourself.*"

—JAMES 2:6–8

SCRIPTURE ADDRESSES ISSUES RAISED by the Black Lives Matter movement. Scripture addresses the devaluation and disposability of black lives through the criminalization of being black. In criminalizing black people for being black, black people are treated as threats by police and other authorities. Criminalized as a group, black people are disproportionately over-policed, over-surveilled, over-arrested, over-litigated, over-sentenced, and over-incarcerated.

James 2, especially verse 6 ("they who drag you into court"), reveals what could be called a decriminalizing gospel of the God who is against prejudicial systems (Jas 2:1; Acts 10:34), names prejudice as sin (Jas 2:9), and requires an anti-prejudicial structure of empowerment (Jas 2:5, 8, 9). This is a gospel demanding the decriminalizing of black people as a group

---

1. An earlier version of this sermon was preached at First Baptist Church of Chicago and Christ Cathedral Church of Christ (Holiness) during February of 2021.

and the erection of a society that values black bodies and lives structurally as well as interpersonally.

Our Scripture text is found in the Letter of James—James, the famous first-century biblical author, Christian theologian, and early church leader. James is the author who has a gift of grabbing us by the collar and seizing our attention. He is an in-your-face kind of writer and teacher. He expects Christians, well, to live like Christians. He expects the church, yes, to act like the church. He expects the gospel to be proclaimed and lived. James is a no-nonsense, brutally honest kind of preacher. James is a theologian of justice and love.

James's letter shocks me! James in chapter 2 shocks me. I'll be honest with you, James shocks me with the subject matter he broaches. He shocks me with the problems he highlights. He shocks me with the solutions he demands.

See James 2:6. It is shocking that the letter condemns oppression (*"Is it not the rich that oppress you?"*). It is shocking that the letter condemns the criminalization of the poor by the rich: Look at the third part of verse 6 (*"they drag you into court"*). It is shocking that a letter in the New Testament denounces the criminalization and oppression of the poor. It is shocking because the criminalization of the poor is not a common theme in every book of the Bible. It is shocking that the first-century church is wrestling with issues that confront the twenty-first-century church.

Stirred by justice, James is dissatisfied with limiting the issue to the realm of feelings, attitudes, and emotions. The Letter of James addresses the sin of criminalization and oppression. The Letter of James exposes the practices of oppression, the systemic nature of oppression. The Letter of James focuses on how the poor are treated and mistreated; how the poor are abused and misused by the courts; how the poor are oppressed.

As a matter of fact, if we updated the language in James and situated the letter in the United States, then James would sound like an essay written by James Baldwin or Malcolm X or Angela Davis or Cornel West or Michelle Alexander or Ibram X. Kendi. Like these writers, James grapples with the first-century version of a criminal justice system that discriminates against the poor and marginalized. Like these writers, James is unafraid to express his emotion or, should I say, his anger, his righteous indignation. Like these writers, James addresses the plight of marginalized people. While our contemporary writers engage African Americans as the subject and racism as the topic, James engages the poor as the subject and criminalization as the topic. While all black people are not poor, the criminalization of the ancient poor and the criminalization of today's black people are similar in many ways.

Stirred by justice, James, in this letter, sincerely wrestles with the high cost, the heavy toll, the deep pain of Christians who are oppressed in the first-century church. James doesn't shy away from the pain. James doesn't shy away from calling oppression: Oppression.

Stirred by justice, James is dissatisfied with a mere change of attitudes, a simple change of feelings and emotions. The Letter of James calls for a change in the behavior: a change in the group behavior of the people in the congregation. The letter calls for group behaviors and practices that are fair and just. The letter calls for just and fair systems.

According to Pedrito Maynard-Reid, a judicial setting is the context for James 2:6. According to his research of the first-century Jewish world and Roman Empire, judges came from the wealthy class, were members of the wealthy class, and often represented the interest of that class.

Go with me to verse 6 of chapter 2 of James: Is it not the rich that oppress you? Is it not they who *drag you into court*?

Look at the latter part of verse 6: "the ones who drag you into court." Look earlier in verse 6: The wealthy, the powerful, who "oppress you" or, according to the Common English Bible translation: "make life difficult for you," for the poor. Sit with verse 6 for a moment. Feel the weight of the text. Carry the burden of the text on your shoulder for a minute. The wealthy, the powerful, who "oppress you," "make life difficult for you," for the poor. The wealthy, the powerful, "the ones who drag you into court."

How do they "oppress you" or "make life difficult for you"? One way is to drag the poor into court as routine practice. Drag them into court on trumped-up charges. Drag them into court for trivial things. We see here that dragging them into court is a strategy to criminalize people, to criminalize the poor. By criminalizing the poor, criminalizing poverty, and weaponizing the court system to crush and to oppress the poor, the powerful can exploit the poor for the benefit of the rich.

How are the poor criminalized? By making it a crime to be poor. The rich erect an economy where the poor are loaned the necessities of life, means of survival, and then they pounce upon the poor to repay their debts, knowing their impoverishment makes repayment nearly impossible.

How are the poor criminalized? By dragging them to court every chance the rich get. The poor are sued for the debts they can't afford to repay. They can't repay because they work in an economy that underpays and overworks them, which, of course, is the real crime; but this "economic crime" is reclassified as legal. Just read the fifth chapter of James where he addresses economic exploitation with brutal honesty.

How are the poor criminalized? By using the court system to keep them poor, keep them down, keep them oppressed, it makes poverty a crime. The imprisonment of a poor family, removal from gainful employment, leads to the further impoverishment of an already impoverished household.

James is not afraid to tell the truth. Is it not the rich that oppress you? Don't the wealthy make life difficult for you? Aren't they the ones who drag you into court?

This is why the Letter of James might possibly echo or reverberate in the writings of James Baldwin, Malcolm X, Angela Davis, Cornel West, Michelle Alexander, or Ibram X. Kendi.

Maybe James Baldwin's "Letter from a Region in My Mind" should be read as a modern Letter of James. Like James, Baldwin tackled the topic of oppression. Like James, Baldwin criticized oppressors. Like James, Baldwin spoke in defense of the oppressed. Like James, Baldwin believed that God was committed to justice.

Do Black Lives Matter?

For way too long, black people have been criminalized for just being black. Criminalized for being poor. Criminalized for being racially different.

For way too long, black people have been criminalized for hanging out on the street corner while being black during the Jim Crow era, for being unemployed in the rural South while being black during the Jim Crow era, for allegedly whistling, while being black, at a white woman during the Jim Crow era.

For way too many times during the early twenty-first century, black people have been criminalized for just being black: jogging while black in an all-white neighborhood in Brunswick, Georgia; for being a twelve-year-old boy playing with a toy gun while black in a playground in Cleveland, Ohio; for sleeping in the bedroom of an apartment in Louisville, Kentucky while black.

Scholars tell us about the school-to-prison pipeline. Some scholars contend that prisons have been planned based on the school performance or, rather, the academic failure, of third-grade black boys. The academic failure of these third-grade boys is used as a predictor of the future size of the prison population.

Research has shown that compared to white people, black people as a group are under-protected by police, under-resourced by the government, under-educated by the schools, under-insured by health insurance, under-represented in Congress, under-paid on the job, and under-funded by philanthropic foundations and government grants. In criminalizing black people for being black, black people are deemed as deserving less, shown to be receiving less, and considered to be valued less.

I understand that if you do the crime, you pay the time. Let this apply to real crimes. But black people pay for crimes they did not commit, for which they were neither accomplices, nor even associated with the offense; their only crime is being black.

Researchers have proven that compared to white people, black people as a criminalized group are over-policed, over-surveilled, over-arrested, over-litigated, over-sentenced, and over-incarcerated. In criminalizing black people for being black, black people are treated as threats by police, threats to the police, and threats police argue that they need to preempt.

Research has calculated the cost of incarceration on the inmates, their families, and their communities:

1. Cost of incarcerating persons (nearly $50 billion annually).

2. Cost of treating the emotional, social, and physical health of incarcerated persons.

3. Cost of treating the emotional, social and physical health of families of incarcerated persons.

4. Cost of withdrawing a parent from parenting; the lost income to the household from the incarcerated person.

5. Cost of antisocial behavior learned by the incarcerated person in prison.

6. Cost of lower life outcomes of the formerly incarcerated (life expectancy, income, housing options, lost voting rights, etc.).

7. Cost of mass imprisonment on social networks and norms.

A Decriminalizing Gospel and Empowering Maneuvers

Is it not the rich that oppress you? Don't the wealthy *make life difficult* for you? Aren't they the ones who *drag you into court*?

James reveals the innocence of the poor as the poor are caught up in a court system that is stacked against them. Before the court, being poor is a criminal offense. The poor are too poor to hire a defense attorney, too poor to dress to impress the judge and jury. The poor are too poor and overworked to find the time simply to research the case with their own resources. Before the court, being poor is a criminal offense. The poor are too under-educated about the legal system to navigate it well. The poor are too under-educated to outsmart a judicial system rigged against them. The poor are too under-educated to mount an effective defense on their own.

James reveals the innocence of the poor as the poor. They face false accusations. They face trumped-up charges. They face the criminalization of poverty.

To the retort that the poor are unworthy of justice because the poor aren't deserving, James proclaims their innocence, their worthiness, their intrinsic value, and even God's preferential option for the poor.

Recall James 2:5: Hasn't God chosen those who are poor by worldly standards . . . ? Hasn't God chosen the poor as heirs of the kingdom he has promised to those who love him?

James exposes that the social reality of criminalizing the poor for being poor contradicts the good news of Christ, and contradicts the gospel's radical message of love.

Is it not the rich that oppress you? Don't the wealthy make life difficult for you? Aren't they the ones who drag you into court?

James exposes how court systems work, how the wealthy hijack court systems to exploit the poor, and how systems of justice get turned into unjust systems.

Justice for James

In James, we hear a gospel that rightly criminalizes the oppressors, the exploiters, the perpetrators of injustice, and decriminalizes the poor. Being poor doesn't make one a criminal. Poverty is the real crime. The exploitation of the poor is a high crime for James. James is against the exploitation of the poor.

James spotlights a judicial system in which the poor are the wrongly arrested, wrongly tried, wrongly convicted, wrongly sentenced, and wrongly imprisoned. James warns the poor: Don't be deceived by the deception of the rich. Not all the poor people caught up in the judicial system and processed as criminals are criminals.

James lets the wealthy know that the church sees their dastardly deeds and the church is strident in broadcasting the truth in the public assembly.

James presupposes how the judicial system should exist as opposed to how it does exist. James takes the covers off a court system rigged to benefit the rich and deployed to crush the poor. James spotlights the criminality of the wealthy accusers and the innocence of the convicted poor.

James frames his analysis with a theology of justice that distinguishes injustice from justice. Justice for James supplies him with the framework to name prejudice, discrimination, and oppression. Justice for James offers him lenses to recognize corrosive vices and constructive virtues.

To paraphrase Ralph Martin: James is woke. In Martin's words, he possesses a "socially sensitized conscience."[2]

With his wokeness, James refuses to proclaim a theology that legitimates the criminalization of the poor for being poor, the exploitation of the poor, the oppression of the poor. With his wokeness, he refuses to lend theological credence to God siding with the powerful and siding against the powerless. Wealth in and of itself is not a sign of the divine approval of how the wealth was acquired or sustained.

Like James, we must be woke. We must refuse to proclaim a theology that legitimates the criminalization of the poor for being poor, the criminalization of black people for being black.

We must be appalled by the scandal of rigged judicial systems. What good to the public are biased courts highjacked by white supremacy? What good to the public are biased courts highjacked by systemic racism? What good to the public are biased courts hijacked by an unjust racial order? When the state denies justice to any race, the state is complicit in the miscarriage of justice by its own criminal justice system. Like James, get woke!

The court-sanctioned and state-sponsored injustice that criminalizes and devalues black lives produces disparities in the surveillance, arrest, litigation, conviction, sentencing, and incarceration of black people

2. Martin, *James*, ixvii.

in addition to compounding racial disparities in life span, life outcomes, health outcomes, education, and quality of life.

What Is the Heart of the Gospel for James?

James proclaims a message that decriminalizes the poor for being poor, denounces the exploitation of the poor as against God's word, and delegitimates the oppression of the poor as the will of God. James proclaims a gospel of justice and love. Poverty is not a sign of the divine punishment upon the poor. Poverty is a system of oppression of one people by another. James values the poor as people, as Christians.

James's letter is an act of defiance, an act of resistance, an act of protest. James proclaims truth that possesses the God-given capacity to change the world.

James points us to a world marked by justice and love. It is love framed by justice that de-marginalizes those on the margins. The poor are people who stand shoulder to shoulder with all people before God, and they should do so before all people.

Yes, "All Lives Matter," but "All Lives" have not been banished to the margins of society. "All Lives" weren't enslaved in the United States. "All Lives" weren't racially segregated in underfunded communities in the United States. "All Lives" weren't barred from the right to vote while being taxed without political representation in government. "All Lives" weren't discriminated against because of their racial classification. "All Lives" weren't racially profiled, disproportionately arrested, litigated, convicted, sentenced, and incarcerated because of their race.

"All Lives" don't fear for their lives because of the color of their skin. Yes, "All Lives Matter," but a generic commitment to "All Lives Matter" in this country has and continues to perpetuate racial inequality, inequity, and disparities.

As James advocated for the poor and was in solidarity with the poor in the first century, we must make a reality: "Black Lives Matter." Black Lives Matter because justice for black people is just basic, the bare minimum.

Yes, we live in James's world of today. Like James, we are dissatisfied with the world as it is, with life as it is: racial inequality, injustice, disparities, unrighteousness, violence, terror. As people, despair overwhelms us, consumes us.

With Kierkegaard, in the words of Vincent Lloyd, we say yes to despair because despair "wipes out false gods and focuses our attention solely on one true God, on a God qualitatively different from the world."[3] Despair exposes the god of capitalism and consumerism, the god of materialism and narcissism, the god of patriarchy and white supremacy.

While we live in James's world of today, as the Church we can glimpse and do work towards James's world of tomorrow, God's world of justice and love.

Elsa Tamez, the Latin American liberation theologian, is correct: James proclaims a "scandalous message."[4]

James Proclaims a Scandalous Message of Justice and Love

James 2:8: Love your neighbor as yourself.

James replaces the dominant society's framework of insider-outsider, powerful-powerless, superior-inferior race, first-class and second-class citizen, and rich-poor with a Christian framework of neighbor-neighbor. Instead of society promoting competition, self-interest, greed, survival-of-the-fittest, domination, oppression, and exploitation, James reintroduces Jesus's transforming message of love.

Love your neighbor as yourself.

We refuse to call the person next to us: threat. We call them neighbor.

We refuse to call the person next to us: enemy. We call them neighbor.

We refuse to call the person next to us: opposition. We call them neighbor.

We call them neighbor, a person in relationship to us and not in opposition. We call them neighbor, a person whose survival is my survival, and my survival is their survival. We call them neighbor, a person whose future is my future, and my future is their future. We call them neighbor, a person whose flourishing is my flourishing, and my flourishing is their flourishing.

---

3. Lloyd, "For What Are Whites to Hope?," 278–79.

4. Tamez, *Scandalous Message of James.*

We call the person next to us: neighbor. We are in relationship to one another with a common destiny. This is an empowering maneuver.

Love your neighbor as yourself.

Among neighbors, the powerful share power generously.

Among neighbors, the powerless exercise power justly.

Among neighbors, power is distributed justly.

Love your neighbor as yourself.

Neighbors are called to participate communally in the life-giving, life-bearing, life-transforming love of God.

Neighbors create neighborhoods, neighborhoods where they are united by justice and the love of God.

Love your neighbor as yourself.

My people and your people become our people together. Together we create neighborhoods of congregations and communities marked by changes in communal behavior: changes in the communal behavior of the congregations and communities as well as changes in the group behavior of the people. The neighborhoods we create together are to be marked by justice and love. This is an empowering maneuver.

In rereading James as a decriminalizing gospel, we glimpse a horizon, which may generate a new horizon in the early twenty-first century, offering a scriptural script for navigating our world.

The advantage of a church driven by justice and love, a church hitched to justice and love, is that it navigates this world with God's world of justice in view. Yes, a church hitched to justice and love might reorient neighborhood after neighborhood and, even the world itself. Yes, a church hitched to justice and love can by the grace of God reorient the world away from oppression, violence, and injustice towards God's world of justice and love. As a people of justice and love, Christians live out of God's future.

A Decriminalizing Gospel as a Word on Target

A decriminalizing gospel spurred by God's future lures us forward, forward towards a just society, forward towards a peaceable society, forward towards God's future.

A decriminalizing gospel of justice and love marks our pursuit of God's tomorrow today. The powerless empower themselves, the silenced unsilence themselves, the marginalized de-marginalizes themselves, the excluded include themselves—all this is done by the grace of God. These are empowering maneuvers.

The decriminalizing gospel encourages us, emboldens us, today to advocate that the society ban the criminalization of the poor and the criminalization of poverty. These are empowering maneuvers.

The decriminalizing gospel encourages us, emboldens us, today to advocate the end to mass incarceration and abolishment of prisons. These are empowering maneuvers.

A decriminalizing gospel shouts no to the status quo of racial surveilling, racial profiling, police brutality. This is an empowering maneuver.

A decriminalizing gospel shouts no to the status quo of racial disparities in arrest, litigation, convictions, sentencing, and incarceration. This is an empowering maneuver.

A decriminalizing gospel shouts no to the status quo of racial inequalities of power, of wealth, of health, of status. This is an empowering maneuver.

The world as we know it fails to be the ultimate act. A decriminalizing gospel proclaims the justice that Christ inaugurates. It lodges this justice in Christ, in God's will for creation, in God's plan for the world. It hitches us to God's justice.

A decriminalizing gospel witnesses God's world-to-come, offers a foretaste of God's world-to-come. In this gospel, we encounter a God who promises that God's future has overwhelmed our present and our past. In this gospel, we glimpse God's horizon of justice where all things are made just in Christ.

A decriminalizing gospel fires up our ecclesial imagination in order to open us up to God's new possibilities for the city, for life, for all people, for all creation, for the world.

The decriminalizing gospel encourages us, emboldens us, today to advocate for a society where all are neighbors and where all neighborhoods are just communities.

Justice grounded in love of God frames the decriminalizing gospel. God's love loves in justice-shaping ways. God's love loves in justice-making ways. God's love loves in justice-changing ways. God's love loves in justice-transforming ways.

Works Cited

Ahn, Ilsup. *Theology and Migration*. Brill Research Perspectives. Theology. Leiden: Brill, 2019.

Alexander, Michelle. *The New Jim Crow: Mass Incarceration in the Age of Colorblindness*. New York: New Press, 2012.

Gilliard, Dominique DuBois. *Rethinking Incarceration: Advocating for Justice That Restores*. Downers Grove, IL: InterVarsity, 2018.

Knapp, Robert C. *Invisible Romans: Prostitutes, Outlaws, Slaves, Gladiators, Ordinary Men and Women—the Romans that History Forgot*. London: Profile, 2011.

Lloyd, Vincent. "For What Are Whites to Hope?" *Political Theology* 17, no. 2 (2016) 178–79.

Martin, Ralph P. *James*. Word Biblical Commentary. Waco, TX: Word, 1988.

Maynard-Reid, Pedrito U. *Poverty and Wealth in James*. Maryknoll, NY: Orbis, 1987.

Tamez, Elsa. *The Scandalous Message of James: Faith without Works Is Dead*. Rev. ed. New York: Crossroad, 2002.

Subject Index

Name Index

Abele, Julian, 235
Abernathy, Ralph, 227
Achtemeier, Paul, 40
Alexander, Michelle, 258, 260
Alkebulan, Adisa, 182n6
Allen, Richard, xxi, 3, 5, 7–8, 9, 250
Alridge, Derrick P., 220, 229
Anderson, Tanisha, 16, 156, 203n4,
    204n6
Andrews, Dale P., 221, 225, 227
Angelou, Maya, 132, 180–81
Anim, Peter Newman, 204–6
Anselm of Canterbury, 145
Arbery, Ahmaud, xix, xx, 171, 186, 242,
    245
Asamoah-Gyadu, 206nn20–21,
    207nn25–26, 210nn41–42,
    211n48, 212n51
Asante-Muhammed, Dedrick, 66n7
Ashe, Bertram, 164
Assimeng, Abraham Anim, 212n49
Augustine of Hippo, 128
Austin, Algernon, 21n19

Bakker, Jim and Tammy, 211
Baldwin, James, 10, 15, 27, 106–7, 141,
    168, 258, 260
Bambaataa, Afrika, 220
Bantu, Vince, xxiii, 191, 202, 203n3
Bantum, Brian, xxiii, 156
Barlund, Dean C., 179n3
Barth, Karl, 147
Bearden, Romarie, 162, 163

Bell, Sean, 52
Berlin, Samantha, 91n5
Berwanger, Eugene, 4n34, 5
Bird, Michael F., 79n12, 80n16
Birzer, Michael, 92
Blackmon, Douglas A., 20n15
Blair, Leonardo, 191n1
Bland, Sandra, 16
Bloom, Joshua, 24n33
Bloomer, Amelia, 251
Blumenbach, Johann Friedrich, 172
Bogel-Burroughs, Nicholas, 93nn19–20
Bonilla-Silva, Eduardo, 141n7
Bor, Jacob, 94n22
Bourdieu, Pierre, xxiv, 217, 218, 222–23,
    226, 229
Bowens, Lisa, xxi, 3, 18n5, 37, 96
Boyd, Todd, 220
Bradford, Sarah H., 252n5
Branch, Taylor, 21n19
Brodess, Edward, 251
Brodhead, Richard, 237
Brown, Henry Box, 96–98
Brown, James, 183
Brown, Michael, 16, 90, 156, 228
Brown, Sterling, 173–74
Bryant, Ma'Khia, 34, 35n1
Burroughs, Margaret, 156, 162
Butler, Judith, 49

Caldwell, Earl, 25nn40–41
Calvin, John, 159
Cannon, Katie Geneva, 36–37

281

Scripture Index

www.ingramcontent.com/pod-product-compliance
Lightning Source LLC
Chambersburg PA
CBHW030921150426
42812CB00046B/469